MY GREATEST DAY
IN BASEBALL

as told to

JOHN P. CARMICHAEL

and other noted sports writers

FORTY-SEVEN DRAMATIC STORIES
BY FORTY-SEVEN STARS

Introduction to the Bison Books Edition
by Jerome Holtzman

University of Nebraska Press
Lincoln and London

♻ The paper in this book meets the minimum requirements of American National
Standard for Information Sciences—Permanence of Paper for Printed Library
Materials, ANSI Z39.48-1984.

First Bison Books printing: 1996
Most recent printing indicated by the last digit below:
10 9 8 7 6 5 4 3 2 1

Library of Congress Cataloging-in-Publication Data
My greatest day in baseball: forty-seven dramatic stories by forty-seven stars / as told to
John P. Carmichael and other noted sports writers; introduction to the Bison Books
edition by Jerome Holtzman.
p. cm.
ISBN 0-8032-6368-6 (pbk.: alk. paper)
1. Baseball. I. Carmichael, John P. (John Peter)
GV873.M9 1996
796.357′0922—dc20
95-40142 CIP

Reprinted from the original 1945 edition by A. S. Barnes & Company, New York.

CONTENTS

ACKNOWLEDGMENTS

These stories were first published in the sports pages of the *Chicago Daily News*,

Credit for pictures, unless otherwise noted, must be given to the *Chicago Daily News*, and may not be reprinted without their permission.

INTRODUCTION

Jerome Holtzman

We should be grateful to John Peter Carmichael for this collection of forty-seven as-told-to stories by some of baseball's best-known luminaries who sat for interviews and recalled their greatest moments in baseball. They are individual recollections but when stitched together become an excellent framework of diamond history, in effect, an antecedent to Larry Ritter's classic *Glory of Their Times*.

I was among the fortunate who not only knew Mr. Carmichael but also worked alongside him. When I was a young sportswriter breaking in on the Chicago baseball beat, he was a veteran and much-decorated sports columnist for the *Chicago Daily News*. I don't know if the "greatest day" series was his idea, or if it flowed from his good friend, Lloyd Lewis, at that time the *Daily News* sports editor. What I do know is, Carmichael always understood the beauty of turning his column over to his subjects.

On many occasions it was their column, not his. The best example of his approach—and for me, it has been unforgettable—occurred almost forty years ago when we were in Tampa, Florida, covering the White Sox during spring training. It was the custom for the writers to meet at the headquarter hotel for five o'clock cocktails; for the next hour or so the happenings of the day were reviewed. Carmichael wasn't anchored to the White Sox and traveled to other camps, usually in the company of fellow columnists. He had been to Bradenton and had interviewed Charley Dressen, the manager of the Milwaukee Braves.

"Charley Dressen gave me a terrific column," Carmichael announced, obviously pleased with his day's production.

And, immediately, it occurred to me that most sportswriters, perhaps all, would have said:

"I wrote a terrific column on Charley Dressen today," giving themselves, not Dressen the credit.

That would have been the natural reaction. But Carmichael knew that Dressen, a good talker, had supplied the column. Carmichael was the host; Dressen was the attraction. I am not suggesting that Carmichael was just a typist. He was among the very best sportswriters of his time, in my view among the best of all time. But like a good baseball manager, he knew when there was no need to interfere.

My Greatest Day in Baseball is the epitome of this sensible and honest approach. Except when moralizing, which is usually a mistake—pontificating is a better word—the best sports columns are entertaining and informative, ideally a combination of both. Essentially an anecdotalist, Carmichael added a third dimension, what can be described as "a gentle ramble."

Readers of the sports pages are knowledgeable. They know what's going on, especially since the advent of television, and, I am convinced, are weary of the shrill daily assaults on players, owners, managers—the so-called "Aw Nuts" school of sportswriting. "Aw Nuts" can be a proper approach if offered sparingly, but many of the practitioners can't play in any other key. They're constantly beating a dead horse. Carmichael was of the "Gee Whiz" genre. He seldom wrote a harsh sentence. If he didn't like somebody—and he certainly had his dislikes—he withdrew and didn't offer access; he ignored them.

Once I asked him why his column was always cheerful, why he was such a nice-guy writer.

His reply:

"The only time I meant to be vicious was against Bill Cox. He owned the Phillies. Judge Landis threw him out for betting on baseball. Cox was an arrogant son-of-a-bitch. When he fired Bucky Harris, his manager, I really blasted him. It was the only time I was mad enough at anyone to do it. I never believed in castigating a lot of people, I don't know why. Maybe it was because I always had a feeling that if you turn out to be wrong, you've done irreparable damage."

Carmichael also abhorred peephole journalism. I recall a story by one of the *Daily News* staffers who was assigned to an owners's meeting at the Edgewater Beach Hotel in Chicago. After listening through an air vent, the reporter presented a running account of some of the dialogue. Carmichael expressed disdain. He insisted it wasn't ethical, that baseball owners were entitled to privacy, same as a meeting of the directors of a corporation.

This book is about events on the field, not behind closed doors. Many historic moments are covered. And all the players aren't portrayed as saints. But the criticism, where it appears, is justified. For example, here is Mordecai "Three Finger" Brown of the Cubs recalling how Christy Mathewson of the Giants, the Great Matty, took the field for the replay of the controversial "Merkle boner" game, which forced a playoff for the 1908 National League pennant:

"I can still see Christy Mathewson making his lordly entrance. He'd always wait until about 10 minutes before game time, then he'd come from the clubhouse across the field in a long linen duster like auto drivers wore in those days, and at every step the crowd would yell louder and louder. This day they split the air. I watched him enter as I went out to the bull pen, where I was to keep ready. [Frank] Chance still insisted on starting [Jack] Pfeister."

Certainly, a revealing glimpse of the aristocratic Mathewson—who at the time of his retirement held the National League record for the most victories. A companion reminiscence of the Merkle game is offered by Johnny Evers, the Chicago second baseman. It was the most controversial game of the twentieth century. Evers reveals the crucial event, in Pittsburgh nineteen days earlier, that prompted the ninth-inning, force-play call by umpire Hank O'Day that denied the Giants of what appeared to be a routine victory.

Carmichael was the co-author of fifteen of these forty-seven chapters. In the original presentation they were in a beautifully illustrated *Chicago Daily News* series. The stories ran in the winter, during the baseball off-season, usually two a week, when the sports pages were empty. In those days, baseball was *the* major sport. Football and basketball were covered but were secondary.

A significant number of contributions were written by "outsiders": Chet Smith of Pittsburgh, for example, was teamed with Honus Wagner, the Pirates's star shortstop. Ernie Mehl of Kansas City was assigned to Satchel Paige, the great black star who for many years made his home in that city. Shirley Povich of Washington interviewed Clark Griffith, the so-called Old Fox who owned and operated the Washington Senators and before that was a big-league pitcher. Similarly, Bill Leiser of San Francisco drew Lefty O'Doul, and New York's Ken Smith did Frankie Frisch.

Carmichael's pieces are among the best. Born in Madison, Wisconsin, on 16 October 1902, the son of the general manager of a dental supply company, he attended Campion Academy in Prairie du Chien, Wisconsin, and Marquette University in Milwaukee. He dropped out of Marquette during his junior year. He did not intend to be a journalist but was supposed to major in accounting and commerce. When I interviewed him in 1972, he explained what had happened:

"I was walking with another fellow, this was when I was at Marquette, going up the hill to Barnett Hall, and I said 'Gee, I hate this eight o'clock class. Why don't they have classes at a civilized hour?'

"He said 'You should have gone into journalism. They don't have any classes until nine or ten o'clock in the morning.'

"The Journalism Building was right across the way. So I left him and enrolled in journalism."

His first newspaper job was covering the morgue as a night-shift cityside reporter for the *Milwaukee Journal*. He switched to the now defunct *Milwaukee Leader* where he remained for two years as a drama critic and reporter. He came to Chicago on a vacation in 1927 and ended up on the sports desk of the old *Herald & Examiner*. He joined the *Daily News* in 1932 and two years later was rewarded with a column.

"Howard Mann was the sports editor and he asked me to think up a name for it," Carmichael recalled. "I said, 'The Barber Shop.'

"He asked me why and I told him 'There is no damn use in putting a column on the sports page with a heading "Inside Sports" or something like that. What the hell, they know it's on sports. I told him I grew up in small towns and the barber shop was the place where everybody settled everything.' "

"The Barber Shop" had a long run, thirty-eight years. Carmichael estimated he had written 11,000 columns. The sports editors of all four Chicago dailies— *Tribune, News, Sun-Times,* and *Chicago Today*—served as co-chairmen of a giant City of Hope testimonial banquet on his retirement in 1972. He died in 1986 at the age of eighty-three.

From the beginning his column was well-received; it wasn't long before he had a national reputation. He was among the country's most prolific and well-traveled sportswriters and was welcome at every stop. Connie Mack and Ted

Williams, among others, repeatedly said he was their favorite sportswriter.

In addition to his column, he wrote hundreds of sidebars and feature stories, along with dozens of lengthy profiles on theatrical personalities, all of which were bannered and took an entire page. The theatre fascinated him. After interviewing Tallulah Bankhead in New York, where she was playing in *The Little Foxes,* she insisted he appear with her and stationed him at a table on the rear of the stage. He was also in constant demand as a speaker.

Except for writing down dates, Mr. Carmichael never took notes. Early on, he discovered the pad and pencil not only slowed the process but were discomfiting and inhibiting to his subjects. This was long before the invasion of electronic journalism. There were no portable tape recorders. To put his subjects at ease, Carmichael worked at developing his memory. When he sat down at the typewriter he was able to reconstruct the dialogue with remarkable accuracy.

Some of the pieces written by others, in spots, are stiff. We can easily detect when the writer is using his words in transmitting the recollections. This is never true with Carmichael. Like Ring Lardner, who was among his Chicago predecessors, Carmichael had a great ear. His piece on Dizzy Dean is a genuine classic, perhaps the best sports story I have read. I still marvel, a half century later, how he did it without taking notes.

After Dean beat Detroit 11-0 in the final game of the 1934 World Series, he recalls a clubhouse conversation with Frankie Frisch, his manager:

"Frisch came by and do you know what he said: 'Anybody with your stuff should have won 40 games instead of a measly 30. You loaf. That's the trouble. Thirty games! You ought to be 'shamed of yourself.'

"Imagine that, and me just winning the Series for him: ol' Diz out there pitchin' outta turn too, don't forget that. He wanted me to pitch although he'd said Bill Hallahan was gonna work the last game. But he came to me the night before and he asked: 'Diz, you wanna be the greatest man in baseball?' I told him I already was, but he didn't even hear me 'cause he went on: 'You pitch that game tomorrow and you'll be tops.' I just told him: 'Gimme that ball tomorrow and your troubles are over.' He wanted me to pitch. I knew that. Hell, I was afraid he would let Hallahan start."

This is sportswriting at its best. If you agree, there is much good reading ahead.

MY GREATEST DAY IN BASEBALL

BABE RUTH
as told to
JOHN P. CARMICHAEL

George Herman Ruth was born February 7, 1894.
Began career with Red Sox in '14. Finished with Braves
in '35.

Nobody but a blankety-blank fool would-a done what I did that
day. When I think of what-a idiot I'd a been if I'd struck out
and I could-a, too, just as well as not because I was mad and I'd made
up my mind to swing at the next pitch if I could reach it with a bat.
Boy, when I think of the good breaks in my life . . . that was one of 'em!

Aw, everybody knows that game; the day I hit the homer off ol'
Charlie Root there in Wrigley Field, the day, October 1, the third
game of that 1932 World Series. But right now I want to settle all argu-
ments: I didn't exactly point to any spot, like the flagpole. Anyway, I
didn't mean to. I just sorta waved at the whole fence, but that was
foolish enough. All I wanted to do was give that thing a ride . . . outta
the park . . . anywhere.

I used to pop off a lot about hittin' homers, but mostly among us
Yankees. Combs and Fletcher and Crosetti and all of 'em used to

1

holler at me when I'd pick up a bat in a close game: "Come on, Babe, hit one." 'Member Herb Pennock? He was a great pitcher, believe me. He told me once: "Babe, I get the biggest thrill of my life whenever I see you hit a home run. It's just like watchin' a circus act." So I'd often kid 'em back and say: "O.K., you bums . . . I'll hit one." Sometimes I did; sometimes I didn't . . . but what the heck, it was fun.

One day we were playin' in Chicago against the White Sox and Mark Roth, our secretary, was worryin' about holdin' the train because we were in extra innings. He was fidgetin' around behind the dugout, lookin' at his watch and I saw him when I went up to hit in the 15th. "All right, quit worrying," I told him. "I'll get this over with right now." Mike Cvengros was pitchin' and I hit one outta the park. We made the train easy. It was fun.

I'd had a lot of trouble in '32 and we weren't any cinches to win that pennant, either, 'cause old Mose Grove was tryin' to keep the Athletics up there for their fourth straight flag and sometime in June I pulled a muscle in my right leg chasin' a fly ball. I was on the bench about three weeks and when I started to play again I had to wear a rubber bandage from my hip to my knee. You know, the ole Babe wasn't getting any younger and Foxx was ahead of me in homers. I was 11 behind him early in September and never did catch up. I wouldn't get one good ball a series to swing at. I remember one whole week when I'll bet I was walked four times in every game.

I always had three ambitions: I wanted to play 20 years in the big leagues. I wanted to play in 10 World Series, and I wanted to hit 700 home runs. Well, '32 was one away from my 20th year and that series with the Cubs was No. 10 and I finally wound up with 729 home runs, countin' World Series games, so I can't kick. But then along in September I had to quit the club and go home because my stomach was kickin' up and the docs found out my appendix was inflamed and maybe I'd have to have it out. No, sir, I wouldn't let 'em . . . not till after the season anyway.

The World Series didn't last long, but it was a honey. That Malone and that Grimes didn't talk like any Sunday school guys, and their

trainer ... yeah, Andy Lot-
shaw ... he got smart in
the first game at New
York, too. That's what started me off. I popped up once in that one,
and he was on their bench wavin' a towel at me and hollerin': "If I
had you, I'd hitch you to a wagon, you pot-belly." I didn't mind no
ballplayers yellin' at me, but the trainer cuttin' in ... that made me
sore. As long as they started in on me, we let 'em have it. We went
after 'em and maybe we gave 'em more than they could take 'cause
they looked beat before they went off the field.

We didn't have to do much the first game at home. Guy Bush walked
everybody around the bases. You look it up and I'll betcha 10 bases
on balls scored for us. Anyway, we got into Chicago for the third
game, that's where those Cubs decided to really get on us. They

were in front of their home folks and I guess they thought they better act tough.

We were givin' them (the Cubs) hell about how cheap they were to Mark Koenig only votin' him a half-share in the series and they were callin' me big belly and balloon-head, but I think we had 'em madder by givin' them that ol' lump-in-the-throat sign ... you know, the thumb and finger at the windpipe. That's like callin' a guy yellow. Then in the very first inning I got a hold of one with two on and parked it in the stands for a three-run lead and that shut 'em up pretty well. But they came back with some runs and we were tied 4 to 4 going into the fifth frame. You know another thing I think of in that game was the play Jurges made on Joe Sewell in that fifth ... just ahead of me. I was out there waitin' to hit, so I could see it good and he made a helluva pickup, way back on the grass, and "shot" Joe out by a half-step. I didn't know whether they were gonna get on me any more or not when I got to the box, but I saw a lemon rolling out to the plate and I looked over and there was Malone and Grimes with their thumbs in their ears wiggling their fingers at me.

I told Hartnett: "If that bum (Root) throws me in here, I'll hit it over the fence again," and I'll say for Gabby, he didn't answer, but those other guys were standing up in the dugout, cocky because they'd got four runs back and everybody hollerin'. So I just changed my mind. I took two strikes and after each one I held up my finger and said: "That's one" and "that's two." Ask Gabby ... he could hear me. Then's when I waved to the fence!

No, I didn't point to any spot, but as long as I'd called the first two strikes on myself, I hadda go through with it. It was damned foolishness, sure, but I just felt like doing it and I felt pretty sure Root would put one close enough for me to cut at, because I was showin' him up. What the hell, he hadda take a chance as well as I did or walk me?

Gosh, that was a great 'feelin' ... gettin' a hold of that ball and I knew it was going someplace ... yes sir, you can feel it in your hands when you've laid wood on one. How that mob howled. Me? I just laughed ... laughed to myself going around the bases and thinking:

"You lucky bum...lucky, lucky" and I looked at poor Charlie (Root) watchin' me and then I saw Art Fletcher (Yankee coach) at third wavin' his cap and behind him I could see the Cubs and I just stopped on third and laughed out loud and slapped my knees and yelled: "Squeeze-the-Eagle-Club" so they'd know I was referrin' to Koenig and for special to Malone I called him "meat-head" and asked when he was gonna pitch.

Yeah, it was silly. I was a blankety-blank fool. But I got away with it and after Gehrig homered, behind me, their backs were broken. That was a day to talk about.

THE BOX SCORE
(October 1, 1932)

NEW YORK	A.B.	R.	H.	P.	A.
Combs, cf.	5	1	0	1	0
Sewell, 3b.	2	1	0	2	2
Ruth, lf.	4	2	2	2	0
Gehrig, 1b.	5	2	2	13	1
Lazzeri, 2b.	4	1	0	3	4
Dickey, c.	4	0	1	2	1
Chapman, rf.	4	0	2	0	0
Crosetti, ss.	4	0	1	4	4
Pipgras, p.	5	0	0	0	0
Pennock, p.	0	0	0	0	1
	—	—	—	—	—
Totals	37	7	8	27	13

CHICAGO	A.B.	R.	H.	P.	A.
Herman, 2b.	4	1	0	1	2
English, 3b.	4	0	0	0	3
Cuyler, rf.	4	1	3	1	0
Stephenson, lf.	4	0	1	1	0
Moore, cf.	3	1	0	3	0
Grimm, 1b.	4	0	1	8	0
Hartnett, c.	4	1	1	10	1
Jurges, ss.	4	1	3	3	3
Root, p.	2	0	0	0	0
Malone, p.	0	0	0	0	0
May, p.	0	0	0	0	0
Tinning, p.	0	0	0	0	0
Gudat	1	0	0	0	0
Koenig	0	0	0	0	0
Hemsley	1	0	0	0	0
	—	—	—	—	—
Totals	35	5	9	27	9

NEW YORK	3	0	1	0	2	0	0	0	1—	7
CHICAGO	1	0	2	1	0	0	0	0	1—	5

Gudat batted for Malone in 7th.
Koenig batted for Tinning in 9th.
Hemsley batted for Koenig in 9th.

Errors—Lazzeri, Herman, Hartnett, Jurges (2). Runs batted in—Ruth (4), Gehrig (2), Cuyler, (2), Grimm, Chapman, Hartnett. Two-base hits—Chapman, Cuyler, Jurges, Grimm. Home runs—Ruth (2), Gehrig (2), Cuyler, Hartnett. Stolen base—Jurges. Double plays—Sewell to Lazzari to Gehrig, Herman to Jurges to Grimm. Struck out—By Root, 4; by Malone, 4; by May, 1; by Tinning, 1; by Pipgras, 1; by Pennock, 1. Bases on balls—Off Root, 3; off Malone, 4; off Pipgras, 3. Hit by pitched ball—By May, 1. Hits—Off Root, 6 in 4 1-3 innings; off Malone, 1 in 2 2-3 innings; off May 1 in 1 2-3 innings; off Tinning, 0 in 2-3 innings; off Pipgras, 9 in 8 innings; off Pennock, 0 in 1 inning. Winning pitcher—Pipgras. Losing pitcher—Root. Umpires—Van Graflan (A. L.), Magerkurth (N. L.), Dineen (A. L.), and Klem (N. L.). Time—2:11. Attendance—49,986.

DIZZY DEAN
as told to
JOHN P. CARMICHAEL

Jerome Herman "Dizzy" Dean has had more birth-places and given names than any other man in baseball. One of them was Jay Hanner Dean, another Jay Hannah —and he has been listed as a native of Lucas, Ark., and Holdenville, Okla. In any event, he was born on January 16, 1911, and is ranked as one of baseball's immortal pitchers. Started his mound saga with St. Joseph in 1930 and joined the Cardinals for a spectacular six-year stretch in 1932. In 1938 "Dizzy" went to the Cubs, and now is a popular radio baseball announcer in St. Louis. He won 141, lost 76 in his big-league history.

As might have been expected, Jerome Hanna Dean did not confine himself to the traditional "Greatest Day in Baseball." He said: "I've had too derned many big days ... lots of 'em."

I just wish my arm was like it was seven-eight years ago. . . . I'd have me a picnic in this league. When I came up every club had three-four .300 hitters who really could powder that ball. Now? Shucks! I'd breeze home any day. I never forget Frank Frisch the day I beat Detroit 11-0 in the last game of the World Series in 1934. We're in the clubhouse, see, celebratin' and I got a rubber tiger, all blown up, and

I'm twistin' his tail and hollerin' like the rest and Frisch came by and stopped and you know what he said?

"Anybody with your stuff should have won 40 games this year instead of a measly 30," he said. "You loaf, that's the trouble. Thirty games! You ought to be 'shamed of yourself." Imagine that, and me just winning the series for him: ol' Diz out there pitchin' outta turn too, don't forget that. He wanted me to pitch although he'd said that Bill Hallahan was gonna work the last game. But he came to me the night before and he asked: "Diz, you wanna be the greatest man in baseball?" I told him I already was, but he didn't even hear me I guess, 'cause he went on: "You pitch that game tomorrow and you'll be tops." I just told him: "Gimme that ball tomorrow and your troubles are over." He wanted me to pitch I knew that. Hell, I was afraid he would let Hallahan start.

That was a big day in my life, I admit it. First World Series and all the excitement,and everybody wild, and two trucks goin' up and down the streets, one playin', "Hold That Tiger" and the other tootlin' the "St. Louis Blues." I saw Babe Ruth and got his autograph, by jingo, and 'taint everybody pitches in a big series and gets Babe's name on a ball too. I liked that ol' Frisch, he was a helluva guy, but he worried all the time. He had nothin' to fret about with ol' Diz out there. You know we was leadin' 11-0 in the ninth with one out and he sent four pitchers down in the bull pen to warm up.

So help me, I thought they must be gettin' ready for the 1935 season. Eleven-nothing I got 'em and that Billy Rogell on base and Hank Greenberg came up. I already struck him out twice, no trouble 'tall, and when he came up in that ninth I hollered over to the Tiger bench, I said: "What, no pinch-hitter?" and Hank looked at me like he'd a liked to break one of them sticks over my head, but hell, he was my meat. He was easy.

You know what that Frisch did? I put two fast balls right past the letters on that Greenberg's uniform and when he missed the second one I hadda laugh. I put my glove up to my face to keep from laughin' right in his face, he looked so funny, and before I could throw any

Branch Rickey

Charlie Grimm

more Frisch came out. He was mad. He said: "Cut out the foolin', we got a lot at stake" and I just stood there and looked at him like he must be outta his mind . . . me leadin' 11-0 with one out in the last of the ninth. Just then Leo Durocher came in from short and he said: "Aw, what the hell, Frank, let the guy have his fun. What's the matter with you?" Well you know what Frisch told me? Yeah . . . he said: "You lose this guy and you're through." Eleven-nothing . . . I can't get over that yet. He was gonna pull me.

That Greenberg couldn't a hit that next pitch if he'd a started to swing when I wound up. Gonna pull me. He didn't even see it and the next guy was Owen and he forced Rogell and the whole thing was over. Them Tigers weren't bad; they gave us a good battle, but they were just pussy-cats with me. I don't like to brag a lot, because folks think I'm a big lunkhead or somethin', but when I had my fast ball, before I broke my toe and couldn't throw it any more, nobody hit me . . . much. You know what I did one day? I pitched a game in Boston and never took a sign or never threw nothin' but fast balls. A whole game, Bill Delancy was catchin'. I told Al Spohrer, the Braves' catcher, before the game that he could tell everybody I was gonna do that too. I beat 'em 10-0 or 13-0 . . . some score that. Just wound up and fogged that ball over.

I'll tell you another day in Boston I got a helluva kick. Remember seein' a big fat guy around with me a lot? Well, he was Johnny Perkins and he worked in a night club around St. Louis and he made this trip with us. He made me a bet I wouldn't strike out Vince DiMaggio the first time he came up. I did and when I went back to the bench I made motions to Perk I'd double the bet the next time. I struck him out again and I put everything back on a third bet and I fanned him three straight times. Then Perkins wanted to make it all or nothin' so I took 'im and when DiMag came up again he lifted a pop foul back of the plate. I thought Ogrodowski was gonna catch it and I ran and hollered: "Let it go, let it go." He couldn't get the ball anyway, as it turned out, 'cause it hit the screen, but I'd a bumped him sure as hell if he'd a got under it. I wanted to win that bet. I struck DiMaggio out next pitch . . . four straight times.

I got a great kick outta the time I was traded to the Cubs, just before the season opened in '38. All ballplayers want to wind up their careers with the Cubs, Giants or Yankees . . . they just can't help it. Seems like they're finally in the big time, although of course the Cubs used to pay derned good wages too, which they don't any more, so you

Frankie Frisch

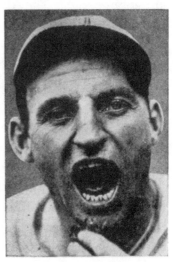

Pepper Martin

couldn't help a guy wantin' to land there. I didn't know anything about it until I came in from the bench during a game with the Browns right in St. Louis . . . spring series, you know . . . and I was walkin' in the clubhouse door and somebody grabbed my arm and it was Clarence Rowland, 'cept I didn't know him then. He said: "Well, Diz, you belong to us now . . . you're a Cub." Hell, I thought he was a fan and kiddin' me and I said: "I'll see you later, bud," and went on inside.

There was a lot of newspapermen and photographers there and I wondered what was going on, but never dreamed a deal for me, and finally Branch Rickey came in and he whispered: "I want to see you in my office after you're dressed," and I said O.K., and then he called for silence and said: "We just want to say we've made a deal with the Cubs and we have traded this man here . . ." and he put an arm on my shoulder, but he should a put it under me 'cause I thought I'd faint . . . "and we don't want you players to feel we're letting you down, because we've got a man to replace.him and we'll still win the pennant."

Well, nobody seemed to know who that man to take my place was, but "Pepper." Martin, he got up on a chair, with a towel around him . . . he'd just come from the shower . . . and he made a helluva speech. He sounds like Mr. Rickey at that. I'd hate to have to listen to both of 'em in the same night. They'd have a guy really dizzy and I ain't kiddin'. He said: "Mr. Rickey, we appreciate you coming in to tell us what you've done and that we ain't going to be too bad off even if Diz here goes, that you still want us to win a pennant and we're all for you and we'll win too." Hell, I knew they couldn't win any ol' pennant without Diz, even if I was only a half a pitcher then, so when they asked me to say something for the newspapermen I said: "Well, Mr. Rickey, I predicted we'd win that flag right here in St. Louis, but now that I'm gone, we'll win it in Chicago and I'll see you get into the world series." How about that, huh, and then we back into it in Chicago? I reminded ol' Branch about that many a time, but I hadda laugh like the devil, 'cause we just made it.

That game I beat Pittsburgh in 1938 (Sept. 27) was just about as big a day as I ever remember. I never had nothin'. I wasn't even supposed

Bill Lee

Gabby Hartnett

to pitch. I was on the inactive list or somethin' and Gabby Hartnett
came in the clubhouse that day and you know he twirls that big seegar
around in that red face of his (I like ol' Gabby, even if I did call him
a pickle-puss in Wichita which he was because he bawled me out right
in front of all the players and people a-gazin' at me and fined me $100)
and he said: "Dean, you're the pitcher" and I said: "Fine," but I
thought he was kiddin' and then Larry French and Herman and them
said: "He ain't foolin' Diz ... you're pitchin'." My God, I couldn't break
a pane of glass and I knew it, but I pitched.

They finally had to get me outta there in the ninth and I was leadin'
2-0 and Bill Lee went in and the first pitch he made was a wild one
and a run scored, but he hung on and they didn't score again and, boy,
I felt like a million. Ol' Diz saved many a game for Cardinal pitchers in
his day and here was a guy who saved one for me and I told him, I
said: "Lee, you're a great man," and he was a helluva guy and a swell
pitcher. I always liked old Gabby, but he shouldn't have yelled at me
in front of all those people in Witchita. They was a-gazin' at me like
I was a freak and I don't stand for bein' shown up by nobody. The fine
was all right.... I didn't get in until 20 minutes to 2 and we had a
midnight deadline ... but he could-a told me on the quiet.

The first game I pitched for the Cubs that year I beat Cincinnati and afterwards some of us went out and had a few beers and such, but I just went along. I didn't know what rules the Cubs had and figured these guys must know what they're doing. We had a helluva time, too, and then I beat the Cardinals and it looked like I'd have a great year, but Diz just didn't have so much left, I guess. But Mr. Wrigley told me not to worry, that he wasn't sorry he bought me and just go ahead and do the best I could and it's too bad I couldn't-a been with the Cubs when I wuz in my prime, because we'd a never got beat and I'd probably been drawin' $50,000 a year and pitchin' my arm off.

How about the time I had the run-in with Ford Frick? I'll never forget that either and I never apologized and never signed a derned letter and his secretary must-a wrote 20 different copies or somethin' for me to sign and I wouldn't. I was in a tough spot, though. See, I wuz pitchin' against Carl Hubbell here in St. Louis and he beat me 4-1. I led into the sixth or seventh and then George Barr, the umpire, called a balk on me; he said I didn't come to a stop before I threw. He was nuts, but anyway they got three runs and ol' Diz never liked to take a beatin'. No time. So I had to go to Belleville, Ill., that night to a banquet . . . promised a friend of mine there . . . and they said I said Frick and Barr were a couple of crooks. 'Course I was still pretty sore by then, too.

That was pretty strong and the Cardinals were goin' East, and when we got to Brooklyn there I was suspended without pay and supposed to apologize. Frick had me up there and waved a lot of telegrams and said this was something terrible, look what all these people had to say, and I told him: "You must live out there and wait till I get some telegrams where I live" and I got some too and they all said I never said nothin' like he was a crook and I wouldn't sign no paper, but I was in a helluva spot and don't you forget it. Frisch was crazy. I got so many laughs listenin' to him I wouldn't a signed even if I'd been wrong and once I told him I had a notion to sue the National League for slander and Frank hit the ceiling. All he wanted me to do was get back in uniform.

Carl Hubbell

So Frick finally saw the error of his ways and I got back, but I had a great time not workin' for a few days. Night-clubbin' every night and a couple of times I ran into ol' Frisch and gave him a big cheery hello and I didn't pitch neither until I made sure I got paid for that time out. Well, it was June 9, 1936, when I put on the uniform and Hubbell'd beaten me May 19 in St. Louis. So here we were again and that Polo Grounds was a madhouse. I was afraid to come out of the dugout. Everybody was yellin' and throwin' things down at our bench and I waited until Frisch said: "You only got five minutes, you better warm up," so I dashed out there by home plate and warmed up and I was almost deaf from the noise when I got through.

I just went out there and pitched a cool three-hitter in the first game of a double-header and beat Hubbell 8-1 and I'd had a shutout only Durocher booted one near the end. Yes sir, ol' Jay Hanna Dean was just in ripe form that day and there was nobody gonna make a monkey outa him. I told that Durocher after the game, I said: "You oughta been more careful on that ball, I wanted to rub it in" and he said: "You rubbed it in enough, don't worry about it . . . the time to boot 'em, if you have to, is when you got runs to spare," which I guess is probably right.

Oh say, I'm forgettin' just about the best day of all, although there was nothin' like that series of 1934, but the afternoon I struck out 17 Cubs wasn't no ordinary day neither. That was July 30, 1933, and no-body's broken the record yet. Frisch had only been manager a couple of days . . . he took Street's job . . . and Guy Bush started against me and nothin' ever occurred to me 'bout this bein' a big day. Hell, Koenig doubled and Herman singled in the first inning and I was losin' 1-0 'fore we ever came to bat. Frisch had two guys warmin' up . . . he didn't know ol' Diz so well then.

We had the biggest crowd in two years in Sportsman's Park, almost 30,000, and I came in off the bench the end of the first inning and Frisch said: "I'm sendin' you to the bull pen next inning if you don't get better" and I told him: "Hell, you worry about gettin' a couple of runs. . . . I just didn't warm up good." Well, Bush was the only man I didn't strike out on the whole Cub team. I didn't know nothin' about it, understand, 'cause I was just a pitchin' away and Jimmy Wilson was catchin' and he never said a word and neither did anybody else. Hell, I might-a broke the record for consecutive strikeouts if somebody'd told me what I was doin', just like I could-a pitched a no-hit game in Brooklyn that time Paul did, 'cept nobody said nothin'. We'd a had a double no-hitter and no brothers ever did that before.

I struck out three men this day in the fifth and the eighth and ninth. Twelve of the 17 swung too at the last one. I never bothered with pitchin' high or low when I was good. . . . I just poured that ball in there, right over the plate. Koenig, Cuyler, Demaree, Hendricks and Jurges each struck out twice and I got that Babe Herman three times. He came up the fourth time and I just threw easy-like and he popped up for a change and he threw his bat away and yelled at me: "You must have a Bible in your pocket, you lucky bush so-and-so" but I didn't. It wuz only ol' Diz on one of his good days. If I'd known I was anywhere near a record I'd a struck out 20 anyway. . . . I just toyed with Bill Jurges a couple of times, figurin' he couldn't hit nothin' anyway.

Never forget the last inning. I struck out Hendricks and Jurges and that made it 16, I found out afterwards. Charley Grimm was makin' faces over on the bench and growlin' at me about bein' a big, dumb Oklahoma busher . . . hee-hee, I never forget he yelled at me: "You look like you live in one of those Oklahoma penthouses" . . . you know what that is, a pigpen with Venetian blinds, and I almost got laughin' and spoiled it all. He sent up somebody named Mosolf to pinch-hit and ol' Wilson met this guy before he got to the plate and I could hear him say: "This is a helluva place to stick you in, kid. . . . I wouldn't be surprised if the first one this dizzy moron threw was right at your ear. He don't like pinch hitters."

Mosolf never took his bat off his shoulder. Wilson'd give me the sign and then he'd straighten up and pound his glove right behind Mosolf's ear and the guy thought surer-'n-hell he was gonna get punctured and I just put three through there. Dean specials with the smoke curlin' off 'em. You'd a thought we won the World Series the way everybody pounded me on the back in the clubhouse and told me what I'd done and I was pretty proud too. But hell, there ain't no use in me tryin' to talk about a special day, 'cause every time I had a ball in my hand, and that suit on, it was my greatest day. The only time you ever feel bad is when you gotta quit.

And with every rose must grow a thorn. "I'd a given anything in the world to have beaten the Yanks that time," said Dean, referring to the World Series game in 1938, with the Cubs, when he led 3-2 into the eighth. "I didn't have nothin'. I had no license to beat anybody. But they could-a cut off my arm in that clubhouse if I'd a won that one. Diz just stubbed his toe one year too soon, in that All-Star game."

TY COBB

as told to
FRANCIS J. POWERS

Tyrus Raymond Cobb joined Detroit in 1905. Twelve times he led the league in batting and he holds the record of 4,191 hits. He stole 892 bases in his major league career.

There was little brotherly love toward the Detroit Tigers when our club arrived in Philadelphia on the morning of September 27, 1907. That old city was baseball mad; it was mad at the Tigers and, judging from my mail, very mad at me. The wildest race the six-year-old American League then had produced was nearing an end and the Athletics were leading the Tigers by a half game. It had been a four-way race all summer with the defending White Sox, Athletics, Tigers and Cleveland jumping in and out of first place. Now the chase had boiled down to a fight between the Tigers and Athletics and would be settled, practically, in the three-game series which was to open the next afternoon. For there were only two series remaining for each club.

The Tigers had come fast that year to be pennant contenders. Hughie Jennings, famous shortstop of the old Baltimore Orioles, had been brought up to manage the team and his "E-yah!" and grass-picking had made him a popular figure. I was on my way to winning my first batting championship and running the bases well. We had tremendous power with Claude Rossman on first and Sam Crawford in center field and I think those Tigers really were the first of the great slugging team that later made the American League synonymous with power. We had some great pitchers but particularly Wild Bill Donovan, one of the finest men ever in the game, who won 25 games and lost only four that season. Ours was a fighting, snarling team that neither asked nor gave gave quarter, patterned after the old Orioles of Jennings and John McGraw.

Philadelphia resented us as upstarts, for Connie Mack still had much of the same team which won the 1905 championship and then had lost to the Giants in that famous World's Series where every game was a shutout. The Mackmen had sensational pitchers in Chief Bender, Eddie Plank, Rube Waddell and Jack Coombs and were a solid defensive team. They were hot to reclaim the championship they had lost to the White Sox the previous season.

We won the first game of the series on September 28, when George Mullin outpitched Chief Bender, and went into first place by a half-game. Then it rained and a double-header was scheduled for September 30. There was the pennant. If we won, we had only Washington and St. Louis ahead while the Mackmen had a series with Cleveland, which stayed in the race until September 27, before getting to the Senators and the "Naps," as Cleveland was called in those days, were certain to give Philadelphia trouble.

When we went on the field to start play there were 30,000 fans looking on. There were 25,000 packed into old Columbia Park that had a capacity of 18,000, and the rest were crowded into windows and on the roofs of houses overlooking the field. There were fans, several rows deep, around the outfield, restrained by ropes and mounted police, and they weren't the least bit friendly. Before that afternoon was finished and we left the park in the autumn dusk with street lights aglow, I had experienced about every thrill that can come in baseball ... or so it seemed to a 19-year-old boy.

Jennings picked Donovan to pitch for the Tigers, leading with our ace, while Mr. Mack started Jimmy Dygert, a spitballer. Mack had

Eddie Plank, the southpaw who always was tough to beat, ready but decided to save him for the second game. You never saw and maybe never heard of a game like this one. It went 17 innings and took three hours and 50 minutes to play. It produced great pitching and poor pitching, long crashing hits and some of the most unusual incidents to be found outside the realm of fiction.

At the end of five innings, Philadelphia led us 7 to 1. The Athletics wasted no time in pounding Donovan. Topsy Hartsel opened with a single and stole second. Socks Seybold walked and Kid Nicholls sacrificed. Harry Davis' hit bounced off Charlie O'Leary's leg and into "Germany" Schaefer's hands but Seybold was safe at second and Hartsel scored. Murphy beat out an infield hit and then Seybold scored on Jimmy Collins' fly and Rube Oldring sent Davis home with a double into the crowd.

Connie Mack (left)

Jennings would have had any pitcher other than Donovan out of the game before that inning finished but Philadelphia was Bill's home town and his dad and relatives always came out to see him work so Hughie never took him out there. It looked like foolish sentiment at that moment, but proved to be a good policy three hours later.

For a few minutes in the second inning it seemed as if we would get them all back. Rossman singled and was safe at second when Dygert threw wild, after fielding Bill Coughlin's smash. Charlie Schmidt sacrificed and then O'Leary hit to the box. Dygert chased Rossman almost to the plate before throwing to Ossie Schreck and then Claude hit the Athletics' catcher so hard he dropped the ball. Dygert walked Donovan but then Rube Waddell came in, and with a pitch that broke from your waist to the ground, fanned the next two batters.

The Athletics got two more in the third, Davis hit a home run in the fifth and Collins and Oldring hit into the crowd for another score and there we were, behind six runs. But as I said before, this Tiger team was a fighting team and we moved back into the game with four runs in the seventh. Two walks and an error filled the bases and then Crawford drove into the left field crowd for two bases. Another scored on my infield out and Crawford raced home while Murphy was making a great play on Rossman. Then we were only two runs behind. The Athletics scored one in their half but we scored in the eighth and went into the ninth still two runs behind.

That ninth is one inning that always will remain bright in my memory. Crawford was on first when I came to bat and I hit a home run over the right fence to tie the score. Right then and there Mr. Mack forgot about saving Plank for the second game and Eddie rushed to the box and retired the next three batters. We went out in front in the 11th when I hit into the crowd after Rossman's single but we couldn't hold the lead and the Athletics tied it, largely because of a wild pitch, at 9-all.

Then the game settled down to a brilliant duel between Donovan and Plank but at the same time produced some of the greatest confusion ever seen on any field. In the 14th inning, Harry Davis hit a long fly to center field that Sam Crawford muffed and it was good for two bases. Our team claimed interference, for a policeman had stepped in front of Crawford as he was following the ball along the ropes. "Silk" O'Loughlin was umpiring behind the plate (there were only two umpires in a game at that time) and it was his play. Both teams gathered around O'Loughlin, arguing and snarling. Finally O'Loughlin called to Tommy Connolly, umpiring at first base: "Was there interference?" Without hesitation, Tommy called: "There was." So Davis was out and that was lucky for us, since Murphy followed with a single after a two-bagger had gone foul by inches.

Rube Waddell

During the argument with the umpires, Rossman and Monte Cross, one of the Athletics' reserve infielders, threw some punches and soon there were players and policemen all over the field. Rossman was tossed out of the game and that started a new argument. Ed Killian, a left-handed pitcher, finished the inning at first base and later Sam Crawford came in from the outfield to play the bag. After the game, Connie Mack was bitter in his denunciation of O'Loughlin and it was one of the few times when he really roasted an umpire.

There was no further scoring, although I got as far as third in our half of the 17th, and at the end of that inning the game was called with the score still 9-all. There was no second game that day; it never was played and the tie meant the championship for us. We left Philadelphia a half game in front and swept through Washington. The Athletics lost one to Cleveland and another to the Senators and we cinched the pennant in St. Louis ... Detroit's first since 1887, when it was in the old National League.

Although I had the thrill of hitting the homer that finally tied the score and making two runs, the star of that game was Bill Donovan. I don't recall a similar exhibition of pitching in my 25 years in the American League. Bill allowed eight runs in seven innings and only one in the next 10 and fanned 11. The modern generation doesn't remember Donovan, but there was a pitcher with great speed, a great curve and a great heart. I'd like to have been half as good a hurler myself and I used to practice pitching and imagine myself out there in a tight spot.

The Athletics made 20 hits that day to our 15 and we had 17 runners left on base to their 13. They made six errors, so during the long afternoon there was just about everything to be found in baseball.

It has been 36 years since that game was played and it is remarkable that any man on either team still should be actively participating in the game. But Connie Mack still manages the Athletics and at 82 is the one active connecting link between the old and present days of baseball. Many of the stars who played that day in Philadelphia's old wooden park are gone: Jennings, Donovan, Rossman, Schaefer, Coughlin and O'Leary of the Tigers and Schreck, Waddell, Plank and "Doc" Powers of the Athletics. But I still can see them hitting, throwing, running and fighting for the pennant as they did on September 30, 1907.

THE BOX SCORE
(September 30, 1907)

DETROIT	A.B.	R.	H.	P.	A.	PHILADELPHIA	A.B.	R.	H.	P.	A.
Jones, lf.	7	1	1	5	0	Hartsel, lf.	9	1	4	3	0
Schaefer, 2b.	9	1	3	3	6	Nicholls, ss.	6	1	2	4	9
Crawford, cf.-1b.	8	2	2	7	0	Seybold, rf.	6	2	1	1	0
Cobb, rf.	8	2	3	1	0	Davis, 1b.	8	3	3	19	1
Rossman, 1b.	7	1	2	13	2	Murphy, 2b.	7	1	4	2	6
Killian, 1b.	0	0	0	1	0	J. Collins, 3b.	7	1	1	3	3
Mullin, 1b.	1	0	0	0	0	Oldring, cf.	7	0	3	3	0
Downs, cf.	1	0	0	2	0	Schreck, c.	4	0	0	9	1
Coughlin, 3b.	7	0	0	1	3	Powers, c.	3	0	0	4	0
Schmidt, c.	1	0	0	3	1	Dygert, p.	0	0	0	0	0
Payne, c.	6	0	1	9	1	Waddell, p.	4	0	0	1	0
O'Leary, ss.	8	1	2	3	1	Plank, p.	4	0	1	2	1
Donovan, p.	7	1	1	3	7	E. Collins	1	0	1	0	0
Totals	70	9	15	51	21	Totals	66	9	20	51	21

E. Collins batted for Oldring in 17th.

DETROIT	0	1	0	0	0	0	4	1	2	0	1	0	0	0	0	0	0	—9
PHILADELPHIA	3	0	2	0	2	0	1	0	0	0	1	0	0	0	0	0	0	—9

Errors—Schmidt, Nicholls, Oldring, Schreck, Powers, Dygert (2). Two-base hits—Crawford, Cobb, O'Leary, Hartsel (3), Nicholls, Davis, J. Collins, Oldring (2). Home runs—Cobb, Davis. Hits—Off Dygert, 1 in 1-3 innings; off Waddell, 7 in 7 2-3 innings; off Plank, 7 in 8 innings. Sacrifice hits—Schmidt, Crawford, Nicholls (2), J. Collins, Powers. Stolen bases—Coughlin, O'Leary, Cobb, Hartsell. Left on bases—Detroit 17, Philadelphia 13. First base on balls—Off Donovan 3, off Dygert 1, off Waddell 1, off Plank 2. First base on errors—Detroit 4. Hit by pitcher—By Plank 1. Struck out—By Donovan 11, by Waddell 7, by Plank 3. Wild pitch—Donovan. Time—3:50. Umpires—O'Loughlin and Connolly.

HANS
WAGNER
as told to
CHET SMITH

John Henry "Hans" Wagner, whose name is written large in golden baseball letters, was rated the greatest shortstop of all time, and once was called "the best ball player that ever trod in spiked shoes" by John J. McGraw. Wagner was born February 24, 1874, at Mansfield, Pa., and at the age of 12 was toiling in the Pennsylvania coal mines. Got his first job in baseball with Mansfield of the Ohio State League when he was 21 and joined Louisville, then of the National League in 1897. Sold, with 14 other players, to Pittsburgh in 1900 and helped win three straight pennants. Still with the Pirates as coach.

When a fellow has played 2,785 games over a span of 21 years it's not the easiest thing in the world to pick out a single contest and say it was his best or that it gave him his biggest thrill. But I was never sharper than in the last game of the World Series our Pirates played with the Detroit Tigers of 1909, and I never walked off any field feeling happier.

It was the afternoon of October 16 and not only a big day for me but for all the sport fans, for on that same afternoon Big Jack Johnson, heavyweight prize-fight champion, knocked out Stanley Ketchel in the 12th round of their battle in San Francisco to retain his crown.

I regard that final game with the Bengals as tops because it meant the end of a grand fight against a bunch of real fighters. I'm still willing to testify that the club of Hughie Jennings and Ty Cobb, of "Wahoo Sam" Crawford and Donie Bush, of Davy Jones and George Moriarity, was a holy terror. And it tickles my vanity to think the Pirates outbattled and defeated them.

Cobb stole two bases in the series, but I was lucky and got six. Cobb made six hits, I made eight.

Ask Ty what happened the day he stood on first and yelled at me, "Hey, Kraut Head, I'm comin' down on the next pitch." I told him to come ahead, and by golly, he did. But George Gibson, our catcher, laid the ball perfect, right in my glove and I stuck it on Ty as he came in. I guess I wasn't too easy about it, 'cause it took three stitches to sew up his lip. That was the kind of a series it was from start to finish. Fred Clarke, our manager, told us we'd better sharpen our spikes since the Tigers would be sure to, and we took him at his word. We were sorta rough, too, I guess.

Cobb surprised the Pirates by playing an unusually clean series, but some of the others weren't so careful.

The trouble started in the first game. Both sides had their jockeys warmed up. The Tigers let us have it and we gave it back to 'em with interest. There was a jawing match on nearly every pitch, and it was a good thing we had two of the greatest umpires who ever worked— Bill Klem and "Silk" O'Loughlin. They were young fellows then, but they knew their business and kept us in line. At least there weren't any riots.

In that first game, Fred Clarke hit a home run off Big George Mullin, who was Detroit's best pitcher that year. I followed Clarke at the

Fred Clarke

plate, and I could see that Mullin was boiling, and anxious to get back at us. I always stood pretty far away from the plate, but this time took every inch I could, figuring Mullin would throw at me. I wasn't wrong. He laid his fast ball right in my ribs. Of course, you can't say a thing like that is deliberate, but our boys reckoned it was, and from that minute the rough-housing was on.

We came into the final game tied up at three apiece. It was played in Detroit, and the night before, the Tiger rooters hired two or three bands to play in front of our hotel and keep us awake, but Clarke fooled 'em by taking us all out to a tavern along the lake shore.

We knew our pitcher was going to be Babe Adams, the kid who had won two of our three victories. Babe was hardly old enough to shave, but Clarke had a hunch on him all along. I'll never forget the look on Adams' face when I told him Clarke wanted him to pitch the opener. He asked me if I wasn't fooling and I told him I wasn't and he hadn't better fool, either, when he got on the mound. What a job he did for us.

I guess I don't have to tell you what the feeling was that last day. "Wild Bill" Donovan, who started for the Tigers, lived up to his name and we got two runs off him in the second. Mullin came in to pitch in the fourth and couldn't find the plate, either. There were two

Wild Bill Donovan

walks and two singles, giving us two more. In the sixth I got my only hit, but it was a three-bagger that drove in Clarke and Tommy Leach, and I kept coming and crossed the plate when Davey Jones made a bad throw from the outfield. We certainly didn't need the run we picked up in the seventh, but it made us eight, and with Adams pitching perfect ball that was the score 8 to 0. But it's far from being the whole story.

On my hit Jones kicked the ball into the overflow crowd, trying to hold it to a double under the ground rules, but O'Loughlin saw him and wouldn't allow it. Another time there was a close play at first and the Tiger runner hit Bill Abstein, our first baseman, in the stomach with his fist. Abstein folded up and Ham Hyatt had to take his place. Another Tiger slid into second and cut Jack Miller on the head and leg. Bobby Byrne, our third baseman, banged into Moriarity so hard that Bobby had to leave the field with a broken ankle, and George, who concealed his injury until the next inning, went to the doctor to have 11 stitches put in his knee. Talk about "bean balls"—they were flying around everybody's head all afternoon.

THE BOX SCORE

(*October 16, 1909*)

PITTSBURGH	R.	H.	P.	A.	DETROIT	R.	H.	P.	A.
Byrne, 3b.	0	0	0	0	D. Jones, lf.	0	1	3	0
Hyatt, cf.	1	0	0	0	Bush, ss.	0	0	3	5
Leach, cf.-3b.	2	2	4	2	Cobb, rf.	0	0	1	0
Clarke, lf.	2	0	5	0	Moriarty, 3b.	0	1	1	0
Wagner, ss.	1	1	3	3	O'Leary, 3b.	0	0	1	1
Miller, 2b.	0	3	3	0	Delehanty, 2b.	0	2	2	3
Abstein, 1b.	1	1	10	0	Crawford, cf.	0	0	4	0
Wilson, rf.	1	0	0	0	T. Jones, 1b.	0	1	9	0
Gibson, c	0	2	2	1	Schmidt, c.	0	1	3	0
Adams, p.	0	0	0	4	Donovan, p.	0	0	0	1
					Mullin, p.	0	0	0	2
Totals	8	9	27	10	Totals	0	6	27	13

PITTSBURGH	0	2	0	2	0	3	0	1	0 — 8
DETROIT	0	0	0	0	0	0	0	0	0 — 0

Error—D. Jones. Hits—Off Donovan, 2 in 3 innings. Three-base hit—Wagner. Two-base hits—Moriarty, Abstein, Leach, Gibson, Schmidt, Miller, Delehanty. Sacrifice hits—Leach. Stolen Bases—Clarke (2), Abstein, Miller. Hit by pitched ball—Byrne, Bush. Struck out—By Adams 1, Mullin 1. Base on balls—Off Adams 1, Donovan 6, Mullin 4. Double play—Bush to Schmidt to Bush. Umpires—O'Loughlin and Klem.

KING CARL
HUBBELL

as told to
JOHN P. CARMICHAEL

"King Carl" Hubbell was one of the most efficient left-handers in the majors, and to prove it the records show he won 253 and lost 154 in 16 years with the New York Giants. Born at Carthage, Mo., on June 22, 1903, started baseball career with Cushing, Okla., in 1923. Mastered the screwball to the point where it was compared to the fadeaway of the immortal Christy Mathewson.

I can remember Frankie Frisch coming off the field behind me at the end of the third inning, grunting to Bill Terry: "I could play second base 15 more years behind that guy. He doesn't need any help. He does it all by himself." Then we hit the bench, and Terry slapped me on the arm and said: "That's pitching, boy!" and Gabby Hartnett let his mask fall down and yelled at the American League dugout: "We gotta look at that all season," and I was pretty happy.

As far as control and "stuff" is concerned, I never had any more in my life than for that All-Star game in 1934. But I never was a strikeout pitcher like Bob Feller or "Dizzy" Dean or "Dazzy" Vance. My style of pitching was to make the other team hit the ball, but on the ground. It was as big a surprise to me to strike out all those fellows as it probably was to them. Before the game, Hartnett and I went down the lineup ... Gehringer, Manush, Ruth, Gehrig, Foxx, Simmons, Cronin, Dickey and Gomez. There wasn't a pitcher they'd ever faced that they hadn't belted one off him somewhere, sometime.

We couldn't discuss weaknesses ... they didn't have any, except Gomez. Finally Gabby said: "We'll waste everything except the screwball. Get that over, but keep your fast ball and hook outside. We can't let 'em hit in the air." So that's the way we started. I knew I had only three innings to work and could bear down on every pitch.

They talk about those All-Star games being exhibition affairs and maybe they are, but I've seen very few players in my life who didn't want to win, no matter whom they were playing or what for. If I'm playing cards for pennies, I want to win. How can you feel any other way? Besides, there were 50,000 fans or more there, and they wanted to see the best you've got. There was an obligation to the people, as well as to ourselves, to go all out. I can recall walking out to the hill in the Polo Grounds that day and looking around the stands and thinking to myself: "Hub, they want to see what you've got."

Gehringer was first up and Hartnett called for a waste ball just so I'd get the feel of the first pitch. It was a little too close, and Charley singled. Down from one of the stands came a yell: "Take him out!"

I had to laugh.

Terry took a couple of steps off first and hollered: "That's all right," and there was Manush at the plate. If I recollect rightly, I got two strikes on him, but then he refused to swing any more, and I lost him. He walked. This time Terry and Frisch and "Pie" Traynor and Travis Jackson all came over to the mound and began worrying. "Are you all right?" Bill asked me. I assured him I was. I could hear more than one voice now from the stands: "Take him out before it's too late."

Well, I could imagine how they felt with two on, nobody out and Ruth at bat. To strike him out was the last thought in my mind. The thing was to make him hit on the ground. He wasn't too fast, as you

Jimmy Foxx

Lou Gehrig

know, and he'd be a cinch to double. He never took the bat off his
shoulder. You could have pushed me over with your little finger. I
fed him three straight screwballs, all over the plate, after wasting a
fast ball, and he stood there. I can see him looking at the umpire on
"You're out," and he wasn't mad. He just didn't believe it, and Hartnett
was laughing when he threw the ball back.

So up came Gehrig. He was a sharp hitter. You could double him,
too, now and then, if the ball was hit hard and straight at an infielder.
That's what we hoped he'd do, at best. Striking out Ruth and Gehrig
in succession was too big an order. By golly, he fanned . . . and on four
pitches. He swung at the last screwball, and you should have heard
that crowd. I felt a lot easier then, and even when Gehringer and
Manush pulled a double steal and got to third and second, with Foxx
up, I looked down at Hartnett and caught the screwball sign, and
Jimmy missed. We were really trying to strike Foxx out, with two
already gone, and Gabby didn't bother to waste any pitches. I threw
three more screwballs, and he went down swinging. We had set down
the side on 12 pitches, and then Frisch hit a homer in our half of the
first, and we were ahead.

It was funny, when I thought of it afterwards, how Ruth and Gehrig
looked as they stood there. The Babe must have been waiting for me

to get the ball up a little so he could get his bat under it. He always was trying for that one big shot at the stands, and anything around his knees, especially a twisting ball, didn't let him get any leverage. Gehrig apparently decided to take one swing at least and he beat down at the pitch, figuring to take a chance on being doubled if he could get a piece of the ball. He whispered something to Foxx as Jim got up from the batter's circle and while I didn't hear it, I found out later he said: "You might as well cut . . . it won't get any higher." At least Foxx wasted no time.

THE BOX SCORE
(*July 10, 1934*)

NATIONAL LEAGUE	A.B.	R.	H.	P.	A.
Frisch, 2b.	3	3	2	0	1
W. Herman, 2b.	2	0	1	0	1
Traynor, 3b.	5	2	2	1	0
Medwick, lf.	2	1	1	0	0
Klein, lf.	3	0	1	1	0
Cuyler, rf.	2	0	0	2	0
Ott, rf.	2	0	0	0	1
Berger, cf.	2	0	0	0	0
P. Waner, cf.	2	0	0	1	0
Terry, 1b.	3	0	1	4	0
Jackson, ss.	2	0	0	0	1
Vaughan, ss.	2	0	0	4	0
Hartnett, c.	2	0	0	9	0
Lopez, c.	2	0	0	5	1
Hubbell, p.	0	0	0	0	0
Warneke, p.	0	0	0	0	0
Mungo, p.	0	0	0	0	0
Martin	0	1	0	0	0
J. Dean, p.	1	0	0	0	0
Frankhouse, p.	1	0	0	0	0
Totals	36	7	8	27	5

AMERICAN LEAGUE	A.B.	R.	H.	P.	A.
Gehringer, 2b.	3	0	2	2	1
Manush, lf.	2	0	0	0	0
Ruffing, p.	1	0	1	0	0
Harder, p.	2	0	0	1	0
Ruth, rf.	2	1	0	0	0
Chapman, rf.	2	0	1	0	1
Gehrig, 1b.	4	1	0	11	1
Foxx, 3b.	5	1	2	1	2
Simmons, cf.-lf.	5	3	3	3	0
Cronin, ss.	5	1	2	2	8
Dickey, c.	2	1	1	4	0
Cochrane, c.	1	0	0	1	1
Gomez, p.	1	0	0	0	0
Averill, cf.	4	1	2	1	0
West, cf.	0	0	0	1	0
Totals	39	9	14	27	14

W. Herman batted for Hubbell in 3rd and took Frisch's place in 7th.
Klein batted for Medwick in 5th.
Ott batted for Cuyler in 5th.
P. Waner batted for Berger in 5th.
Vaughan batted for Jackson in 5th.
Martin batted for Mungo in 5th.

Cochrane ran for Dickey in 6th.
Averill batted for Gomez in 4th.

```
AMERICAN LEAGUE  0   0   0   2   6   1   0   0   0 — 9
NATIONAL LEAGUE  1   0   3   0   3   0   0   0   0 — 7
```

Errors—Berger, Gehrig. Runs batted in—Frisch, Medwick (3), Cronin (2), Averill (3), Foxx, Simmons, Ruffing (2), Traynor, Klein. Two-base hits—Simmons (2), Averill, Cronin, Foxx, W. Herman. Three-base hits—Averill, Chapman. Home runs—Frisch, Medwick. Stolen bases—Gehringer, Manush, Traynor, Ott. Double play—Lopez and Vaughan. Bases on balls—Off Hubbell 2, Gomez 1, Warneke 3, Mungo 2, Ruffing 1. J. Dean 1, Harder 1, Frankhouse 1. Struck out—By Hubbell 6, Gomez 3, Warneke 1, Mungo 1, Harder 2, J. Dean 4. Pitching records—Hubbell 2 hits, 0 runs in three innings; Warneke, 3 hits, 2 runs in 1 (none out in fifth); Mungo, 4 hits, 6 runs in 1; J. Dean, 5 hits, 1 run in 3; Gomez, 3 hits, 4 runs in 3; Ruffing, 4 hits, 2 runs in 1 (none out in fifth). Left on bases—American League —12. National League—5. Winning pitcher—Harder. Losing pitcher—Mungo. Umpires— Pittman (N. L.); Moriarty (A. L.); Owens (A. L.); Stark (N. L.). Time of game—2:44.

Of course the second inning was easier because Simmons and Cronin both struck out with nobody on base and then I got too close to Dickey and he singled. Simmons and Foxx, incidentally, both went down swinging and I know every pitch to them was good enough to hit at and those they missed had a big hunk of the plate. Once Hartnett kinda shook his head at me as if to say I was getting too good. After Dickey came Gomez and as he walked into the box he looked down at Gabby and said: "You are now looking at a man whose batting average is .104. What the hell am I doing up here?" He was easy after all those other guys and we were back on the bench again.

We were all feeling pretty good by this time and Traynor began counting on his fingers: "Ruth, Gehrig, Foxx, Simmons, Cronin! Hey, Hub, do you put anything on the ball?" Terry came over to see how my arm was, but it never was stronger.' I walked one man in the third ... don't remember who it was ... but this time Ruth hit one on the ground and we were still all right. You could hear him puff when he swung. That was all for me. Afterwards, they got six runs in the fifth and licked us, but for three innings I had the greatest day in my life. One of the writers who kept track told me that I'd pitched 27 strikes and 21 balls to 13 men and only five pitches were hit in fair territory.

CHARLES GRIMM
as told to
HAL TOTTEN

Charles John Grimm was famed for his amazing defensive play around first base with Pittsburgh and Chicago in the National League, although he made his big league debut with the Athletics in 1916. Joined the Pirates in 1919 and went to the Cubs in 1925, eventually becoming manager in 1932. Left Chicago to take over the Milwaukee Brewers in 1941. Returned as Cub manager May 5, 1944. Born in St. Louis on August 28, 1899, and still possesses a showplace country home at Normandy, Mo.

I'll pick a day in 1932 to talk about. One of the greatest events of my life occurred that year. On August 2, I was appointed manager of the Cubs. And if that isn't enough to make 1932 stand out by itself in my life, it'll do until something better comes along.

Our club had moved into first place during the first month of the season and we'd stayed there until along about the middle of July. Then Pittsburgh took over and we dropped to second.

We had an idea all along that we were good enough to win that pennant, but the going had been tough in spots. However, we were in

31

good position. The Cubs played their first series for me in Philadelphia and we won three out of four. We went to New York and knocked off two out of three and we were pretty near the top.

So we moved to Pittsburgh for a single game before going to St. Louis. We were only a half a game out with a chance to get back on top. Guy Bush pitched a whale of a game that day and we won out in the 10th, 3 to 2. That put us in first place, and they never got us out of there.

Down in St. Louis we won two out of three again, and that gave us eight out of 11 since the first of the month.

We had a terrific series at home with Boston. One game went 19 innings and another 15. But we won three out of four. Next came the Phillies and we took them four straight. Three more from the Dodgers. And then came our big test—the New York Giants.

Well, the first day we beat 'em a double header. Then we took two more, and we felt we were really gonna go places. The fifth game was the big one. If we swept this series, we were certain nothing could stop us. We went out there that day feeling that this was the most important game of all—the biggest one of the season. A win here, and we'd show our heels to everybody. That day was the day.

I started right out to give 'em the best we had. Our pitcher was Lon Warneke. But it just wasn't Warneke's day. He walked Joe Moore. Then Hughie Critz singled to right-center and Moore was on third. Up came Terry. The boys on the bench were giving him both barrels. And that Big Lug drives one clear to the fence between Johnny Moore and Kiki Cuyler for a triple. Two runs came home.

Ott hit one toward right. Billy Herman got his glove on it but couldn't hold it, so it went for a hit and Terry scored. Freddie Lindstrom lined one over Herman's head for another single. And that was all for Lon.

Bud Tinning at that time was our ace relief pitcher. Time and again he'd stepped in and stopped many a rally. He had done practically all our relieving for us. So I figured if we were going to lose, we'd lose with our best.

Bud went in and he stopped that rally cold—got the next three men. They picked up another run in the second when Critz came through again—this time with a double—and Terry drove him in with a single. Maybe the fans were down a little by then, but we weren't. The boys were still talking it up—never quiet a minute.

We started rolling in the third. Herman scratched a hit past Terry and Cuyler smashed one clear over Lindstrom's head in center for three bases to score him. Ole Riggs Stephenson drove Ki across with a double to the wall in left-center. That made it 4 to 2. The Giants got another in the fourth on a single by Vergez, a couple of infield outs and an error.

In the last half Mark Koenig slashed one down the right-field line for a triple. Now—Tinning had been going good but I had Bob Smith ready, and he'd shut the Giants out on Saturday. So I sent Hemsley up to bat for Bud. Rollie was thrown out, but we got the run home. We were still two runs behind. Still the boys were yelling their heads off.

It went that way until the eighth inning. Stephenson walked and with two out I went up there bound and determined to get that base hit—I was praying I could tie into one. Well, I did—a

Bill Terry

Kiki Cuyler

double—and Stevie scored. I had the tying run on second, so I called Stan Hack out to run for me. Then I began to look for some speed at the plate, as well as power, so I sent Marvin Gudat up to bat for Gabby. Marv had been a great pinch hitter for us all year—drove in run after run. But this time they got him out.

Then came the ninth. Koenig was out, but Demaree batted for Smith and singled. Herman flied out, but English singled to right. Cuyler got his fourth hit of the day—a single to center to tie the score. Just about then it started to rain a little. Terry jerked Fitzsimmons and sent in Herman Bell. He walked Stevie to fill the bases and Critz made a great play to get Moore just as Woody was crossing the plate.

This time I sent in Guy Bush. He had been a great clutch pitcher for us—as I said, he pitched us into first place in Pittsburgh. But Bush had a helluva time. He walked Marshall and hit Vergez. It was raining hard when O'Farrell came to bat for Bell and darned if Joe didn't hit him, too. Moore singled and the bases still were full. Bush made a wild pitch and Vergez scored and the runners moved up. Then that pesky little Critz came up and got his fourth hit—a single to center to score two more runs.

I began to look for another pitcher. Grimes was the number one man, but he'd worked so hard in one game of the series that I didn't want to warm him up. So I sent out good old LeRoy Herrmann with that freak underhand delivery of his. While he was getting ready Terry got another hit. But Stevie made a great recovery, threw to English, and his relay cut down Critz at the plate. Then I called in Herrmann. And we had rain, rain, and more rain! He got 'em out when Ott flied to Stevie.

I'll admit that when they got those runs, we didn't have a word to say. But that play at the plate gave us heart. When the boys came in Woody English let out a yell.

"Come on," he hollered, "we've still got our big inning left. Let's go out and beat 'em."

They sent old Sam Gibson in—and he got the first two men out. But Koenig crashed the next pitch over the right-field wall.

Then came one of the strangest plays of the year—and perhaps the one that won us the pennant. Taylor had gone in to catch for us in the eighth and naturally had my place in the batting order—sixth. Demaree had batted for Smith in the ninth and so our pitcher was still batting ninth.

For some reason—I'll never know why—Taylor went up to bat when it was Herrmann's turn. And instead of waiting until he had done something and then protesting a man batting out of turn—which they should have done—Terry and the Giants rushed the plate and argued that he was in the wrong place. Umpire Magerkurth heard 'em out, and then ruled that Taylor could bat. And he singled.

THE BOX SCORE
(*August 31, 1932*)

NEW YORK	A.B.	R.	H.	P.	A.
Joe Moore, lf.	5	2	1	4	0
Critz, 2b.	6	2	4	1	5
Terry, 1b.	6	1	5	13	0
Ott, rf.	6	0	2	2	0
Lindstrom, cf.	5	0	1	2	0
Hogan, c.	5	0	0	3	1
Marshall, ss.	4	1	1	3	5
Vergez, 3b.	4	2	2	1	3
Fitzsimmons, p.	2	0	0	0	2
Bell, p.	0	0	0	0	0
O'Farrell	0	1	0	0	0
Gibson, p.	0	0	0	0	0
Totals	43	9	16	*29	16

CUBS	A.B.	R.	H.	P.	A.
Herman, 2b.	6	2	3	4	5
English, 3b.	6	1	2	0	3
Cuyler, rf.	6	2	5	2	1
Stephenson, lf.	3	1	1	7	2
John Moore, cf.	5	0	0	2	0
Grimm, 1b.	4	0	3	11	1
Hack	0	0	0	0	0
Taylor, c.	1	1	1	1	0
Hartnett, c.	2	0	0	1	0
Gudat, 1b.	2	0	0	1	0
Koenig, ss.	5	2	2	1	3
Warneke, p.	0	0	0	0	0
Tinning, p.	1	0	0	0	2
Hemsley	1	0	0	0	0
Smith, p.	1	0	1	0	3
Demaree	1	1	1	6	0
Bush, p.	0	0	0	0	0
Herrmann, p.	0	0	0	0	0
Jurges	1	0	0	0	0
Totals	45	10	19	30	20

* Two out when winning run was scored.
O'Farrell batted for Bell in 10th.

Hack ran for Grimm in 8th.
Hemsley batted for Tinning in 4th.
Demaree batted for Smith in 9th.
Jurges batted for Herrmann in 10th.

NEW YORK	3	1	0	1	0	0	0	0	0	4 — 9
CUBS	0	0	2	1	0	0	0	1	1	5 — 10

Errors—Koenig, Tinning. Runs batted in—Terry (3), Ott, Cuyler (5), Stephenson, Hemsley, Grimm, Joe Moore, Critz (2), Koenig, English. Two-base hits—Critz, Stephenson, Grimm. Three-base hits—Terry, Cuyler, Koenig. Home runs—Koenig, Cuyler. Sacrifices—Fitzsimmons (2). Double plays—Herman to Koenig to Grimm, Critz to Marshall to Terry, Fitzsimmons to Marshall to Terry, Hogan to Marshall to Terry; Stephenson to Koenig to Taylor. Left on bases—New York 10, Chicago 9. Bases on balls—Off Warneke 1, Fitzsimmons, 2; Bell, 1; Bush 1. Struck out—By Fitzsimmons, 3; Smith, 1. Hits—Off Warneke, 4 in no innings; Fitzsimmons, 14 in 8 1-3 innings; Tinning, 4 in 4; Bell, none in 2-3; Smith, 5 in 5; Gibson, 5 in 2-3; Bush, 2 in none; Herrmann, 1 in 1. Hit by pitcher—By Bush 2. Wild pitches—Fitzsimmons, Bush. Winning pitcher—Herrmann. Losing pitcher—Gibson. Umpires—Magerkurth and Quigley. Time—2:15.

Then again they should have argued. But maybe because it was raining or something, the Giants figured their lead was safe and they wanted to get it over, so they said nothing. Herman singled. Somebody yelled at Gibson: "You'd better get this ball game over before Cuyler comes up." You see, Cuyler used to hit him like he owned him—he just couldn't get him out. Well, English singled, Taylor scored—and there was Cuyler at the plate. Everybody on the bench was up now. "Hey, Gibson," they yelled. "Here's Cuyler. What are you going to do with him!"

Well, Gibson pitched; and the ball started out toward right center in the rain. Farther and farther it went! Higher and higher! Lindstrom climbed the fence. He reached for it. but it dropped over his head and it went into the bleachers for a home run. We spotted 'em four runs in the 10th, and then scored five ourselves to win. And we went into the clubhouse, a happy bunch of guys, soaking wet.

And just to keep the record clear—Taylor did bat out of turn—and I, as manager of the ball club, didn't know it, either.

Herman Bell

Johnny Evers, Fred Merkle, and Al Bridwell

JOHNNY EVERS

as told to

JOHN P. CARMICHAEL

*Johnny Evers, one of the game's greatest infielders,
began career with Cubs in 1904. Went to Braves in 1914
and was with Phils in 1917 when his playing days ended.
Managed Cubs in 1921 and White Sox in 1924.*

It is 36 years now since the day Fred Merkle didn't touch second,
but it could be 135 and I'd never forget what happened. I can't
get around much any more with this bum leg, so sitting in this chair
day after day there's nothing much to do but live in the past. You
know most of the stories afterward said Umpire Hank O'Day walked
off the field without saying a word as the fans came down on the diamond under the impression New York had won 2-1. But he didn't. He
stayed right there and waited for me to make the play and told me the
Giant run didn't count.

The Merkle affair occurred Sept. 23, 1908, but it was 19 days earlier,
at Pittsburgh, that we really won the game at New York. The same play
came up against the Pirates and O'Day was the umpire then too.
Mordecai Brown was pitching for the Cubs and he'd shut out the Bucs
three straight times earlier in the season. This day they hadn't scored

off him again in nine innings, making it 36 frames he'd held them run-less, but we couldn't get anything off Vic Willis either. In the 10th we got beat.

Fred Clarke was on third, Wagner on second and Gill on first with Wilson at the plate. Wilson singled to center and Jimmy Slagle threw the ball back to the infield as Clarke, of course, went on home. But Gill didn't go to second. He ran off the field. I got the ball and hollered to O'Day to look. He wouldn't. I stood on second and yelled that the run didn't count ... that Gill was the third out, but Hank refused to listen. "Clarke scored before the out could have been made," he told Manager Frank Chance and pushed his way to the dressing room.

Ol' Hank was mad at me anyway for an argument we'd had in St. Louis a few weeks before and you could tell that his whole attitude was he'd be damned if that little squirt Evers was going to get him in another jam. But just the same he was a good umpire ... if you didn't tell him so too often ... and he realized later what had happened and in the long run we got the break when we needed it most in New York. As everybody knows, we couldn't have won the pennant if we hadn't.

There were only about 10 points between the Giants and us by Sept. 23. This was the last game of the series and McGraw sent Christy Mathewson to the mound. Jack Pfiester was pitching for us. O'Day and Bob Emslie were the umpires and there were 25,000 fans there easily. In the fifth inning we got in front when Joe Tinker hit a home run. It really was just a line drive to the outfield but Donlin tried to make a shoestring catch and the ball rolled past him and Joe got all the way around. In the next inning the Giants tied it as Herzog beat out a slow roller to Steinfeldt at third and got to second when Harry made a bad throw to first. Up came Donlin and squared himself for missing Tinker's ball with a single that scored Herzog.

So that's the way we stood going into the ninth and to show you what a pitcher's battle it was, Tinker handled 14 chances that game and I had 11 which was as many as I had in any game all season. Matty set us down one-two-three in our half and New York put on a rally. With one out, Devlin singled and McCormick slashed one right at me. It was just slow enough so the best Tinker and I could do was to get Devlin at second. Still there were two gone even if McCormick was safe. Up came Merkle. He was just a rookie at that time and probably wouldn't have been playing if we hadn't had a southpaw working, but McGraw wanted to get as much right-handed hitting into his lineup as possible and anyway Fred Tenny had a bum ankle and could use extra rest, so Merkle was at first.

Well, he singled and McCormick went to third. Al Bridwell was the next hitter and he singled to center. That's where the fun began.

Artie Hofman threw the ball in as McCormick went home and Merkle jogged halfway to second. I had my eye on him, saw him stop, glance around at the fans pouring out of their seats, and start for the clubhouse beyond right field. Hofman's throw had gone over Tinker's head and rolled over to where Joe McGinnity, the Giant pitcher, was standing. Joe'd been coaching on third and he knew what was in our minds as Tinker and I raced for the ball. He got it first, but before he could get rid of the thing, Joe and I had him and we wrestled around there for what seemed to be five minutes. Of course it wasn't.

We grabbed for his hands to make sure he wouldn't heave the ball away but he broke loose and tossed it into the crowd. I can see the fellow who caught it yet...a tall, stringy middle-aged gent with a brown bowler hat on. Steinfeldt and Floyd Kroh, a young pitcher we'd added to our staff during the summer, raced after him. "Gimme the ball for just a minute," Steinfeldt begged him. "I'll bring it right back." The guy wouldn't let go and suddenly Kroh solved the problem. He hit the customer right on top of that stiff hat, drove it down over his eyes and as the gent folded up, the ball fell free and Kroh got it. I was yelling and waving my hands out by second base and Tinker relayed it over to me and I stepped on the bag and made sure O'Day saw me. As I said before, he was waiting for that very play...he remembered the Pittsburgh game...and he said: "The run does not count." Then he walked away. But he made no attempt to continue the game in the confusion.

Joe McGinnity

Umpire Hank O'Day

There was hell a-poppin' after that. Emslie refused to take a stand for or against O'Day. "I didn't see the play," he insisted and that's all he'd say. Mathewson and a couple of the Giants dashed for the clubhouse and tried to get Merkle back to second, but I was standing there with the ball before they got him out the door. They saw it was too late, although McGraw kept hollering that the Giants had won and the fans, who only knew the Cubs were trying to pull off some trick, gave us a good going over. A couple of park "fly cops" which McGraw had scattered around to "protect" the visiting players took a few pokes at Chance under the guise of keeping the crowd back and there must have been five fist fights going on as we finally got out of there.

Inside the clubhouse we made a horrible discovery. It was the custom of the club in those days for some player, usually a pitcher, who was sure of not seeing service during the game, to take charge of a bag in which we placed our money and valuables for safekeeping while in uniform. Kroh had been the man in charge this day and he'd left the bag near the bench while he went in pursuit of the ball. Then he'd forgotten all about it, and of course it was gone when he tried to find it. We lost about $200 in cash and $5,000 in jewelry.

But at least we won the game, eventually . . . that is we played it off Oct. 8 and Brown won, 4-2. President Harry Pulliam of the league backed O'Day in his decision, but the Giants protested so vigorously and long that the board of directors finally had to settle matters. I'm not so sure they would have decided in our favor at that, but Jack Ryder, the old Cincinnati writer, who is dead now, broke into the meeting and delivered a helluva speech in our favor, claiming there was no choice but to play the game over and vowing that the league would make itself a laughingstock if it let the Giants get away with a pennant on a bonehead play.

So it turned out all right for us, but one day during the off-season I ran into Roger Bresnahan, who caught Matty that afternoon, and the Giant catcher showed me a medal. It was one of 28 which John T. Brush, Giant owner, had struck off for each member of the team and showed a ballplayer with a bat in his hand and another throwing a ball and the inscription read:

"The Real Champions, 1908."

THE BOX SCORE
(September 23, 1908)

CHICAGO	R.	H.	P.	A.	NEW YORK	R.	H.	P.	A.
Hayden, rf.	0	0	1	0	Herzog, 2b.	1	1	1	1
Evers, 2b.	0	1	4	7	Bresnahan, c.	0	0	10	0
Schulte, lf.	0	0	1	0	Donlin, rf.	0	1	2	0
Chance, 1b.	0	1	11	1	Seymour, cf.	0	1	1	0
Steinfeldt, 3b.	0	0	1	0	Devlin, 3b.	0	2	0	2
Hofman, cf.	0	1	0	0	McCormick, lf.	0	0	1	0
Tinker, ss.	1	1	8	6	Merkle, 1b.	0	1	10	1
Kling, c.	0	1	0	1	Bridwell, ss.	0	0	2	8
Pfiester, p.	0	0	1	0	Mathewson, p.	0	0	0	2
Totals	1	5	27	15	Totals	1	6	27	14

NEW YORK	0	0	0	0	1	0	0	0	0 — 1
CHICAGO	0	0	0	1	0	0	0	0	0 — 1

Errors—Steinfeldt, Tinker (2). Home run—Tinker. Sacrifice hits—Steinfeldt, Bresnahan. Double plays—Tinker to Chance (2), Evers to Chance, Mathewson to Bridwell to Merkle. Bases on balls—Off Pfiester 2. Hit by pitcher—By Pfiester 1. Struck out—By Mathewson 9. Time—1:30. Umpires—O'Day and Emslie.

BUCK WEAVER

as told to
HAL TOTTEN

George "Buck" Weaver was ranked as the greatest third baseman of all time, although he was also a short-stop with the White Sox. Came up from San Francisco in 1912 and "retired" in 1920, after a history as one of the game's daredevils.

Back in the winter of 1913 and '14, Charles Comiskey and John McGraw took a couple of ball teams around the world. I was on one of them and we were playin' for keeps—ridin' each other and there were plenty of hard feelin's.

Well, we hit Cairo, Egypt, and things got so bad we almost had a free-for-all right there. We got to ridin' Fred Merkle and Fred Snodgrass and callin' 'em boneheads and the whole National League team got up in arms about it. Finally McGraw got in his two-bits' worth— and that's the start of my story.

He started tellin' us off—and when McGraw told somebody off, they usually stayed told. But not us.

"Go-wan," I yelped at McGraw. "You got a powder-puff ball club. You're yellow. You ain't got the guts of a canary bird. I only hope we get you guys in a World Series. Then we'll show you what a real fightin' ball club is—you and your yellowbellies."

Now, remember—I'm just 28 years old. And here I am pullin' that kind of stuff on McGraw. Well, we ironed out that trouble. But none of us forgot about it. And you can bet McGraw didn't, either. So we go along and we get to the 1917 season. We win the pennant in the American League and the Giants win the National. It looks like we're due for the big blowoff.

Well, we were ready for 'em. You know, before you go into a World Series, you scout the other club mighty careful—and I don't mean just how to pitch to 'em and how to play 'em, either. You go over every man on the club and you figure which ones you can ride and which ones you can't. There's no use ridin' a guy if it only makes him play harder and better. So you want to know which ones to get "on" and which ones to lay off of.

We had our meetin' before the first game and we had everyone on that Giant team pegged. We knew just how to handle all of 'em. Then,

Art Fletcher

John McGraw

just before we went out on the field, somebody had an idea. We knew they were expectin' a pretty rough ridin'. They probably were set for it and gunnin' for us. So why not give 'em a surprise—take 'em unawares? We agreed among ourselves not to say a word to any of 'em, no matter what happened or what they said.

The minute they came on the field, they started on us. They called us all the dirty so-and-so's and filthy such-and-suches you could think of. We never even looked at 'em. We didn't answer 'em, just looked the other way. Boy, then they gave it to us plenty.

"Thought you were a fightin' ball club," they'd holler. "Who're the yellowbellies now? Fightin' ball club? Hell!!!"

But still we didn't open our mouths. And we win the ball game, 2 to 1, when Happy Felsch hit a home run in the fourth innin'. Well, it worked all right that day, so we did the same thing the next day. They gave it to us worse than ever then—they were mad and they tried to take it out on us. But we let 'em alone and we won that one easy, 7 to 2.

So we got to New York and on the train we figure to go on the same way down there. They weren't quite so noisy when we played that third game. But they showed us a big left-hander named Rube Benton and he could hit a 10-cent piece with a curve ball or a fast ball that day, that's how perfect he was. He shut us out, 2 to 0.

The next day they shut us out again, 5 to 0, with another southpaw, Ferdie Schupp, and they got chesty again. Called us a candy ball club and a lot of other things. Still kept our mouths shut.

But on the train that night we were wild. They had us on the ropes. We'd kept it in so long that we just had to get it out of us. So we decided that the next day we'd let loose. And that's the day I'm pickin' as my greatest in baseball—October 13, 1917.

We went out to the ball park early, took the files and sharpened our spikes till they were like razors. We were goin' in there cuttin'. There was only one guy who didn't sharpen his spikes—that was Eddie Collins. Why? Well, he was a different type of ball player. He never went in for that sorta stuff because he figured they might come back at him and he'd get hurt playin' there in the infield. He was a great guy to look out for himself. If there was a tough gent comin' down to second, he'd yell for the shortstop to take the play.

When we went out on the field to take our hittin' practice, the whole Giant team was down the right field line throwin' the ball around and warmin' up. We still didn't say anythin'. Dave Danforth, the old southpaw, was on the mound to pitch battin' practice, and I went up there first. I signed to Dave to give me one low and outside and I reached out and smacked it on a line down among the Giant players. I wanted to knock a couple of 'em cold, and none of us yelled for 'em to look out.

They stopped warmin' up and turned around to look at me. Dave gave me another in the same place and I cracked that one down there too. Right away they started yellin' and wanted to know what was the big idea. Then I made my speech. I told 'em I was goin' to flatten a couple of 'em; that they thought they were a fightin' ball club; well, we'd show 'em a REAL fightin' team. I hit seven or eight line drives right down that line. But by the third one they were all off the field and sittin' down. And they stayed sittin' down until I got out of there.

Well, that started the ball rollin'. Every one of us gave it to 'em. Each of us had picked our man, and we gave him our very special attention. I had Art Fletcher, McGraw's scrappy shortstop, and I had him crazy.

We talked to 'em and they raged at us; we called 'em yellow and everything else we could think of. In the first inning "Buck" Herzog was forced at the plate and he tried to kick the ball out of Ray Schalk's hands with his spikes. He didn't. We

Eddie Collins and Buck Herzog

went into every base with our spikes in the air—and we reminded 'em how sharp they were. When they'd tag us out, they'd grab the ball with both hands and slam it down on us. That was all right with us.

They got two runs in the first innin' but it only made us talk louder. We got one back in the third, but they got two more runs in the fourth and were leadin' us 4 to 1. We just got rougher. In the fifth innin' Felsch slid hard into first base and Holke and Herzog charged him and Heine Zimmerman ran clear across the diamond and tried to jump on him. Then Fletcher made a rush at him, but Happy stood his ground and it looked like they were gonna tangle, but Umpire Klem got between 'em and McGraw pulled Fletcher off.

In the sixth I was on first and Ray Schalk got a hit. I started for third and at second base Herzog and Fletcher were both in the way. I just crashed between 'em and went on to third. We figured on knockin' 'em down first and then hollerin' to the umpires afterward. We hollered but they wouldn't let me score. I did a minute later anyway. They got another run in the seventh. But we put on a big rally in the seventh and scored three runs to tie it up. They folded up right there.

We won it in the eighth with three more runs and we had 'em crazy wild. Shauno Collins singled and McMullen sacrificed him along. Eddie Collins singled him home and on the hit and run, Jackson singled to right and Eddie went to third. Zim took the throw and tried to get Jackson at second and threw wild so Collins scored.

The boys on the bench were on Zim and he started for our dugout, but Umpire Evans pulled him back. Felsch singled and scored Jackson. Hap went down to second and went in with his spikes in the air. Fletcher stepped out of his way but took the ball in both hands and smashed it down on Happy's stomach. Clarence Rowland, our manager, followed Fletcher all the way to first base and they had a helluva argument for four or five minutes until the umps broke it up. Rowland challenged Art—invited him to meet him under the stands after the game; but Art never did.

Well, that was all. We won the game 8 to 5. And the next day we knocked 'em off again 4 to 2 to win the series. We showed 'em who was the fightin' ball club, and we showed 'em good.

And you wanta know somethin' I'll never forget? Remember what I told you about that argument in Cairo? Well, after the last out in the last game of the '17 series, what happens but John McGraw comes tearin' across the field straight at me. He sticks out his hand and he says: "I wanta shake your hand, kid. You're the best, and I wanta take my hat off to you."

THE BOX SCORE
(October 13, 1917)

WHITE SOX	A.B.	H.	P.	A.	NEW YORK	A.B.	H.	P.	A.
J. Collins, rf.	5	1	1	0	Burns, lf.	4	1	3	0
McMullin, 3b.	3	0	1	4	Herzog, 2b.	5	1	0	1
E. Collins, 2b.	4	3	1	4	Kauff, cf.	5	2	2	0
Jackson, lf.	5	3	3	0	Zimmerman, 3b.	5	1	1	2
Felsch, cf.	5	3	0	0	Fletcher, ss.	5	1	2	3
Gandil, 1b.	5	1	10	1	Thorne, rf.	0	0	0	0
Weaver, ss.	4	1	2	2	Robertson, rf.	5	3	2	0
Schalk, c.	3	1	9	0	Holke, 1b.	5	0	11	0
Russell, p.	0	0	0	0	Rariden, c.	3	3	3	1
Cicotte, p.	1	0	0	0	Sallee, p.	3	0	0	2
Risberg	1	1	0	0	Perritt, p.	0	0	0	0
Williams, p.	0	0	0	0					
Lynn	1	0	0	0					
Faber, p.	0	0	0	1					
Totals	36	14	27	12	Totals	40	12	24	9

Risberg batted for Cicotte in 6th.
Lynn batted for Williams in 7th.

NEW YORK	2	0	0	2	0	0	1	0	0 — 5	
WHITE SOX	0	0	1	0	0	1	3	3	* — 8	

Runs—J. Collins, E. Collins (2), Jackson (2), Felsch, Gandil, Weaver, Burns (2), Zimmerman, Fletcher, Rariden. Errors—J. Collins, Gandil, Weaver (3), Williams, Herzog, Zimmerman, Fletcher. Hits—Off Russell, 2 in 1-3 inning; off Cicotte, 8 in 5 2-3 innings; off Williams, 2 in 1 inning; off Salee, 13 in 7 1-3 innings. Two-base hits—Kauff, Felsch, Fletcher, Gandil. Struck out—By Cicotte 3, by Sallee 2.

LEFTY GOMEZ

as told to
JOHN DROHAN

Vernon "Lefty" Gomez was and is one of the real characters of baseball. He was born at Rodeo, Calif., on November 26, 1910, and at 18 started his career with Salt Lake City; hitting the Yankees in 1930 and staying on as one of New York's ace hurlers until 1942, when he went to the Boston Braves. Won six world series games for the Yanks against no defeats and was the winning pitcher in three of six All-Star games, losing only one. Released to Washington, but quit baseball for radio broadcasting.

To tell the truth, in relating my biggest baseball day, I'm torn between two loves. I'm something like the Old Soak who never knew whether his wife told him to take one drink and come home at 12, or take 12 and come home at 1. Of course, there have been complaints? I've been a pitcher. On the other hand, there was a hot day last August in Washington—and can it get hot there—when I got four for five, as they say down at the clubhouse.

I'd like to dwell a bit on that, because those days have been rare in my career. But inasmuch as I've drawn my best salary checks for pitching, rather than hitting, I'll pass it up, much as I dislike to. However, the fact I got four for five might have had something to do with Bucky Harris resigning his job a few weeks later.

Searching the old cerebellum, I think my biggest thrill in baseball was my first World Series game. It was against the Chicago Cubs in the second game of the 1932 series.

Red Ruffing had won the first game, 12-6 from Guy Bush at the Yankee Stadium and I was to work the second against Lon Warneke, the Arkansas Humming Bird.

Joe McCarthy had us hopped up to pour it on the Cubs and lick 'em quick. He'd got the old heave-ho from the Cubs only two years before, and was anxious to get back at them. He figured he hadn't got such a good shake in Chicago and often said he'd like to get even. This was his chance.

Revenge couldn't be as sweet to him as if Rogers Hornsby had stayed as manager of the Cubs. Hornsby had succeeded McCarthy as manager of the Cubs in 1931 and then had been given the old heave-ho in his turn in August, '32. That had brought in Charley Grimm as Cub manager, and the club has turned it on hot to come down the stretch whooping and hollering and kicking everybody out of their way to grab the flag in one of baseball's best stretch drives.

The Yanks under Huggins had swept the World Series four straight from the Pirates in '27 and again from the Cards in '28, and McCarthy naturally wanted to do what Miller had done. We figured we could do it, for while Grimm had Jurges, Herman, Koenig and English with him on the infield, Cuyler, Stephenson and Demaree in the outfield, Hartnett catching and Warneke, Root, Malone, Bush, Grimes and Jakie May pitching, we had what we thought was a much stronger club, with Dickey catching, Gehrig on first, Crosetti at short, Lazzeri at second, Sewell at third, Babe Ruth, Sam Chapman and Earle Combs in the outfield and Red Ruffing, Wilcy Moore, Johnny Allen, George Pipgras and myself.

There was a lot of talk, as the second game came up, about the kid-competition between Lon Warneke and me—two bean poles. Both of us were sophomores; he was 23, I was 21; he had won 22 that summer for the Cubs, I had managed to get by with 24 for the Yanks.

Babe Ruth was 37 and beginning to slow down in the field, but he could still flatten the ball and had hit 41 homers that year.

I remember how Ed Barrow, our general manager, kept after me all my first and second years to put on weight. It scared him when he looked at me, for I weighed only 152, which was thin enough for my height, over 6 feet. Barrow figured I couldn't last.

At the end of the first season he told me, "About 25 years ago we had a pitcher around here named Jack Chesbro, the first pitcher ever to win 16 straight games in the American League. If you'd only put on more weight you could make the fans forget Chesbro."

I wasn't any fatter my second year, '32, but I could fire the ball through a two-inch plank. Barrow, however, kept after me, and I knew during the series that I'd have to spend the winter at a health resort in California Barrow had picked out—a sort of old ladies' home where I was to fatten up.

Incidentally, I did come back to start the '33 season 20 pounds fatter and they put me to rooming with Pat Malone, whom McCarthy had bought from the Cubs, who was a fat man.

That '33 season I won only 16 and lost 10 and instead of making the fans forget Chesbro I was making 'em forget Gomez, so that winter of '33-35 I took off so much weight I showed up in '34 spring training thinner than Bill Powell—and won 26 games and lost five for an .839 percentage, the best I ever hung up.

Anyway, on September 29, 1932, when I went against Lon Warneke and the Cubs, I was thin and felt good.

I had a break, for Warneke showed up wild and kept putting men on for us to bat around, while I found I could get the ball where I wanted and where the Cubs didn't. That afternoon I fanned eight and walked only one. Guy Bush had been wild in the first game of the series and in these first two games we got 10 walks which turned into nine runs.

As I remember it, the Cubs didn't even threaten mildly after tying the score in the third, for we went ahead with a couple more in our half and wound up winning 5-2.

It wasn't any closeness of score or suspense that made it my biggest baseball day; it was simply that it was my first World Series game and I won it.

I remember Gabby Hartnett hitting one down the left field line and Ben Chapman, the fastest man in the American League, scooping up the ball and firing it to second in time for Crosetti to be waiting with it when the old "Milford Freight" came steaming into the bag.

When the rest of the Yanks got through slapping ol' Lon around about all he had left was his chaw of terbacker. And even that was pretty well used up. But if I didn't hit Lon he didn't hit me. So I guess we're even in that respect.

That one game was my only chance in the '32 series. The Babe fixed the third one up for us in Chicago by waving toward the bleachers in center field and

Lon Warneke

then whacking one of Charley Root's pitches in there. Pipgras pitched us to a 7-5 win, and the next day Wilcy Moore beat Bush, Warneke, Jakie May, Bud Tinning and a great many other gentlemen whose names escape me, 13-6.

The whole series was pretty enjoyable for me. I was going with June O'Dea, prima donna of the Broadway show, "Of Thee I Sing," at the time and, hanging around the theater saw the show so often I felt I could act myself. So when bookers came to me after the series I signed up without a quiver for vaudeville monologues on a 12-week booking. I lasted three weeks, but the audiences didn't.

I knew so little about show business that one afternoon at Loew's State in New York, when the manager said, "There won't be anybody here for the supper show," I started to skip that show as a matter of course. He caught me as I was leaving for the Rodeo over at Madison Square Garden and drove me back into my dressing room, where I put on my Yankee uniform and went out and gave my monologue to three stews, two of whom were asleep when I started and the third soon was.

The year 1932 I am safe in saying saw an end to my career in the theater.

CLARK GRIFFITH

as told to
SHIRLEY POVICH

Seventy-five years young, the "Old Fox" broke into baseball in 1887 with Bloomington, Ill. As pitcher, player-manager and mogul, Clark Griffith starred with Pop Anson's Chicago Nationals, helped organize the American League, brought the Washington Senators to renown in a 56-year career.

The day, bless it, was the 10th of October, 1924. Of all the 10,000 afternoons I have spent in a ball park during the last 57 years as a player, manager and club owner, that afternoon is my pet.

Calvin Coolidge was President of the United States and, incidentally, he was setting a new record for White House attendance at a World Series. Only a mild baseball fan to that point, Mr. Coolidge was in a Griffith Stadium box seat for the third time during the series. He was caught up in the excitement that swept on the heels of Bucky Harris' pennant victory with my Senators, the first pennant ever won by Washington.

It was the day the Senators were battling John McGraw's Giants in the seventh game of the World Series.

Bucky Harris, a great manager, had pulled the sixth game out of the fire by singling in the tying and winning runs.

The baseball writers had called it "Griffith's Folly" when I named the 27-year-old Harris manager of my club before the start of the 1924 season. He had only been a manager for two years and he was rated as only an ordinary second baseman. But I liked his fight. He had showed me a lot of fire. I liked Harris from the day I first saw him at Buffalo, where I scouted him personally. He knew I was in the stands watching him and he made eight hits in a double-header that afternoon, although he wasn't supposed to be much of a hitter. But he was aching to get a chance in the big leagues.

I knew Bucky could take care of himself in the series even when he had to match wits with John McGraw. I liked his cockiness. He told me he thought he knew as much baseball "as that old buzzard McGraw," even if it was his first year as a manager. Bucky didn't ask his team to go out and win for him. He showed 'em how. Here's the kind of a competitor Harris was: He had hit only one home run all season, because he wasn't a home-run hitter.

Yet, in the World Series, he clouted two homers that won ball games for us. He had hit only .268 in the summer and batted in only 58 runs in 544 times at bat, yet in 33 times at bat in the series he hit .333 and drove in seven runs.

Despite the fact that we had tied up the series with the Giants in that sixth game, there was sadness in Washington for Walter Johnson, finally getting his chance in a World Series, had been beaten in two starts.

The afternoon before the final game Johnson came to my office to pick up some seventh-game tickets and he was depressed. I tried to cheer him by telling him we were counting on him to pull us through in the seventh game if we needed a relief pitcher. I made him promise to go home to his farm and rest overnight, to get away from the handshaking he always had to do when he stayed downtown. Walter said he would swap his World Series share for one more crack at the Giants.

Incidentally, I never knew until after the series that it cost Walter Johnson $500 to get into the park for the series game. Before the series, "friends" from all over the country had asked Johnson to buy series tickets for them. He bought about $2,000 worth to accommodate them. A lot of those persons didn't show up to claim the tickets Walter bought. When he went out to the mound to pitch the opening game he had $500 worth of tickets to the games in his locker. He was so kind-hearted, he had kept them right up to game time and was stuck with 'em despite the fact they would have brought five times what he had paid.

Well, to get up to the seventh game with the Giants, Bucky Harris had come to my house the night before with the plan that made base-ball history.

"Tell me, if you think I'm crazy," Bucky said, "but I've got an idea how we can get a big edge on the Giants tomorrow." And then he un-folded his idea. "This Bill Terry is murdering us," said Bucky, "and McGraw is sure-pop to have him in there at first base if we start a right-hander. Terry loves right-handed pitching. He's got six hits in 12 times at bat so far against our right-handers. Against left-handed pitching McGraw will play George Kelly at first base.

"Here's my idea," recited Harris. "George Mogridge is the fellow who figures to beat the Giants tomorrow, but if we start him and have to shift to a right-hander, McGraw will switch on us and bench Kelly and put Terry in there. I'm going to start Curly Ogden, a right-hander, and that will get Terry in their line-up, and then I'm going to lift Ogden

Bucky Harris and Freddie Lindstrom

after he pitches to one batter and put in Mogridge. McGraw won't leave Terry in there against Mogridge, and we ought to be rid of him for the day."

That strategy sounded logical enough to me, even if it was a bit radical at first glance. I told Bucky I liked the idea. If he had nerve enough to try it, I was going along with him.

The trick worked. McGraw did let Terry stay in there and take two turns at bat against the left-handed Mogridge, but in the sixth inning, after he failed to get a hit, McGraw put in Bob Meusel to pinch hit for Terry, despite the fact that Terry at the time was the leading hitter of the series with a .429 average. That got Terry out of the way, and Kelly was at first base for the rest of the game.

For three innings it was 0-0, and then Bucky Harris homered. The 31,667 fans went hysterical, but in the sixth the Giants got three runs off Mogridge and Fred Marberry. Going into the eighth, we were still behind 3 to 1. Jess Barnes, the Giants' big right-hander, was doing a job on us, holding us to four hits, and the two runs we needed looked impossible. I left my box seat to be ready to escort President Coolidge from the park and had just reached the steps near the Washington dugout when things began to happen. With one gone, Leibold pinch hitting for Taylor, doubled. I watched the rest of the inning from the steps, too superstitious to move. Ruel, who up to that point in the series hadn't made a hit, singled down his pet third-base alley to put the tying run on base, Leibold holding up at third. Tate, hitting for Marberry, walked. McNeely flied out and Harris was next up.

If any World Series ever belonged to one man this one belonged to Harris. He banged Barnes' first pitch for a clean single to left and tied up the ball game at 3 to 3. Those fans wanted to tear my Stadium down.

The ovation for Harris, though, was nothing compared to what happened a few minutes later after the Giants finally got us out. As the Giants went to bat in the ninth the park was in a fearful uproar because Walter Johnson was walking to the mound. Utter strangers were hugging each other in the stands because Walter was getting one more chance in the series. It was his ball game now, with the score tied at 3-3 going into the ninth.

I never saw such a grim face as Johnson's when Harris gave him the ball and patted him on the back. Walter couldn't talk. I actually saw him gritting his teeth. He grabbed that ball so hard the white showed through his knuckles. I was still watching the game from the dugout steps, still too superstitious to move. For four innings I stood there as Johnson, always in trouble, pulled out by fanning Giants in the clutch—five he struck out in four innings. Up to the 12th we couldn't score either. Then what happened—and that is the high spot of my 55 years in baseball.

Muddy Ruel, batting .050 with one hit in 20 times at bat, popped a high foul in back of the plate. As Hank Gowdy, the Giant catcher, reached for it he stepped on his mask and went down in a heap, dropping the ball. Muddy expressed his gratitude by immediately doubling to left.

Bucky let Johnson hit for himself, and Travis Jackson fumbled Walter's grounder, putting Johnson on first. But Ruel was held at second. Then along came Earl McNeely, for whom I had paid Sacramento $50,000 earlier in the season.

McNeely then contributed the famous "pebble hit." I can still see Freddie Lindstrom poised to take McNeely's grounder on a nice big hop for the second out. And I can still see the panic on Lindstrom's face when the ball took a devilish hop high over his head for a freak single.

That was the hit that won the World Series, with Muddy Ruel scoring from second after what

President Calvin Coolidge

seemed an eternity of running the 180 feet from second base to the plate. Muddy was no speed demon.

Walter Johnson and Muddy Ruel (left)

MUDDY
RUEL
as told to
LLOYD LEWIS

One of baseball's little fellows who spent 17 years in big league baseball, Herold D. "Muddy" Ruel is still at it —coaching White Sox pitchers. Muddy was born in St. Louis on February 20, 1896, and started his baseball life with the Browns in 1915, moving to the Yankees in 1917, and then to the Red Sox (1921), Washington (1923) and Detroit (1931). Although rated too slight for catching, Ruel was in 149 games in 1924 and then caught seven in the world series. Lifetime batting average was .277.

I have either been playing ball or coaching big league clubs since 1915, but in that time, which will soon be a third of a century, I never saw a day in baseball like that of October 10, 1924, in Griffith Stadium, Washington.

It was the seventh game of the World Series between the Senators and the Giants and my 156th of the year. I had caught 149 for Washington in the pennant fight, and although we only had a mediocre ball club we had won it by keeping the team together, that way, day after day, same lineup—Goose Goslin and Sam Rice playing 154 games in the outfield, Joe Judge 140 on first, Peckinpaugh 155 at short, Bucky Harris 143 at second—a tough, determined ball club, paced by the boy-manager, Harris, who would get hit by pitched balls to get to first and who would knock fielders out of his way to get to second.

The series had started on high, with the Senators' immortal Walter Johnson smothered by telegrams, letters, handshakes, sentimental publicity because this was his first pennant—his first World Series. The great man had never been on a flag winner before, and the whole country seemed to be whooping for him but betting on the Giants.

Even the Giants, looking at us with tolerance and amused confidence, spoke well of the great Walter. They could afford to. They figured the series was in the bag. They had in the outfield the really terrific Ross Youngs, a .355 hitter, and Meusel, another .300 man; Hack Wilson, a murderous freshman hitter, and George "Highpockets" Kelly with an average of .323 and 21 home runs to his credit that season. When southpaws worked against the Giants, Kelly went back to first, his old post, but against right-handers McGraw used a kid named Bill Terry on the bag, a pitcher whom he was converting into a slugger. Great kids the Giants had, an 18-year-older, name of Freddie Lindstrom, on third; a sophomore, aged 20, name of Travis Jackson, on short, and nobody but Frankie Frisch, aged 24, on second.

The whole club had hit .300 for the season, had pulled a pitching staff of Nehf, Bentley, McQuillan, Ryan, Jess Barnes and Jonnard through to a flag. They had Hughie Jennings, the "ee-yah" coach, on third, and McGraw scowling from the bench—an awesome club, but not to us. We Senators were tough, too.

The pressure should have been terrific on us, for the City of Washington was wild with its first flag. Even President Coolidge came out to the first game to root, in his own restrained way, for Walter Johnson.

Walter was in the evening of his career, 37 years old, and getting so he'd tire in the late innings, and I'd seen that fast one coming in a shade slower than in other years. The Giants had licked him the first game, tagged him for 14 hits, 4-3 in 12 innings.

The big, swarthy kid, Bill Terry, got three for five off Walter that day and Art Nehf, Ross Youngs and Kelly had hammered out two runs in the 12th inning to win.

But old Tom Zachary—he wasn't old, just looked so sage and crafty and cunning that he'd been called "Old Tom" from his second year —he stepped out and beat the Giants 4-3 in the second game.

The third game we lost 6-4, but Mogridge had pulled us back in the fourth game by holding the Giants to six hits and four runs while we got seven runs across. Johnson tried again in the fifth game and lost. The kid Terry was still hammering him—had four hits in seven times up off Walter in two games. And Lindstrom hit Walter that day as if he owned him—four for five.

That looked like curtains for us, but Old Tom Zachary didn't think so, and pitching slow and tormentingly, beat the Giants in the sixth game 2-1, to square it at three all. That brought us up to the payoff, October 10—and Washington was wilder than ever.

We talked before the game and figured we had to get Terry out of there, so Harris announced Curley Ogden, a second-string right-hander to start. That meant McGraw would start Terry, who was a left-hand hitter, on first and use Long George Kelly in the outfield.

It worked, and after Ogden had pitched to two batters, Harris took him out and sent Mogridge, a southpaw, who held them till the sixth, when they tired him out by waiting for walks. With two on and Terry up, McGraw jerked his young first baseman and sent in Meusel.

We had done it! We had got Terry out of the game, and Kelly would now go to first, but we were still in trouble and Harris sent Mogridge off the hill and brought in Fred Marberry, the greatest relief pitcher I ever saw. He was a second-year man, 24 years old, and a character. On the mound he'd grab at the ball, paw the ground with his spikes, fume, fret, wave his big shoes in the batter's face and blaze a fast one through. But the Giants weren't bothered by his big feet that inning and, helped by errors by Judge and Oscar Bluege, they scored three.

In the eighth Liebold doubled for us and I was up. I hadn't made a hit in the whole series, and I could feel the crowd sigh as I came to the plate. I singled. Then with two out Harris bounced a sharp one a little to Lindstrom's left. It hopped over Freddie's head and, coming in behind Liebold, I scored the tying run.

The yell from the crowd wasn't any louder or longer, however, than a few minutes later when Walter Johnson came out to pitch the ninth. Washington was crazy for him to get even for the two lacings the Giants had given him.

He had to face the top of the Giants' batting order, with Lindstrom, his kid Nemesis, leading off. He got Freddie, but that dad-gummed Frisch hit a triple to center. The ball seemed never to stop rolling and I was crazy for fear Frisch would come clear home. With him on third, Ross Youngs came up. He'd crouch at the plate and poise himself like lightning about to strike, his eyes boring in on a pitcher, tense as a violin string. I'll never forget that big white bat of his hanging over my head as I crouched behind the plate. We walked him.

Kelly up, with everybody thinking about those 21 homers of his. Walter threw. Strike one. Youngs went with the pitch to second and Frisch was ready to break for home if I threw. I bluffed it, hoping to trap Frankie. That one run on third was important for it could win for them. Two runs were no worse, so I let Youngs steal. But Frisch was thinking right along with me and wouldn't be betrayed. He knew, too, that if I did throw to second Harris would run in and cut it off and throw home, and nobody in the history of baseball ever could make that play better than Bucky. So Frisch stuck to the bag and we went back to work on Kelly. Walter threw twice more, and I can see yet that ball streaking in through Kelly's swing for "Strike Three."

That left Meusel up, two down. Johnson got him to ground out.

We got Barnes out of there in our half of the ninth, but Hughie McQuillan kept us from scoring and he and Johnson kept the plate free till the last of the 12th. Johnson fanned Kelly again in the 11th after Groh had singled and Youngs had walked once more—fanned Kelly and Frisch, too—with the stands a real inferno of noise.

Miller started our 12th going out at first. I hit a high foul over the plate and everybody said, "Two outs," but Hank Gowdy, the Giants catcher, stepped on his mask, stumbled, dropped the ball, and on the next pitch, like a sinner forgiven, a lifer pardoned, I doubled—my second hit of the whole series.

Walter hit sharp to Jackson's right and I made as if to run past Travis, then turned and scuttled back to second. Jackson fumbled the ball. Two on, one out. The fans were really giving tongue now. They couldn't believe things like this happened.

McNeely up. He bounced one sharply but straight to Lindstrom, who was about 12 feet from third base. Running hard, I figured all I could do on a sure out like that would be to throw myself to the left, into the diamond in front of Freddie and try to get him to try and tag me instead of throwing to first. I saw Freddie hold his hands ready at his chest for the ball, then I saw him jump up. The ball had hit a pebble and bounced away over his head. I swerved back into the base line, tagged third and came home with the winning run. Meusel had no chance to get me. It was over. We were in!

THE BOX SCORE
(October 10, 1924)

NEW YORK	A.B.	H.	P.	A.		WASHINGTON	A.B.	H.	P.	A.
Lindstrom, 3b.	5	1	0	3		McNeely, cf.	6	1	0	0
Frisch, 2b.	5	2	3	4		Harris, 2b.	5	3	4	1
Youngs, cf.-lf.	2	0	2	0		Rice, rf.	5	0	1	0
Kelly, cf.-1b.	6	1	8	1		Goslin,, lf.	5	2	3	0
Terry, 1b.	2	0	6	1		Judge, 1b.	4	1	12	1
Meusel, lf.-rf.	3	1	1	0		Bluege, ss.	5	0	1	7
Wilson, lf.-cf.	5	1	4	0		Taylor, 3b.	2	0	0	3
Jackson, ss.	6	0	1	4		Miller, 3b.	2	0	1	1
Gowdy, c.	6	1	8	0		Ruel, c.	5	2	13	0
Barnes, p.	3	0	1	2		Ogden, p.	0	0	0	0
Nehf, p.	0	0	0	0		Mogridge, p.	1	0	0	0
McQuillan, p.	0	0	0	0		Marberry, p.	1	0	1	0
Groh	1	1	0	0		Liebold	1	1	0	0
Southworth	0	0	0	0		Tate	0	0	0	0
Bentley, p.	0	0	0	0		Shirley	0	0	0	0
						Johnson, p.	2	0	0	1
Totals	44	8	*34	15		Totals	44	10	36	14

* One out when winning run scored.
Meusel batted for Terry in 6th.
Groh batted for McQuillan in 11th.
Southworth ran for Groh in 11th.

Liebold batted for Taylor in 8th.
Tate batted for Marberry in 8th.
Shirley ran for Tate in 8th.

| NEW YORK | 0 0 0 0 0 3 0 0 0 0 0 0—3 |
| WASHINGTON | 0 0 0 1 0 0 0 2 0 0 0 1—4 |

Errors—Kelly, Jackson, Gowdy, Bluege (2), Taylor. Runs—Youngs, Kelly, Wilson, Harris, Ruel (2), Liebold. Runs batted in—Harris (3), McNeely, Meusel. Double plays—Kelly to Jackson, Frisch to Kelly, Johnson to Bluege to Judge. Bases on balls—Ogden, 1; Mogridge, 1; Marberry, 1; Bentley, 1; Johnson, 3. Struck out—By Ogden, 1; Mogridge, 3; Marberry, 3; McQuillan, 1; Barnes, 6; Johnson, 5. Hits—Ogden, 0 in 1-3 inning; Mogridge, 4 in 4 2-3; Marberry, 1 in 3; Johnson, 3 in 4; Barnes, 6 in 7 2-3; Nehf, 1 in 2-3; McQuillan, 0 in 1 2-3; Bentley, 3 in 1 1-3. Winning pitcher—Johnson.

TRIS SPEAKER

as told to

FRANCIS J. POWERS

Tris Speaker during his score of years in the majors compiled a batting average of .345 for 2,789 games. Played in three World Series. Elected to Hall of Fame in 1936.

I'll always think of the 1912 season as one of the greatest in major league history. That's natural for it was in 1912 that I first played with a pennant winner and world's championship team, and there are no greater thrills for a young player. Our Boston Red Sox, managed by Jake Stahl, a former University of Illinois star, won the American League pennant while the New York Giants were the winners on the National League side.

There were a couple of great teams. The Red Sox won 105 games that season for a league record that stood until the Yankees won 110 in 1926. And the Giants came home with 103 victories and no other National League winner since touched that total until the Cardinals won 106 in 1942. Joe Wood won 34 games for us, almost one-third of our total and 10 of them were shutouts.

Many a time I have heard "Smoke" say in our clubhouse meetings, "get me two runs today and we'll win this one." Woody won 16 in a

Red Murray

Christy Mathewson

row and beat Walter Johnson after the Big Train had won a similar string and no one has beaten those marks although they have been tied. We had Duffy Lewis and Harry Hooper in the outfield and there never were any better, Larry Gardner at third, Heinie Wagner at short and Buck O'Brien and Hugh Bedient on the pitching staff, just to mention some of our stars.

While Wood (and Johnson) made pitching history in the American League that summer Rube Marquard was writing an unequaled chapter in the National. The gangling, wry-necked left-hander won 19 straight and no one has come along to wipe out that performance. Those Giants were a hard hitting, fast running team with the likes of Josh Devore, Red Murray, Buck Herzog, Chief Meyers and Fred Merkle and had great pitchers in Christy Mathewson, Marquard, Jeff Tesreau and Red Ames.

In the opening game of the World Series Woody beat Tesreau, 4 to 3. I guess maybe John McGraw figured "Smoke" would beat any of his pitchers so he held Marquard and Mathewson back; although Tesreau was a great pitcher. The second game went 11 innings to a six-all tie with Matty pitching for the Giants and Bedient, Ray Collins and Charlie Hall, who died a few weeks ago, working for Boston. In the third game the Giants made it all even with Marquard getting a 2-1 decision over O'Brien. Then Wood and Bedient beat Tesreau and Mathewson in terrific 3-1 and 2-1 duels and we were ahead three games to one and it looked as if the series was about finished.

But the Giants weren't through by any means. In the sixth game, Marquard beat O'Brien and Collins and in the seventh, the Giants took a toe hold and pounded Wood out of the box and kept on hammering O'Brien and Collins to win 11-4. So the series went into its eighth game on October 16 and that's where I had my biggest day.

McGraw called on Christie Mathewson with the chips down and that was natural for Matty still was in his prime; his fadeaway was tough to hit and he knew every angle of the pitching business. Since Wood already had worked three games, and had been beaten the day before Stahl couldn't send him back, so he started Bedient.

The game quickly took the form of a magnificent pitcher's battle and I don't think Matty ever was much better than that autumn afternoon. He turned us back with machinelike precision for six innings and by that time the one run the Giants had scored in the third began to look awful big. I got a double into right field in the first inning but through six innings that was about our only scoring chance. The Giants got their run when Devore walked, advanced on two outs and scored when "Red" Murray hit a long double. That the Giants weren't another run to the good in the fifth was due to one of the greatest catches I ever saw. Larry Doyle hit a terrific drive to right that appeared headed for a home run but Harry Hooper cut it off with a running, leaping catch that was easily the outstanding play of the series.

Boston tied the score in the seventh due to confusion among the Giants. Stahl hit a Texas leaguer toward left and it fell safe when Murray, Fred Snodgrass and Art Fletcher couldn't agree on who was to make the catch. Wagner walked and then Stahl sent Olaf Hendrickson up to bat for Bedient. Now Hendrickson was one of the greatest pinch hitters ever in the game; like Moose McCormick of the Giants. He was

John McGraw

Rube Marquard

one of those rare fellows who could go up cold and hit any sort of pitching. Matty worked hard on Hendrickson but the Swede belted a long double that scored Stahl. Then Joe Wood came in to pitch for us.

The score still was one-one going into the 10th and the Giants tried their best to put the game away in their half. Murray doubled again and he was the tough man for us all through the series and raced home on Merkle's single. So there we were behind again with the last chance coming up.

Once more the breaks and big breaks went our way. Clyde Engle batted for Woody and reached second when Snodgrass muffed his fly in center field. Hooper flied out and Yerkes worked Matty for a pass. And I was the next batter.

It looked as if I was out when I cut one of Matty's fadeaways and lifted a high foul between the plate and first base. The ball was drifting toward first and would have been an easy catch for Merkle. I was going to yell for Meyers to make the catch for I didn't think he could, but before I could open my mouth I heard Matty calling: "Meyers, Meyers."

Meyers chased the ball but it was going away from him and finally Merkle charged in but he was too late and couldn't hold the ball. Fred was blamed for not making the catch and the term "bonehead" was thrown at him again, recalling his failure to touch second base in 1908. I never thought Merkle deserved any blame at all. It was Matty who made the blunder in calling for Meyers to try for the catch.

That gave me a reprieve and I didn't miss the second chance. I got a good hold of a pitch for a single to right that scored Engle and the game was tied again. Then Matty walked Lewis, purposely, for Duffy always was a money hitter, filling the bases. With Gardner at bat the Giant infield played in close on the chance of cutting Yerkes off at the plate. But Gardner was another who did his best when the chips were on the table and crashed a long fly that sent Yerkes home with the deciding run.

THE BOX SCORE
(October 16, 1912)

NEW YORK	A.B.	R.	H.	P.	A.	BOSTON	A.B.	R.	H.	P.	A.
Devore, rf.	3	1	1	3	1	Hooper, rf.	5	0	0	3	0
Doyle, 2b.	5	0	0	1	5	Yerkes, 2b.	4	1	1	0	3
Snodgrass, cf.	4	0	1	4	1	Speaker, cf.	4	0	2	2	0
Murray, lf.	5	1	2	3	0	Lewis, lf.	4	0	0	1	0
Merkle, 1b.	5	0	1	10	0	Gardner, 3b.	3	0	1	1	4
Herzog, 3b.	5	0	2	2	1	Stahl, 1b.	4	1	2	15	0
Meyers, c.	3	0	0	4	1	Wagner, ss.	3	0	1	3	5
Fletcher, ss.	3	0	1	2	3	Cady, c.	4	0	0	5	3
McCormick	1	0	0	0	0	Bedient, p.	2	0	0	0	1
Mathewson, p.	4	0	1	0	3	Hendrickson	1	0	1	0	0
Shafer, ss.	0	0	0	0	0	Wood, p.	0	0	0	0	2
						Engle	1	1	0	0	0
Totals	38	2	9	*29	15	Totals	35	3	8	30	18

* Two out when winning run scored.
McCormick batted for Fletcher in 9th.
Shafer went to shortstop in 10th.

Hendrickson batted for Bedient in 7th.
Engle batted for Wood in 10th.

NEW YORK	0	0	1	0	0	0	0	0	0	1—2
BOSTON	0	0	0	0	0	0	1	0	0	2—3

Errors—Doyle, Snodgrass, Speaker, Gardner (2), Stahl, Wagner. Two-base hits—Murray (2), Herzog, Gardner, Stahl, Hendrickson. Sacrifice hit—Meyers. Sacrifice fly—Gardner. Stolen base—Devore. Struck out—By Mathewson, 4; by Bedient, 2; by Wood, 2. Bases on balls—Off Mathewson, 5; off Bedient, 3; off Wood, 1. Hits—Off Bedient, 6 in 7 innings; off Wood, 3 in 3 innings. Winning pitcher—Wood. Umpires—O'Loughlin (A. L.), Rigler, (N. L.), Klem (N. L.) and Evans (A. L.). Time—2:39. Attendance—17,034.

I was in other World Series, but outside of the game between Cleveland and Brooklyn in 1920, when Bill Wambsganss made his unassisted triple play, I can't recall any when there was more drama and when there were more unusual incidents. It was a great thrill for me to manage the Cleveland Indians to the 1920 world's championship, with my mother looking on; but from strictly a playing angle, that single off Matty was my biggest moment.

Al Simmons batting

AL SIMMONS

as told to

JOHN P. CARMICHAEL

Aloysius Harry "Al" Simmons was born May 22, 1903, in Milwaukee, Wis., as Aloysius Szymanski. He leaped off the prairie diamond to stardom as an outfielder-fence buster for the Philadelphia Athletics (1924-32), leading the American League in batting in 1930-31 with averages of .381 and .390. Also played for the White Sox and Detroit and holds the major league record for most consecutive years of batting in 100 or more runs per season —nine. Now coach-player with Athletics.

When that 1930 season was over and we had won our second straight pennant I understand Clark Griffith told Connie Mack: "I went back and checked up on Al Simmons this year. He hit 14 home runs in the eighth and ninth innings and every one figured in the ball game. We were never the same after he licked us in that double-header." So Connie gave me a three-year contract for $100,000, which he didn't intend to do at all. But that's more like the end, not the beginning, of this particular day.... Memorial Day, 1930!

The Senators were in town for morning and afternoon games. They were leading the league by four games and we were second. What's more, they wanted to make so sure of knocking us off twice and really getting a strangle hold on first place that they'd sent Pitchers Ad Liska and "Bump" Hadley into town 48 hours ahead of the team to get fully rested for the big day. Liska worked the opener against "Lefty" Grove, but we weren't worried, because Mose never had lost a morning game in his career ... that's a fact ... and he always asked to pitch them.

Well, we were brand-new world champions, of course, and we had a good crowd on hand, but we weren't doing so well near the end of the affair. Liska was one of those semi-underhand pitchers with a little of this and that and not much of anything, but he had us off stride and was ahead 6-3 into the ninth with two out, nobody on base and Grove up. Naturally Grove didn't hit. Connie sent Spencer Harris up to swing for him and he got a single. Then Dibs Williams hit safely and old man Simmons was on the spot. I'd already gone four for the collar and those Philly fans could be tough every so often. Some of 'em were yelling "Three out" and: "How about another pinch hitter?" and I was thinking, "Boy, we better win that second game," when Liska cut loose.

The ball was right in there and didn't break and I really swung. It landed in the left-field seats, the score was tied and the customers were all for me now. We couldn't do anything more and went into extra innings. I got a double in the 11th, but we didn't score. I singled in the 13th and didn't get home. In the 15th I hit another two-bagger ... four straight hits, mind you, after going out easily four times in a row. Jimmie Foxx came up and hit a twisting roller down the third-base line ... topped the ball. He beat it out by a half step and on the play I went to third and rounded the bag as if I might try to score. I got caught in a run-down. Well, there I was, scrambling around and cursing myself for blowing a chance to get the game over, but finally I dove for third and was safe. Just as I lit I felt something go haywire in my right knee.

Standing on the bag I could feel it swelling up under my uniform and by the time "Boob" McNair singled and I scored the winning run it was becoming stiff. We went inside and got the clothes off and the damn thing was twice its normal size. Connie Mack couldn't believe his eyes. "How did you do it?" he kept asking. I didn't know myself . . . didn't hit anything but the ground. He put in a call for Dr. Carnett, our club physician. I can't remember his first name . . . and he's dead now . . . but he was one of the outstanding doctors in the East and a great ball fan. He came in and ordered cold compresses on it.

"You've broken a blood vessel," he said, "but it'll be all right."

We didn't have so much time between games, because that opener had taken too long, so there was nothing to do but sit around and order a little lunch. The outgoing crowd was all mixed up with the incoming customers and, of course, a lot of those who figured to see only the morning game were so het up that they turned right around outside the gates and bought their way back in again. Meanwhile the swelling in my knee was going down, but it hurt and finally Mr. Mack said to Carnett: "He can't play any more today, I suppose," and Doc said no. "You'll probably want to take him to a hospital," said Connie and Carnett agreed.

"But not today," he said. "I came out here to see a double-header and I'm going to see it. You . . ." and he addressed Mr. Mack . . . "can put him back in a uniform and let him sit on the bench. He can't run, but he might come in handy as a pinch hitter. What's more . . . if a spot comes up, I want him in there, too. I'll take care of the knee later, but at the moment I'm a rabid fan and assistant manager."

Out we went for the second game and the fans were in a great state when they saw Harris going to left instead of me. Only a few knew anything had happened and they couldn't understand why I was benched after driving in three runs and scoring the last one. I think George Earnshaw was going for us and Hadley for them and he got off just as good as Liska had in the first game. Came the seventh inning and we were behind 7-3. We sent up a pinch-hitter for Joe Boley and he got on and then there was a base on balls and a hit and the bags were loaded. Suddenly I saw Connie look down the line and crook that finger at me.

"Looks like this is the time and the place," he said. "This is what Dr. Carnett meant and you know what he said. Walk around the bases if you can."

I picked out a bat and there I was for the second time in the same day in the clutch. Hadley told me afterwards: "I never wanted a place to put somebody so much in all my life, but we were full up." He seemed to take a long time and finally pitched and it was outside for a ball. He tried another in the same spot and I let it go. Then he changed up on me and tried for a strike.

My bat caught it just right . . . where you know that even if the ball is caught, you've hit it solid. This one came down in the left-field stands, too, and the score was 7-7. I hobbled around the bases and got back to the bench and Connie was sitting up straight, his eyes bright like a bird's, and he said: "My, that was fine, Al!" We won in the ninth and down came Carnett and lugged me off to the hospital.

THE BOX SCORE
(May 30, 1930)

WASHINGTON	A.B.	R.	H.	P.	A.		PHILADELPHIA	A.B.	R.	H.	P.	A.
Loepp, cf.	4	0	1	1	0		Bishop, 2b.	4	1	0	2	3
Goslin, lf.	6	0	0	3	0		Haas, cf.	5	0	0	8	0
Judge, 1b.	5	1	0	13	0		Cochrane, c.	3	1	1	6	0
Meyer, 2b.	6	1	1	3	0		Perkins, c.	0	0	0	1	0
Cronin, ss.	5	2	1	1	6		Williams	0	1	0	0	0
Bluege, 3b.	5	1	2	2	3		Quinn, p.	2	0	0	0	3
Ruel, c.	4	1	2	7	1		Simmons, lf.	7	3	3	3	0
Liska, p.	4	0	1	0	3		Foxx, 1b.	7	0	6	12	1
Marberry, p.	1	0	0	0	0		Miller, rf.	3	0	0	4	0
West, cf.	1	0	0	4	0		Dykes, 3b.	6	0	0	0	2
Rice, rf.	6	0	1	4	0		Boley, ss.	2	0	0	1	1
							McNair, ss.	3	0	2	1	1
							Grove, p.	2	0	0	0	2
							Harris	1	1	1	0	0
							Schang, c.	2	0	0	1	0
Totals	47	6	9	*38	13		Totals	47	7	13	39	13

* Two out when winning run scored.

Williams batted for Perkins in 9th.
Cramer batted for Boley in 8th.
Harris batted for Grove in 9th.

WASHINGTON	0 1 0 0 0 4 0 1 0 0 0 0 0—6
PHILADELPHIA	2 0 1 0 0 0 0 3 0 0 0 1—7

Errors—Ruel, Cochrane, Boley. Two-base hits—Foxx (2), Simmons. Three-base hits—Foxx, Ruel. Home runs—Cochrane, Simmons. Stolen base—Cronin. Sacrifices—Haas (2), Grove. Double plays—Foxx to McNair. Bases on balls—Liska, 7; Margery, 3; Grove, 4. Struck out—Liska, 3; Marberry, 3; Grove, 6; Quinn, 1. Hits—Liska, 7 in 8 2-3 innings; Marberry, 6 in 4; Grove, 9 in 9; Quinn, none in 4.

HANK GOWDY

as told to

FRANCIS J. POWERS

Hank Gowdy, a native of Columbus, Ohio, was the first major leaguer to enlist in the World War I and became a sergeant during his service in France. A coach with Cincinnati when World War II broke out, Gowdy sought service again and was commissioned a major. In this war, at 55, Hank has been athletic officer at Fort Benning, Ga.

Gowdy in the First World War

On July 15, 1914, the Boston Braves were in last place—13 games behind the New York Giants, who were defending champions. When the season closed on October 7, those same Braves were in first place, 10½ games ahead of the Giants in the runner-up spot. Over a span of 77 games, the Braves won 61 in the fastest, most furious sprint the game ever has known. George Stallings became the Miracle Man.

Every day was a great day during that drive and especially for Hank Gowdy, playing his first season as a regular in the big time. I'd come up in '10 with the Giants as a first baseman and McGraw traded me to the Braves the next season. I kicked around between Boston and

Buffalo for two seasons and it was only in 1913 that I turned to catching.

You remember, even the younger fans, how the Braves won the pennant. How they came from last place on the pitching of Dick Rudolph, Lefty George Tyler and Bill James. We began to climb only after Stallings decided to work those three in order and there was little break in their continuity for the remainder of the season. James won 26 games, Rudolph 27 and Tyler 16 over the campaign. We had other pitchers, but it was the THREE who won the pennant.

Despite our great winning drive, the Braves were strictly under-dogs as they set out to play the Philadelphia Athletics in the World Series. The A's were back in the king row with their fourth pennant in five seasons and they had great batting, great speed and fine pitching. They had the $100,000 infield of McInnis, Collins, Barry and

Gowdy as a major in Second World War

Rabbit Maranville

Baker and Bullet Joe Bush had come up to join Chief Bender, Eddie Plank and other veterans on the pitching staff.

I guess fans underestimated the Braves,

Johnny Evers

outside of our pitching, and we didn't have much of a hitting team. But it was a fighting team from Stallings to the bat boy. The keymen of the team were Johnny Evers, who came to Boston after being fired as manager of the Cubs and, although a graying veteran, played sensationally, and Rabbit Maranville, the kid shortstop. Big Charlie "Butch" Schmidt was on first and we went into the series with Charlie Deal on third because "Red" Smith, our regular, was hurt. And Deal played the series as George Rohe did for the White Sox against the Cubs in 1906. We used five outfielders, Herbie Moran, Possum Whitted and Joe Connolly against right-handers, with Les Mann and Ted Cather playing against southpaws.

I'll settle for the third game as my biggest thrill, but I'd better tell you about the first two games.

We opened with Rudolph while Connie called on Chief Bender, who was one of the craftiest pitchers ever in the game. Dick allowed five scattered hits; we made 11 off the Chief and Herb Wykoff, who finished. I got three for three. I got a double in the second to drive in our first run and later scored on Mann's single. In the fifth I opened with a long triple and Maranville batted me home. The second game was a masterpiece. Bill James allowed just two hits, by Collins and Schang, and we won 1-0 in the ninth when Deal doubled, stole third and scored on Mann's single.

So now we're up to that third game. By this time the betting had shifted. Fans all over the country were pulling for the Braves. Stallings went with Tyler while Mack, after losing with Bender and Plank, called out young Bush.

The Athletics moved out in front right at the start when Danny Murphy doubled, went down on Rube Oldring's sacrifice and scored when Connolly muffed Collins' fly. We got that run right back in the second, when Maranville walked and stole and I doubled into the left-field bleachers. Both teams scored a run in the fourth and that was all until the 10th. Tyler and Bush staged one of the finest, tightest duels you'd ever want to see.

Tyler weakened a bit in the 10th and the Macks scored two runs. That put the Braves in a big hole. Our last bats were coming up and while we had an edge on the A's, we couldn't afford to give them any rope. And the Braves' first batter was Gowdy. Bush threw me one I liked and I swung and there went a home run into the centerfield bleachers. We were back in the game. That shook Bush a bit for he walked Moran; then Evers singled and Herbie scored on Connolly's fly and the score was all even again.

Bill James then went to the box for us and pitched two scoreless innings. In our half of the 12th, I was the leadoff man again. This time I bounced a double into the left-field bleachers, but when I reached second, Stallings had Les Mann ready to run for me. Larry Gilbert, who later became a great minor league manager, batted for James and walked. Then Moran bunted. Bush fielded the ball and threw wild into left and Mann scored. There was the game and the series. Nothing could stop us after that third victory.

You easily can understand my thrills in that game and what made it more thrilling was the fact that my mother and father were there to see me get those hits. When sportswriters crowded into the clubhouse, Stallings told them: "Help yourself to anything you want to say. If you want to make it four straight, I'm with you."

We made George's confidence stand up the next day when we won 3-1. Dick Rudolph pitched another great game while we bunched hits off Bob Shawkey and Herb Pennock, a couple of Connie's youngsters, in the fourth and fifth innings. There never was another man like Stallings and there never was another team like his Braves. And for me there never was another series like it.

THE BOX SCORE
(October 12, 1914)

PHILADELPHIA	A.B.	R.	H.	P.	A.	BOSTON	A.B.	R.	H.	P.	A.
Murphy, rf.	5	2	2	2	0	Moran, rf.	4	1	0	2	0
Oldring, lf.	5	0	0	1	0	Evers, 2b.	5	0	3	3	5
Collins, 2b.	4	0	1	1	4	Connolly, lf.	4	0	0	1	0
Baker, 3b.	5	0	2	4	4	Whitted, cf.	5	0	0	2	0
McInnis, 1b.	5	1	1	18	0	Schmidt, 1b.	5	1	1	17	1
Walsh, cf.	4	0	1	1	0	Deal, 3b.	5	0	1	2	3
Barry, ss.	5	0	0	0	7	Maranville, ss.	4	1	1	2	3
Schang, c.	4	1	1	6	1	Gowdy, c.	4	1	3	6	0
Bush, p.	5	0	0	0	5	Mann	0	1	0	0	0
						Tyler, p.	3	0	0	1	5
						Devore	1	0	0	0	0
						James, p.	0	0	0	0	2
						Gilbert	0	0	0	0	0
Totals	42	4	8	*33	21	Totals	40	5	9	36	19

* None out when winning run scored.

Mann ran for Gowdy in 12th.
Devore batted for Tyler in 10th.
Gilbert batted for James in 12th.

PHILADELPHIA	1	0	0	1	0	0	0	0	0	2	0	0	—	4
BOSTON	0	1	0	1	0	0	0	0	0	2	0	1	—	5

Errors—Schang, Bush, Connolly. Two-base hits—Murphy (2), Gowdy (2), McInnis, Deal, Baker. Home run—Gowdy. Sacrifice hits—Oldring, Moran. Sacrifice flies—Collins, Connolly. Stolen bases—Collins, Evers, Maranville (2). Double play—Evers to Maranville to Schmidt. Struck out—By Bush, 4; by Tyler, 4; by James, 1. Bases on balls—Off Bush, 4; off Tyler, 3; off James, 3. Hits—Off Tyler, 8 in 10 innings; off James, 0 in 2 innings. Winning pitcher—James. Umpires—Klem (N. L.), Dinneen (A. L.), Byron (N. L.), and Hildebrand (A. L.).

ED WALSH

as told to
FRANCIS J. POWERS

Ed Walsh, 63 years old now, is superintendent of the water filtration plant in Meriden, Conn. A native of Wilkes-Barre, Pa., Walsh started pitching for Meriden in 1902 and after a few seasons in the minors was finally drafted by the White Sox, where he became one of the American League greats.

Did you ever see Larry Lajoie bat? No. Then you missed something. I want to tell you that there was one of the greatest hitters—and fielders, too—ever in baseball. There's no telling the records he'd made if he'd hit against the lively ball. To tell you about my greatest day, I'll have to go back there to October, 1908, when I fanned Larry with the bases full and the White Sox chances for the pennant hanging on every pitch to the big Frenchman.

That was October 3, and the day after I had that great game with Addie Joss and he beat me 1 to 0 with a perfect game; no run—no hits—no man reached first. There was a great pitcher and a grand fellow, Addie. One of my closest friends and he'd been one of the best of all time only for his untimely death two years later. That game was a surprise to both of us for we were sitting on a tarpaulin talking about having some singing in the hotel that night, when Lajoie, who managed Cleveland, and Fielder Jones told us to warm up. A pitcher never knew when he'd work in those days.

I don't think there'll ever be another pennant race like there was in the American League that year. All summer four teams, the Sox, Cleveland, Detroit, and St. Louis, had been fighting and three of 'em still had a chance on this day. When Joss beat me the day before it left us two and one-half games behind the Tigers and two behind the Naps (as Cleveland was called in honor of Lajoie). We had only four games left to play.

It was a Saturday and the biggest crowd ever to see a game in Cleveland up to that date jammed around the park. Jones started Frank Smith for us and we got him three runs off Glenn Liebhardt and were leading by two going into the seventh. I was in the bull pen, ready for anything because, as I said, we had to win this one.

As I recall it George Perring, the shortstop, was first up for Cleveland and he went all the way to second when Patsy Dougherty muffed his fly in the sun. I began to warm up in a hurry. Nig Clarke batted for Liebhardt and fanned and things looked better. Smith would have been out of trouble only Tannehill fumbled Josh Clarke's grounder and

Larry Lajoie

couldn't make a play. Clarke stole second and that upset Smith and he walked Bill Bradley. I rushed to the box and the first batter I faced was Bill Hinchman. Bill wasn't a champion hitter but he was a tough man in a pinch. I knew his weakness was a spit ball on the inside corner so I told Sully (Billy Sullivan) we'd have to get in close on him. I did. My spitter nearly always broke down and I could put it about where I wanted. Bill got a piece of the ball and hit a fast grounder that Tannehill fielded with one hand and we forced Perring at the plate.

So, there were two out and Larry at bat. Now if the Frenchman had a weakness it was a fast ball, high and right through the middle. If you pitched inside to him, he'd tear a hand off the third baseman and if you pitched outside he'd knock down the second baseman. I tried him with a spit ball that broke to the inside and down. You know a spit ball was heavy and traveled fast. Lajoie hit the pitch hard down the third base line and it traveled so fast that it curved 20 feet, I'd guess, over the foul line and into the bleachers. There was strike one.

My next pitch was a spitter on the outside and Larry swung and tipped it foul back to the stands. Sully signed for another spitter but I just stared at him; I never shook him off with a nod or anything like that. He signed for the spitter twice more but still I just looked at him. Then Billy walked out to the box. "What's the matter?" Bill asked me. "I'll give him a fast one," I said, but Billy was dubious. Finally, he agreed. I threw Larry an overhand fast ball that raised and he watched it come over without ever an offer. "Strike three!" roared Silk O'Loughlin. Lajoie sort of grinned at me and tossed his bat toward the bench **without** ever a word. That was the high spot of my baseball days, fanning Larry in the clutch and without him swinging.

Well, we came home to finish out the season with three games against the Tigers. We still were in the race but we needed three straight for the flag. We got the first two. In the opener, Doc White beat the Tigers 3-1 and held Cobb and Claude Rossman hitless. I pitched the second and beat 'em 6-1 and allowed only four hits and that was my 65th game and 40th win of the season. And that left us a half game out of first and Cleveland was out of the race when it dropped the first game of a double-header to the Browns.

That brought it down to the final day of the season. We heard that Hughie Jennings and Harry Tuthill (Detroit trainer) had sat up to 4 o'clock in the morning putting hot towels on Bill Donovan's arm, trying to get it in shape to pitch. At game time we weren't sure Bill would pitch for he was visiting under the stands with Joe Farrell when Jennings came by and told him to warm up.

Most of us thought Jones would start Smith against the Tigers for he really had them handcuffed and always could be expected to pitch his best against them. We were startled rather than surprised when Jones said "Doc" White would pitch.

When Jones came in, I asked: "Are you going to pitch Doc?" He said "yes." Then I said, "That's a great injustice to a fine young man. You know White needs his full rest to be effective. I'll pitch if you want me to (I'd pitched in 65 games, my arm felt great and another game wouldn't hurt me). The man you should pitch is Smith . . . but you're mad at him."

I couldn't argue Jones out of starting White and "Doc" didn't last long. I'll never forget that first inning. Matty McIntyre singled. Donie Bush was hit by a pitched ball but the umpires wouldn't let him take first because he hadn't tried to duck the pitch. Then Donie fanned. There was a crowd around in the outfield and Sam Crawford hit a terrific drive into the fans for two bases. And then Cobb—Cobb the man who never could hit White—tripled, cleaning the bases.

I got down to the bull pen in time to get warmed up a bit and after Cobb's hit, Jones sent me to the box. The Tigers scored two more before I could stop them and then I pitched through the fifth. Then when I came to the bench, I threw my glove in the corner. "What's the matter with you?" Jones asked. "I'm through," I said. "Now you'll have to pitch Smith, the man who should have started. Smith finished but the Tigers beat us 7-0 and there went the pennant. Donovan allowed only two hits and fanned nine and we dropped to third place when the Naps won from St. Louis.

I like to think back to the White Sox of those days. In 1906, we won the pennant and beat the Cubs in the World Series. Next season we were in the pennant race until the last days of September and in 1908 we fought them down to the final day of the season. There never was a fielding first baseman like Jiggs Donahue in 1908 when he set a record for assists. Sullivan was a great catcher, one of the greatest. It was a great team, a smart team. But the tops of all days was when I fanned Lajoie with the bases filled. Not many pitchers ever did that.

THE BOX SCORE

(October 8, 1908)

CHICAGO	R.	H.	P.	A.	CLEVELAND	R.	H.	P.	A.
Hahn, rf.	0	1	0	0	J. Clarke, rf.	0	0	1	0
Jones, cf.	0	0	1	0	Bradley, 3b.	0	0	1	0
Isbell, 1b.	1	2	11	1	Hinchman, lf.	0	1	2	0
Dougherty, lf.	0	0	0	0	Lajoie, 2b.	1	2	1	0
Davis, 2b.	1	1	3	2	Stovall, 1b.	1	2	8	1
Parent, ss.	0	1	4	4	Bemis, c.	0	1	8	1
Sullivan, c.	1	2	8	4	Birmingham, cf.	0	1	2	0
Tannehill, 3b.	0	1	0	4	Perring, ss.	0	1	3	5
Smith, p.	0	0	0	1	Liebhardt, p.	0	0	1	2
Walsh, p.	0	0	0	0	Rhoades, p.	0	0	0	2
					N. Clarke	0	0	0	0
Totals	3	8	27	16	Totals	2	8	27	11

N. Clarke batted for Liebhardt in 7th.

CHICAGO	0	2	0	0	0	1	0	0	0 — 3
CLEVELAND	0	1	0	0	0	0	0	1	0 — 2

Errors—Dougherty, Tannehill (2), Bemis. Stolen bases—Davis, Sullivan (2), Perring, Bemis, J. Clarke. Two-base hits—Lajoie (2), Parent, Stovall. Sacrifice hits—Stovall, Liebhardt. Double play—Perring to Stovall. Hits—Off Liebhardt, 6 in 5 innings; off Rhoades, 2 in 2 innings; off Smith, 6 in 6 1-3 innings; off Walsh, 2 in 2 2-3 innings. Struck out—By Smith 4 (Bradley, Hinchman, Stovall, N. Clarke); Walsh 4 (Lajoie, Perring, Rhoades, J. Clarke); Liebhardt 6 (C. Hahn, Davis 2, Parent 2, Smith); Rhoades 2 (Jones, Tannehill). Bases on balls—Off Smith 3, Liebhardt 3. Wild pitch—Liebhardt.

Bill Dickey, Joe McCarthy and Spud Chandler

BILL DICKEY
as told to
JOHN P. CARMICHAEL

*William Malcolm Dickey was born in Basthrop, La.,
June 6, 1907. Spent three seasons in the minors before
joining the Yankees in 1928. Has appeared in eight World
Series. The 1944 season would have been Dickey's 17th
as a major leaguer, but he was then a member of Uncle
Sam's Navy.*

My biggest day? Well, I used to think it was the afternoon in
1932 when Babe Ruth didn't hit me right on the chin. I put
a raw egg in one of his spikes before a game and you can imagine
what happened when he set that big dog of his down inside. He
really was "red" when he pulled the foot out, with egg drippin' all
over and he looked around the clubhouse and yelled:

"I can whip the man that did that."

Well, nobody answered and the Babe got madder 'n' madder and
growled around and finally I said: "I did it, Babe," and he glared at
me and took a couple of steps toward my locker and suddenly started
to laugh and said: "Aw, to hell with it" and changed socks and shoes.
He'd a been a pretty big guy to tangle with.

A day I remember for the laugh we all got was in '30 when Bob Shawkey had the club and "Lefty" Grove was pitchin' against us. To me he was the fastest man I ever saw and he was having a field day against the Yanks. "Red" Ruffing was sittin' on the bench and just for fun he kept telling everybody: "I can't understand how you guys don't hit him. He's just nice and fast . . . boy, I like to hit those kind of pitchers. Sure wish I was in there today."

Finally we got the bags loaded in the eighth with two out and Shawkey looked down the line and motioned to Ruffing. "I know you want to take a crack at Grove," said Bob, "so pick up a bat and go up there." We all gave "Red" a big hand when he walked to the plate. Then we sat and watched. Grove threw three times. Ruffing hardly got a good look at any of 'em. He was back in a minute without ever getting the bat off his shoulder . . . three strikes and out!

That World Series of '38 with the Cubs was a honey . . . especially the day that Hack and Jurges collided going after a ground ball and Lou Gehrig scored from first base. I can still see "Diz" Dean chasin' the ball back on the grass while your left fielder (Carl Reynolds) stood around and watched. But I guess when you come down to it, this last World Series . . . the last game when I hit a home run . . . is the biggest day of all.

One of the newspapermen in the clubhouse afterwards hollered at Joe McCarthy: "Hey, Joe, how about ol' Bill Dickey there," and Joe reached over and slapped me on the back and said: "Bill and I have come a long way . . . we practically started together on the Yanks." That's about right, too . . . it was the eighth series for both of us and we won out seven times. Joe and I were the old-timers of them all.

You know the Yanks are supposed to beat everybody, all the time. Nobody thinks it strange or remarkable when we win; they take it for granted. If we lose they figure it was accidental and something must be wrong. I rather thought the Cards had a better team, during the season, than we did although I thought we could beat them in the series. But they had a great pitcher in Mort Cooper, one of the sharpest, most consistent hitters I ever saw in Stan Musial and a regular floating ghost at short. That skinny Marion is a wonder. Phil Rizzuto, who was with us in '42, was the only shortstop I ever saw as good on slow-hit balls.

The '43 series was a tough one and some of those games could have changed scores very easily. Take that second one in which Cooper beat us 4-3. We had one run home in the ninth, a man on third and nobody out when I came to bat. I hit the hardest ball, for me, of the whole series. Caught it good . . . but it was a line drive right into the hands of Klein. Five feet either side and I'd a been on first with another run home and still no outs.

Then there was the ninth inning of the fourth game, with Russo leading 2-1. There was one gone when Marion doubled and the tying run was on second. They sent up that third-string catcher . . . oh, wait a minute, Sam Narron . . . to hit and we got two strikes on him in a hurry. Then I decided to waste one and called for a high, outside fast ball. I didn't expect him to hit at it . . . didn't want him to, in fact, because I was only setting him up for another curve. But for some reason I caught Crosetti's eye just after giving Russo the sign and motioned Frank over toward second a few steps.

It was a good thing I did, because Narron hit that outside pitch . . . pretty smart down toward second base and if Frank hadn't been over there, it'd been a hit and we'd a never got Marion at home. Even as it was Crosetti had to make a quick stop and throw. That was a hard hit ball and it was good strategy to send a fellow like Narron up because we didn't know anything about him or what he couldn't hit. Hell, he'd hardly played all season.

I think even if we'd lost next day, the fifth game, we still would have won the series but maybe it's just as well it didn't go any longer. You remember Cooper striking out five of us in a row at the start, including me, and he was fast. You could see he'd made up his mind to throw everything he had into that last effort and we got some good breaks along the way. That play Crosetti made on Klein to start the fourth or fifth inning. . . . I don't see how he ever got to the ball, but he did and it got their leadoff man out of the way and gave us a margin to operate on.

Johnny Hopp

Then the next frame Kurowski led off and bunted safely toward third on the first pitch. I was a little afraid of "Spud" Chandler losing his control, because I didn't think he was as sharp in either series game as in most of his season starts and sure enough he got wild and walked Ray Sanders on four pitches. There were two men on, nobody out, and no score in the game. Up came Johnny Hopp, a left-handed hitter to boot, and Chandler threw three straight balls to him.

McCarthy wig-wagged me to go out to the mound and see what happened. "Spud" said he wasn't tired or anything; he just didn't want to give Hopp a clean shot. But I told him to "come on and get the ball over" and called for a sinker. It was good for strike one, just around the knees, and, naturally, Hopp didn't swing. After all, Chandler had thrown seven straight balls. I took a chance he wouldn't even cut at the 3-1 pitch and asked for a curve. It was called strike two, so it was 3-2 and the next pitch was "for the money."

It was . . . but for our money. I signaled for a fast ball and Chandler threw one at least a foot off the plate, outside. The bases should have been loaded with nobody gone. I don't know why Hopp swung at the ball, but he did . . . and fanned. There was one of the two big breaks of the whole series in our favor; that one and the day in New York when Lindell knocked the ball out of Kurowski's hands. Anyway, with Hopp gone, we got the next two easily.

There were two out in the sixth when Keller bounced the ball between first and second for a hit and I came up. I wasn't trying to outguess Cooper. I wasn't trying to hit the ball out of the park either. I wanted a fast ball and I only wanted to meet it squarely, just so it would go safe. Well, I got it . . . and hit it good, but not hard. At least I didn't think so, but when I was running to first I saw the ball heading for the roof and Earl Combs (Yank coach) yelled at me: "You got one, Bill." But the only thing I thought was: "We'll get a run, anyway, for 'Spud' and maybe it'll be enough." Then I saw Art Fletcher (at third) wavin' his cap and I knew it was a home run and we had two runs.

It didn't mean so much at the time; it wasn't until that night, when I was in bed that I began to realize I'd won the game and the series with one blow and we were champions again and I'd had a pretty darn good season for an old man who'd been playing up there 16 years.

THE BOX SCORE
(October 11, 1943)

ST. LOUIS	A.B.	R.	H.	P.	A.	NEW YORK	A.B.	R.	H.	P.	A.
Klein, 2b.	5	0	1	3	1	Crosetti, ss.	4	0	1	0	5
Garms, lf.	4	0	0	1	0	Metheny, rf.	5	0	1	1	0
Musial, rf.	3	0	0	1	0	Lindell, rf.	0	0	0	0	0
W. Cooper, c.	2	0	1	6	0	Johnson, 3b.	4	0	1	1	2
O'Dea, c.	2	0	2	2	0	Keller, lf.	3	1	1	1	1
Kurowski, 3b.	4	0	2	3	3	Dickey, c.	4	1	1	7	0
Sanders, 1b.	3	0	1	7	2	Etten, 1b.	3	0	1	11	1
Hopp, cf.	4	0	0	1	0	Gordon, 2b.	2	0	0	6	6
Marion, ss.	3	0	1	2	3	Stainback, cf.	3	0	1	0	0
M. Cooper, p.	2	0	0	0	1	Chandler, p.	3	0	0	0	2
Walker	1	0	1	0	0						
Lanier, p.	0	0	0	0	1						
Dickson, p.	0	0	0	1	0						
Litwhiler,	1	0	1	0	0						
Totals	34	0	10	27	11	Totals	31	2	7	27	17

Walker batted for M. Cooper in 7th.
Litwhiler batted for Dickson in 9th.

ST. LOUIS	0	0	0	0	0	0	0	0	0—0
NEW YORK	0	0	0	0	0	2	0	0	0—2

Errors—Crosetti, W. Cooper. Runs batted in—Dickey (2). Earned runs—New York 2. Left on bases—New York 9, St. Louis 11. Double plays—Crosetti to Gordon to Etten, Klein to Marion to Sanders. Struck out—Chandler 7, M. Cooper 6, Lanier 1. Bases on balls— Chandler 2, M. Cooper 2, Lanier 2, Dickson 1. Hits—Off M. Cooper, 5 in 7 innings; Lanier, 2 in 1 1-3; Dickson, 0 in 2-3. Wild pitch—M. Cooper. Losing pitcher—M. Cooper. Umpires —Rommel (A. L.), Reardon (N. L.), Rue (A. L.), Steward (N. L.). Time—2:24.

WAITE HOYT
as told to
FRANCIS J. POWERS

Waite Charles Hoyt's first full season in the majors was with Red Sox in 1919. He was traded to the Yankees in 1920. Born in Brooklyn on September 9, 1899, threw and batted right-handed, and holds, jointly with Chief Bender, the record for total games won in world series— six. Pitched in seven world series. Now is baseball announcer in Cincinnati.

I'm another whose greatest day was against the New York Giants and John McGraw. It was the second game of the 1921 World Series between the Giants and Yankees; New York's first nickel series and the first of the late Miller Huggins' six championship teams. The Yanks finally had "arrived" to challenge McGraw and his Giants for the supremacy of baseball right on Broadway where they had ruled so long. And it still was George M. Cohan's Broadway. As a native

New Yorker and only 22, you can imagine my jubilation. I had come to the Yanks that spring from the Red Sox and had won 19 games, so I was sure Huggins would start me in the series.

I was keen to get a crack at the Giants. Besides the natural ambition to pitch in a series I had other reasons. I had been quite a pitcher in the New York Public School League and when I was only 16, my father signed a contract for me with McGraw. But McGraw didn't keep me around long. In the next three seasons I was with six minor league clubs and came back to the big leagues when the Red Sox bought me from New Orleans in '19. That was one extra reason I wanted to pitch.

Another reason developed the day before the series opened. That year the Yanks were tenants in the Polo Grounds, renting, while Col. Jack Ruppert and Capt. Til Houston planned their magnificent stadium just across the river. The Giants took their workout from 10 to 12 in the morning and then we had the field. I was warming up in the bull pen, getting ready to pitch in batting practice when I heard a hard, rasping voice at my elbow.

"So that's the young punk who expects to beat us." It was Ross Youngs talking to Frankie Frisch and if there ever was a player who typified the old Giants it was Youngs, the Texas outfielder who died all too early. It was strictly a rib, plain and unsparing, but at the time I took it as a personal insult and promised myself I'd beat those fellows.

"Hug" opened the series with Carl Mays on the mound, going against "Shufflin'" Phil Douglas. Mays' underhand delivery was sharp that afternoon and he beat the Giants 3-0. After the game "Hug" said: "You go tomorrow." My opponent was Art Nehf, a great left-hander, and we tangled three times before the series was finished. I admit I was nervous as I warmed up. There were photographers milling around, sports writers asking questions and fights in the grandstands, for New York was taking its subway series seriously. It seems to me there was a lot more belligerency in those days than now.

I got by the first inning although those first three Giant hitters, George Burns, Dave Bancroft and Frisch looked pretty terrifying. In the second, I made Youngs look bad on slow balls. I still can see Ross. crouched at the plate, his jaws set and eyes like slits. I made Earl Smith, the big and rough catcher, look worse. I began to get confidence. I had spells of wildness but I kept turning the Giants back, inning after inning. Johnny Rawlings, the fast little second baseman, clipped one that bounced over Mike McNally's head at third, and in the ninth, Frisch rifled a clean single to right. That was all the hitting the Giants did that day.

The Giants did everything they knew to get me out of the box, to get me up in the air. They even read the advertisements in the newspapers. Shortly before the series opening, I had signed a testimonial for some brand of soap. The Giants had seen the ads. McGraw never missed a trick. Once, after grounding out, when I was on my way back to the bench a cake of soap came flying out of the Giant bench and landed at my feet. That was too much. I picked up the soap and with plenty of speed fired it back and it just shaved McGraw's ear. Man, those Giants really singed my hair with their retorts—uncourteous. But it was no go; the Giants couldn't bother me that day.

Really, it was the Giants who were jittery, and they helped us to our three runs with some poor play, for we made only three hits. We got on in the fourth, when Ward opened with a Texas Leaguer, McNally hit to Nehf and both runners were safe when Art made a wild throw to Bancroft. A pass to Wally Schang filled the bases and when I grounded to Rawlings, he threw to first and Ward scored.

We got the other two in the eighth. Frisch muffed Peck's fly after some confusion with Banny, and Ruth forced Rog. When Meusel singled to center, Babe went right into third and beat Burns' throw by a hair while Bob traveled on to second. Wally Pipp hit to Rawlings and once again Johnny threw to first while Babe scored. On Nehf's next pitch, Meusel broke for home and scored when Oil Smith muffed the ball.

I went back at the Giants and Nehf in the fifth game and won 3-1, to make the series all even. But they got me in the eighth and deciding game on a 1-0 count. I pitched a full 27 innings in the series without allowing an earned run and technically that tied the record set by Christy Mathewson in the 1905 series against the Athletics, when every game was a shut-out, although ours was an eight-game series. While we lost the series, I was pretty happy with my pitching, partic-ularly since it was against the Giants.

Now I'm going back a bit and tell you how I came back to the majors, after getting out of organized baseball and pitching for the Baltimore Drydocks. I was the property of New Orleans when Ed Barrow, then managing Boston, bought my contract. I signed on the

John McGraw

27th of July, 1919, with the understanding I would get a chance to pitch and not wind up as a bench jockey, which was a custom in those days.

After I had been with the Red Sox for three days, Barrow told me I'd work the next day. A nice opponent he threw me. The Tigers with Ty Cobb, Harry Heilmann and Bob Veach. I developed a head-ache that evening and it lasted through the next day, until game time. The game was important to me not only because it was my first start, but because I had argued with Barrow that I could win in the Ameri-can League if I had the chance. Here was the chance.

I got the first two Tigers; then one reached first. Cobb up. In those days there was no whitewashed ring for the batter on deck and two-three batters could stand around swinging bats, riding the pitcher and doing almost anything to unhinge him. Cobb started on me while Veach was batting. When he came up instead of standing in the batter's box, he stood on top of the plate with his back to me and held a long conversation with Schang.

When Ty finally faced me, standing in his half crouch, I backed off the rubber. Then I threw him a slow ball that he missed a foot. The crowd (all 3,000 of it) booed and Ty didn't like that a bit. He snarled something about a "fresh busher" but didn't do anything that turn. Boston was leading 1-0 in the eighth when Cobb tripled, scoring the tying run. I was learning about him rapidly.

I wasn't nervous by that time but I pitched as if I were in a coma and my prayers were as strong as my arm. So the game went into the 13th. In our half, Erve Scott reached first, with one out, and McNally ran for him. Schang hit to short and the shortstop (not Donie Bush, for Moriarity had chased him early in the game) threw to first. But McNally didn't stop at third. He lit right out for home and seemed trapped by Catcher Eddie Ainsmith and Third Baseman Bobby Jones. Suddenly Mike shot for the plate, running headlong over Ainsmith, who didn't have the ball. The game was over and I had won my first American League start, 2-1. Cobb, Heilmann and Moriarity had a fight on the way to the clubhouse but that didn't interest me—I was walking on air.

THE BOX SCORE
(October 6, 1921)

GIANTS	A.B.	R.	H.	P.	A.	YANKEES	A.B.	R.	H.	P.	A.
Burns, cf.	3	0	0	1	0	Miller, cf.	3	0	0	1	0
Bancroft, ss.	4	0	0	3	3	Peckinpaugh, ss	3	0	0	3	1
Frisch, 3b.	4	0	1	3	2	Ruth, lf.	1	1	0	0	0
Youngs, rf.	2	0	0	2	0	R. Meusel, rf.	4	1	1	1	0
Kelly, 1b.	4	0	0	12	2	Pipp, 1b.	3	0	0	14	0
E. Meusel, lf.	2	0	0	0	0	Ward, 2b.	4	1	1	4	7
Rawlings, 2b.	3	0	1	2	2	McNally, 3b.	3	0	0	0	3
Smith, c.	3	0	0	1	1	Schang, c.	2	0	0	4	2
Nehf, p.	2	0	0	0	3	Hoyt, p.	3	0	1	0	2
Totals	27	0	2	24	13	Totals	26	3	3	27	15

GIANTS	0	0	0	0	0	0	0	0	0—0
YANKEES	0	0	0	1	0	0	0	2	*—3

Errors—Frisch, Smith, Nehf. Stolen bases—Ruth (2), R. Meusel. Double plays—Frisch to Rawlings, Rawlings to Kelly to Smith, McNally to Ward to Pipp. Struck out—By Hoyt 5. Bases on balls—Off Nehf 7, Hoyt 5. Passed ball—Smith. Umpires—Moriarity (A. L.), Quigley (N. L.), Chill (A. L.), Rigler (N. L.). Time—1:58. Attendance—34,939.

GABBY
HARTNETT
as told to
HAL TOTTEN

Charles Leo "Gabby" Hartnett was the official noise-maker for the Chicago Cubs from 1922 until he left as manager in 1938. Gabby made his debut with the Cubs on their Catalina Island spring training base in 1922 and became one of the game's most competent catchers, as well as one of its most powerful hitters. Gabby was born at Woonsocket, R. I., December 20, 1900, and in 17 years as a big leaguer he hit a grand .299.

D o you know how you feel when you're real scared, or something BIG is going to happen? Well, that's the way I felt for one terrific minute of my biggest day in baseball—and I don't believe you'll have to guess very much as to just which day that was.

It was in 1938, September 28, the day of "the home run in the dark." But as a matter of fact, that day—that one big moment—was the climax of a series of things that had gone on for a week or more. And every one of those incidents helped to make it the biggest day in all my years in the major leagues.

The week before—on Sunday—you'll remember we had played a double-header in Brooklyn. We lost the first game 4 to 3, and we were leading the second game by two runs along about the fifth inning. It was muddy and raining and was getting dark fast. Then big Fred Sington came up with a man on base and hit a home run to tie the score.

It was too dark to play any more, so they called the game and it ended in a tie. Now—every game meant a lot to us just then. We were three and a half games behind. Winning was the only way we could hope to catch the Pirates and we were scheduled in Philadelphia the next day. So we couldn't play the game off then.

But Larry MacPhail wanted to play it. We had an open date for travel at the end of the series in Philly, and he wanted us to go back to Brooklyn and play off the tie. The boys wanted to play it, too. They figured we could win it and gain on the Pirates.

Well, I could't make up my mind right away, so I asked MacPhail to give me 24 hours to decide. He said he would. But I'd been figuring —you see, we had to win all three games in the series with Pittsburgh if we were to win the pennant. And I had to think of my pitchers. I had to argue with the whole ball club—they wanted to play.

But I stuck my neck out and turned it down. I'll admit that I didn't feel any too easy about it. But I had to make the decision. And I felt that we might lose that game just as easy as we could win it. So I took that chance.

Well, we sat for three days in Philly and watched it rain. Of course, Pittsburgh wasn't able to play in Brooklyn, either, and they were three and a half games in front of us. On Thursday we played the Phils twice and beat 'em both times, 4 to 0 and 2 to 1. Lee won his 20th game of the season in that first one—and his fourth straight shutout. Clay Bryant was the pitcher in the second. But Pittsburgh beat Brooklyn twice, so were still three and a half back.

The next day we won two again—and we had to come from behind to do it. Rip Collins put the second one on ice by doubling in the ninth with the bases full to drive in three runs just as they posted the score showing that Cincinnati had beaten the Pirates. That put us within two games of the leaders. We were really rollin'.

Mace Brown

Then we came home and on Saturday we played the Cardinals—and beat 'em 9 to 3. But the Pirates won, too. On Sunday it was the same thing —we both won. Monday Pittsburgh wasn't scheduled, so the Pirates were in the stands at Wrigley Field as we played the final of the series with St. Louis. Bill Lee was scored on for the first time in five games, but we won 6 to 3. Then came the big series—with the lead cut to a game and a half.

I stuck my neck out in the very first game of the series. Several times, in fact. I started Dizzy Dean on the mound. He hadn't pitched since September 13 and hadn't started a game since August 13. But how he pitched! Just a slow ball, control, and a world of heart.

We got him out in front in the third when Collins tripled and Jurges drove him in with a single. For five innings Dean was great. Then he seemed to tire. Lloyd Waner grounded out in that inning, and Paul Waner fouled out. Rizzo singled, but Vaughan popped to Herman. Still, I noticed that he didn't have as much on the ball.

Probably I was the only one to notice it—except maybe Diz himself. I began to worry a bit and I made up my mind right then and there that no matter how anything else was going, the minute Dean got in trouble, I was going to get him out of there. We got another run the last half of that inning. And Diz got through the seventh and eighth, although it took a great play by Dean himself to cut down a run at the plate in the eighth.

When the ninth came around I decided to play safe and started Lee warming up in the bull pen. Bill wasn't usually a good relief pitcher, but he was the best pitcher in the league, and that was a spot for the best we had.

Dean hit Vaughan to start the ninth and I was plenty uneasy. But Suhr popped out, and Jensen batted for Young and forced Arky at second. Then came little "Jeep" Handley and he hit one clear to the wall in left center for a double. That put the tying runs on second and third, and that was my cue.

Todd was up. He always hit Dean pretty good, even when Diz had his stuff—and Diz didn't have a thing then. Not only that, but Todd never hit Lee very well. So even though Lee hadn't been a steady relief pitcher, I called him in. My neck was out again. What if Todd hit one? What if Lee had trouble getting started—after all, he'd been working day after day. But—well, when it gets to the place where it means a ball game, you've got to make a change, even if the hitter socks one into the bleachers.

I'll say this for Dean—he never complained about that. He walked right in and said I'd done the right thing—that he'd lost his stuff and his arm didn't feel so good. So Lee came in. The first pitch was a strike. Todd fouled the next one off. Then Lee cut loose with as wild a pitch as I ever saw and Jensen scored. Handley went to third with the tying run. My hunch didn't look so good. But Lee wound up again; he pitched; and Todd swung and struck out. We'd won the game and were only a half game out of first place.

That brings us up to the big day. We scored in the second inning on a couple of errors. But Pittsburgh went ahead with three in the sixth. We tied it up in our half. But the Pirates got two in the eighth and led, 5 to 3. In our half Collins opened with a single and Jurges walked.

Lazzeri batted for Lee, who had gone in again that day, and doubled, scoring Rip. They walked Hack. Then Herman drove in Jurges to tie it up again, but Joe Marty—who had run for Tony—was thrown out at the plate by Paul Waner. A double play ended that round.

It was very dark by then. But the umpires decided to let us go one more. Charlie Root got through the first half of the ninth all right. In our half Cavarretta hit one a country mile to center, but Lloyd Waner pulled it down. Reynolds grounded out. And it was my turn.

Well—I swung once—and missed; I swung again, and got a piece of it, but that was all. A foul and strike two. I had one more chance. Mace Brown wound up and let fly; I swung with everything I had and then I got that feeling I was talking about—the kind of feeling you get when the blood rushes out of your head and you get dizzy.

A lot of people have told me they didn't know the ball was in the bleachers. Well, I did—maybe I was the only one in the park who did. I knew it the minute I hit it. When I got to second base I couldn't see third for the players and fans there. I don't think I walked a step to the plate—I was carried in. But when I got there I saw George Barr taking a good look—he was going to make sure I touched that platter.

THE BOX SCORE
(September 28, 1938)

PITTSBURGH	A.B.	H.	P.	A.	CUBS	A.B.	H.	P.	A.
L. Waner, cf.	4	2	1	0	Hack, 3b.	3	0	3	1
P. Waner, rf.	5	2	3	1	Herman, 2b.	5	3	2	2
Rizzo, lf.	4	1	1	0	Demaree, lf.	5	0	2	0
Vaughan, ss.	2	1	2	6	Cavarretta, rf.	5	0	2	0
Suhr, 1b.	3	1	6	0	Reynolds, cf.	5	1	5	0
Young, 2b.	2	0	1	1	Hartnett, c.	4	2	4	1
Th'v'w, 2b.	0	0	1	2	Collins 1b.	4	3	5	0
Handley, 3b.	4	2	2	1	Jurgess, ss.	3	1	4	4
Todd, c.	4	0	9	0	Bryant, p.	2	0	0	0
Klinger, p.	4	0	0	2	Russell, p.	0	0	0	0
Swift, p.	0	0	0	0	Page, p.	0	0	0	0
Brown, p.	0	0	0	0	French, p.	0	0	0	0
Manush	1	1	0	0	Lee, p.	0	0	0	1
					Root, p.	0	0	0	0
					O'Dea	1	0	0	0
					Lazzeri	1	1	0	0
					Marty	0	0	0	0
Totals	33	10	*26	13	Totals	38	12	27	9

* Two out when winning run scored.
Swift replaced Klinger in 8th.
Brown replaced Swift in 8th.
Manush batted for Young in 8th.

Russell replaced Bryant in 6th.
French replaced Page in 8th.
Lee replaced French in 8th.
O'Dea batted for Russell in 6th.
Lazzeri batted for Lee in 8th.
Marty ran for Lazzeri in 8th.

PITTSBURGH	0	0	0	0	0	3	0	2	0—5
CUBS	0	1	0	0	0	2	0	2	1—6

Errors—P. Waner, Vaughan, Handley, Todd. Runs—Rizzo, Vaughan (2), Suhr (2), Hart-nett (2), Collins (3), Jurges. Runs batted in—Rizzo, Handley (3), Collins, Hack, Manush, Lazzeri, Herman, Hartnett. Home runs—Rizzo, Hartnett. Two-base hits—L. Waner, Hart-nett, Collins, Lazzeri. Wild pitch—Lee. Struck out—By Klinger, 6; Bryant, 1; Page, 1. Bases on balls—Off Klinger, 2; Swift, 2; Bryant, 5; Page, 1. Winning pitcher—Root. Losing pitcher—Brown.

That was the shot that did it. We went into first place. And while we still had the pennant to win, we couldn't be headed. We won again the next day for Bill Lee, easy—10 to 1. The heart was gone out of Pittsburgh. And we clinched the pennant down in St. Louis the next Saturday when we won and Pittsburgh lost to Cincinnati.

Hartnett after his "twilight homer."

FRANKIE
F. FRISCH

as told to
KEN SMITH

Frankie F. Frisch, now manager of the Pittsburgh Pirates, was the famous "Fordham Flash" when he came up with the New York Giants in 1919, jumping directly from the campus to a second-base job in the National League. Went to Cardinals in 1927 and became manager in 1933 to 1937. Hit .316 in 19 years.

I finally got to sleep on the night of October 8, 1934, in my hotel in Detroit. The next day was the most important day of my whole baseball career so far, and I knew it.

When I had been a fresh kid, with John J. McGraw's Giants in the 1921, '22, '23 and '24 World Series, I never fretted about anything. Slept like a baby and played with an abandon I wish I had had in the three Series during the '30s. McGraw and the older men like Dave Bancroft, Heinie Groh and Casey Stengel did the worrying in the old days. A young squirt isn't afraid of anything. Life's a breeze and every day is a lark.

But in the 1930, '31 and '34 Series, the responsibility was terrific. This stuff you hear about old codgers mellowing and losing the competitive urge is the bunk. It grows stronger with age, especially when you are playing second base and managing the Gashouse Gang.

Well, we were even-Stephen at three games apiece, in the 1934 Series —the Cardinals against the Tigers. You can imagine how I would feel if we blew this, of all Series, after such a Donnybrook as we had been through in the first six games. I lay there in the sheets, figuring pitches for Mickey Cochrane, Charley Gehringer, Goose Goslin and Hank Greenberg, knowing that here was the one big game of my life whether I played a personal part in the playing end, or not, I don't have to thumb back and say: "Let's see, now, which WAS my biggest day?"

You can imagine what was on my mind lying there before the seventh and deciding game. Dizzy Dean had won the first for us in Detroit, 8-3. Schoolboy Rowe, who had a tremendous year with the Tigers, had beaten us the second game, 3-2, the Schoolboy retiring 22 batters in a row starting with the fourth inning. Paul Dean had won the third battle, but the Tigers had taken the fourth and fifth, and the city of Detroit was beginning to lay the red carpet for a championship celebration.

Dizzy Dean

Then Paul came back and won the sixth game with a single, 4-3, I'll never forget old Dizzy hugging Paul in the dressing room after the game, wresting him and yelping, "You're the greatest pitcher the Dean family ever had," and then Diz would pound everybody else on the back and brag about his kid brother. Diz had announced at the start of the year "me and Paul will win 50 games," and they'd darn near done it, Dean winning 30 and Paul 19. Diz had said they'd murder the Tigers in the Series, too, and now they had between them won three games—the only ones we had taken.

I remember John Carmichael coming up to me in the confusion of that dressing room after the sixth game and asking, "Dean tomorrow —the other Dean?" and me sitting there, all in from the strain, and answering "If I last till tomorrow, maybe. It'll be Dean or Wild Bill Hallahan."

Carmichael took one look at Diz charging around the room with a white pith helmet—the kind Englishmen wear on tiger hunts—and hollering how he'd take the seventh game tomorrow. Carmichael said, "Wild horses can't keep Dean off that mound tomorrow, Frank."

I looked. Dizzy had a rubber tiger, a Detroit souvenir, by the tail and was whacking Bill DeLancey over the head with it and then throwing it into the showers at Pepper Martin. I knew inside me Diz would pitch it. He had a terrible head cold and only two days before had been knocked out running the bases, but there'd be no use fighting against it—he was the boy and the chips were sure down.

Incidentally the wolves had been on me for putting in Dizzy to run for big, slow Virgil Davis in that fourth game—the time Diz went into second so high and hard that Charley Gehringer, trying for a forceout, hit Diz in the head. But I didn't mind the criticism. We were out to win. We were the Gashouse Gang and I knew Diz would give 'em something to worry about running bases as well as pitching.

Well, morning came for the big game and then at the park Diz took the ball and warmed up with what looked like 50,000 Tiger fans hooting at him, and him grinning and yelling at each of us Cards who passed, "I'll shut 'em out. Get me a couple of runs: that's all. I'll blank the blank-blank blankety-blanks."

Dizzy said he'd shut 'em out and he did. And with the score 0-0 to start the third he singled and stretched it to get to second.

Pepper Martin, the Wild Horse, was up next and he hit a slow hopper to Greenberg and went down so fast he beat the throw. Three years before Pepper had driven Mickey Cochrane crazy running bases in the Series between the Athletics and the Cards and now he did it again.

Then Auker walked Rothrock and the bases were full. And I was up.

Joe Medwick

I couldn't let the rest of them make an old man out of the playing-manager, so I doubled and all three of 'em came in.

That was all for Auker and in came Schoolboy Rowe. Our bench stood up and gave him the "How'm-I-doin'-Edna?" chant. He had asked that during a radio interview, throwing in a little message to his girl, and the papers had been riding him about it. Rip Collins welcomed Rowe with a double and I scored. Then De-Lancey doubled and Rip scored—and away went Schoolboy with a lot of others besides us asking Edna how he was doin'.

We kept on hitting, and Cochrane, who was fit to be asylumed by this time, kept bringing in more pitchers. Dizzy got his second hit of the inning by racing like Pepper to first on a slow grounder, bringing DeLancey in. By the time the inning was over we had seven runs and I figured maybe Dizzy would be winded by all that hitting and base running he'd done in the inning, but, heck, no. He beat the rest of the team out to position and could hardly take time to make his warmup throws.

The Tigers were sore with that score standing against them and Dizzy holding them helpless. They called us plenty of names, but we had the fanciest name-callers in the game and poured it right back and, I suppose, more so.

It was like playing ball at the foot of Vesuvius. And in the sixth came the eruption. Pepper started by singling and, seeing Goslin in left juggle the throw momentarily, he went on to second. Rothrock and I went out, but Medwick lammed the ball against the screen for a double and kept on to third, sliding in hard. Marv Owen on third got the ball and stepped on Medwick's leg. Joe kicked up from his position on his back and hit Owen in the chest. They started to fight, and both teams boiled out. The panic was on, but nothing to what happened after the umpires had quieted everybody down and got the inning played out. As Medwick went out to left field the Tiger fans met him with cushions, bottles, lemons, and some of them took off their shoes and tried to bean him. They tried to climb the 18-foot wire fence to murder him. For 15 minutes the game was stopped and finally Commissioner Landis told Cochrane and me to bring Owen and Medwick up to his box. He asked Medwick, "Did you kick him?" and Joe said "You're darn right, I did!" They wouldn't shake hands and the noise got worse. Cochrane would run out and beg the bleachers to be good, but they would have none of his advice. So Landis put both Medwick and Owen out of the game and we went on to finish it.

So it ended 11-0. Dizzy had done what he said he'd do and we'd done more than he asked us.

THE BOX SCORE
(*October 9, 1934*)

ST. LOUIS

	A.B.	R.	H.	P.	A.
Martin, 3b.	5	3	2	0	1
Rothrock, rf.	5	1	2	4	0
Frisch, 2b.	5	1	1	3	5
Medwick, lf.	4	1	1	1	0
Fullis, lf.	1	0	1	1	0
Collins, 1b.	5	1	4	7	2
DeLancey, c.	5	1	1	5	0
Orsatti, cf.	3	1	1	2	0
Durocher, ss.	5	1	2	3	4
J. Dean, p.	5	1	2	1'	0
Totals	43	11	17	27	12

DETROIT

	A.B.	R.	H.	P.	A.
White, cf.	4	0	0	3	0
Cochrane, c.	4	0	0	2	2
Hayworth, c.	0	0	0	1	0
Gehringer, 2b.	4	0	2	3	5
Goslin, lf.	4	0	0	4	0
Rogell, ss.	4	0	1	3	2
Greenberg, 1b.	4	0	1	7	0
Owen, 3b.	4	0	0	1	2
Fox, rf.	3	0	2	3	0
Auker, p.	0	0	0	0	0
Rowe, p.	0	0	0	0	0
Hogsett, p.	0	0	0	0	0
Bridges, p.	2	0	0	0	1
Marberry, p.	0	0	0	0	0
G. Walker	1	0	0	0	0
Crowder, p.	0	0	0	0	0
Totals	34	0	6	27	12

G. Walker batted for Marberry in 8th.

ST. LOUIS	0	0	7	0	0	2	0	0	0 — 11	
DETROIT	0	0	0	0	0	0	0	0	0 — 0.	

Errors.—Collins, White, Gehringer, Goslin. Two-base hits—Rothrock (2), Fox (2), Frisch, DeLancey. Three-base hits—Medwick, Durocher. Runs batted in—Frisch (3), Collins (2), Martin, Rothrock, Medwick, J. Dean, DeLancey. Stolen base—Martin. Double play—Owen, Gehringer, Greenberg. Base on balls—Off Auker 1 (Rothrock), off Hogsett 2 (Orsatti, Martin), off Marberry 1 (Orsatti). Struck out—By Auker 1 (Martin), by Bridges 2 (J. Dean, DeLancey), by Crowder 1 (Rothrock), by J. Dean 5 (Greenberg (3), Bridges, White). Pitching records—Auker 6 hits, 4 runs in 2 1-3 innings; Rowe 2 hits in 1-3 inning; Hogsett 2 hits, 1 run in 0 inning (pitched to 4 batters); Bridges 6 hits, 4 runs in 4 1-3 innings; Marberry 1 hit, 0 run in 1 inning; Crowder 0 hits, 0 runs in 1 inning. Left on bases—St. Louis 9, Detroit 7. Earned runs—St. Louis 10, Detroit 0. Caught stealing—Orsatti. Losing pitcher— Auker. Umpires—Geisel (A. L.) home plate; Reardon (N. L.) first base; Klem (N. L.) third base. Time of game—2:19.

(Wide World)

Cy Young

CY YOUNG
as told to
FRANCIS J. POWERS

Denton True Young was born at Gilmore, Ohio, on March 29, 1867, and still lives in the same section of the Buckeye state, at the little town of Paoli. During his long major league career he pitched for Cleveland, Boston and St. Louis in the National, and Boston and Cleveland in the American League. He was one of the first players elected to Baseball's Hall of Fame.

A pitcher's got to be good and he's got to be lucky to get a no-hit game. But to get a perfect game, no run, no hit, no man reach first base, he's got to have everything his way. There've been only six perfect games pitched in the big leagues since 1880.

I certainly had my share of luck in the 23 years I pitched in the two big leagues because I threw three no-hitters and one of them was perfect. You look at the records and you'll find that Larry Corcoran, who pitched for the Chicago Nationals "away back when," was the only other big leaguer ever to get three no-hitters and none of them was perfect.

So it's no job for me to pick out my greatest day in baseball. It was May 5, 1904, when I was pitching for the Boston Red Sox and beat the Philadelphia Athletics without a run, hit or man reaching first. I'll be 78 next month, but of all the 879 games I pitched in the big leagues that one stands clearest in my mind.

The American League was pretty young then, just four seasons old, but it had a lot of good players and good teams. I was with St. Louis in the National when Ban Johnson organized the American League and I was one of the many players who jumped to the new circuit.

Jimmy Collins, whom I regard as the greatest of all third basemen, was the first manager of the Boston team and in 1903 we won the pennant and beat Pittsburgh in the first modern world's series.

Before I get into the details of my greatest day, I'd like to tell something about our Red Sox of those days. We had a great team. Besides Collins at third we had Freddie Parent at short, Hobe Ferris at second and Candy La Chance on first. You find some real old-timer and he'll tell you how great those fellows were.

In the outfield were Buck Freeman, who was the Babe Ruth of that time, Patsy Dougherty, who later played with the White Sox and Chick Stahl. Bill Dineen was one of our other pitchers and he'd licked the Pirates three games in the world's series the fall before.

Every great pitcher usually has a great catcher, like Mathewson had Roger Bresnahan and Miner Brown had Johnny Kling. Well, in my time I had two. First, "Chief" Zimmer, when I was with Cleveland in the National League, and then Lou Criger, who caught me at Boston and handled my perfect game.

As I said, my greatest game was against the Athletics, who were building up to win the 1905 pennant, and Rube Waddell was their pitcher. And I'd like to say that beating Rube anytime was a big job. I never saw many who were better pitchers.

I was real fast in those days but what very few batters knew was that I had two curves. One of them sailed in there as hard as my fast ball and broke in reverse. It was a narrow curve that broke away from the batter and went in just like a fast ball. And the other was a wide break. I never said much about them until after I was through with the game.

There was a big crowd for those times out that day. Maybe 10,000, I guess, for Waddell always was a big attraction.

I don't think I ever had more stuff and I fanned eight, getting Davis and Monte Cross, Philly shortstop, twice. But the boys gave me some great support and when I tell you about it, you'll understand why I say a pitcher's got to be awfully lucky to get a perfect game.

The closest the Athletics came to a hit was in the third when Monte Cross hit a pop fly that was dropping just back of the infield between first and second. Freeman came tearing in from right like a deer and barely caught the ball.

But Ollie Pickering, who played center field for Mr. Mack, gave me two bad scares. Once he hit a fly back of second that Chick Stahl caught around his knees after a long run from center. The other time Ollie hit a slow roller to short and Parent just got him by a step.

Patsy Dougherty helped me out in the seventh when he crashed into the left field fence to get Danny Hoffman's long foul; and I recall that Criger almost went into the Boston bench to get a foul by Davis.

Most of the other batters were pretty easy but all told there were 10 flies hit, six to the outfield. The infielders had seven assists and I had two and 18 of the putouts were divided evenly between Criger and La Chance.

Well, sir, when I had two out in the ninth, and it was Waddell's time to bat, some of the fans began to yell for Connie Mack to send up a pinch hitter. They wanted me to finish what looked like a perfect game against a stronger batter.

But Mr. Mack let Rube take his turn. Rube took a couple of strikes and then hit a fly that Stahl caught going away from the infield.

You can realize how perfect we all were that day when I tell you the game only took one hour and 23 minutes.

We got three runs off Waddell and when the game was finished it looked like all the fans came down on the field and tried to shake my hand. One gray-haired fellow jumped the fence back of third and shoved a bill into my hand. It was $5.

The game was a sensation at the time. It was the first perfect game in 24 years, or since 1880, when both John M. Ward and Lee Richmond did the trick. It also was the second no-hitter ever pitched in the American League. Jimmy Callahan of the White Sox pitched the first against Detroit in 1902 but somehow a batter got to first base.

During my 23 years in the big leagues I pitched 472 games in the National League and won 291, and then I went into the American League and won 220 there. So all told I worked 879 games and won 511 and far as I can see these modern pitchers aren't gonna catch me.

By the way, you might be interested to know that in my last big-league game I was beaten 1-0 by a kid named Grover Cleveland Alexander.

THE BOX SCORE
(*May 5, 1904*)

BOSTON	A.B.	R.	H.	P.	A.	ATHLETICS	A.B.	R.	H.	P.	A.
Dougherty, lf.	4	0	1	1	0	Hartsel	1	0	0	0	0
Collins, 3b.	4	0	2	2	0	Hoffman, lf.	2	0	0	2	1
Stahl, cf.	4	1	1	3	0	Pickering, cf.	3	0	0	1	0
Freeman, rf.	4	0	1	2	0	Davis, 1b.	3	0	0	5	0
Parent, ss.	4	0	2	1	4	L. Cross, 3b.	3	0	0	4	1
La Chance, 1b.	3	0	1	9	0	Seybold, rf.	3	0	0	2	0
Ferris, 2b.	3	1	1	0	3	Murphy, 2b.	3	0	0	1	2
Criger, c.	3	1	1	9	0	M. Cross, ss.	3	0	0	2	3
Young, p.	3	0	0	0	2	Schreck, c.	3	0	0	7	0
						Waddell, p.	3	0	0	0	1
Totals	32	3	10	27	9	Totals	27	0	0	24	8

```
ATHLETICS     0  0  0   0  0  0  0   0  0—0
BOSTON        0  0  0   0  0  1  2   0  *—3
```

Error—Davis. Two-base hits—Collins, Criger. Three-base hits—Stahl, Freeman, Ferris. Sacrifice hit—La Chance. Left on bases—Boston 5. Double plays—Hoffman to Schreck, L. Cross to Davis. Struck out—By Young 8, Waddell 6. Time—1:23. Umpire—Dwyer. Attendance—10,267.

Fred Fitzsimmons

FRED
FITZSIMMONS

as told to

JOHN P. CARMICHAEL

Fred L. Fitzsimmons was born July 28, 1901 in Misha-waka, Ind. Began his major league career with the Giants in 1925 and traded to Brooklyn on June 11, 1937, remaining with the Dodgers until July 27, 1943, when he was named manager of the Phillies. Off the ball field, Freddie is owner of a vast chicken ranch near Arcadia, Calif.

The Dodgers were sprawled along the front of their Ebbets Field dugout that early September afternoon, talking about their impending Western tour...their last of the 1941 season. "Where do we go first?" asked Manager Leo Durocher just to refresh his memory. He was told Chicago...then St. Louis...and then Cincy, Pittsburgh and Philly in that order. Leo nodded and suddenly turned toward Freddie Fitzsimmons. "You're opening against the Cards," he barked. "Be ready...!"

So here I was with 10 days notice (said Fitzsimmons) and when the day came around I never was less ready. However, at the time we weren't too much worried about the Cardinals because we had a three-game lead leaving home and less than two weeks to go. But when we reached St. Louis, things had changed. We dropped a double-header to the Cubs on Sept. 10 and that same day those guys (the Cards) won a pair, so the chips were down in the Redbird series. Our lead was down to one game. We just had to win the opener there the next day.

A pitcher shouldn't worry, because it doesn't do any good and I've often told youngsters that, but I didn't sleep too sound the night before that game. I didn't fool myself that I was a great pitcher any longer, but our staff wasn't in good shape and Leo put it up to me. If I got beat, it meant the Cards had wiped out the last bit of our lead and they were finishing at home while we had to go all the way on the road.

I remember our clubhouse meeting that day . . . Leo put a little extra bite into his words . . . he told us this was "it" and we couldn't afford to lose. The Cards were pretty confident when we got onto the field. They knew I was going to work and they'd keep calling over: "Oh, you're the ace of Durocher's staff, huh, Fitz?" and "You're an old man, Freddie, we feel sorry for you" and things like that. It's all part of the game, of course, and I didn't blame 'em for feeling pert because they just about had us over the barrel.

The crowd got on us, too, especially Joe Medwick, who used to play there. "You're right where you belong . . . with the Bums . . . Joe," a guy hollered as we cut across the field. I was walkin' alongside Joe and he said: "My public, Fitz . . . listen to the cheers. Would I like to hit one today." I thought to myself: "I hope you hit a couple, Joe-boy, because I got a feelin' we'll need all we can get." Ernie White was to pitch for them and he could do pretty well against a left-handed hitting club like we were. Our power was Reiser, Camilli and Walker . . . all southpaws.

Durocher came out when I was warming up and asked how I felt and I told him fine, but I could see Corriden (Coach John Corriden) watching me throw and he kinda wrinkled his nose a couple of times as though he didn't like what he saw. I didn't have a thing . . . no stuff . . . and my knuckler wouldn't drop. You know I always used to tell the plate umpire before I went out to pitch: "Remember, my knuckle ball doesn't float like some of 'em. It breaks down like a spitter, so don't call it too soon." This day it wasn't doing anything but just hanging

in the air, but I went to Umpire Al Barlick at the plate anyway and
said:

"Don't forget . . . watch my knuckler close . . . it drops."

That was about the last friendly word Barlick and I spoke for the
afternoon. The game started and White let loose as if he intended to
scare us right out of the park. He retired nine Dodgers in order and
fanned five of the first six. He was plenty fast and our boys were so
anxious to hit they were swinging at his motion instead of waiting for
the ball to get there. Then in the third inning, the Cards got two runs,
I tried a knuckler on Jimmy Brown and he hit it into left field. Medwick was so nervous he fumbled and you know those Redbirds . . .
boom! Brown was into second head-first.

Well, Hopp bunted and Camilli came up with the ball but I didn't
get to first fast enough for the play and he was safe. Then Padgett
singled Brown home and, after an infield out, Crespi hit safely and
Hopp scored. Durocher gave me a slap on the pants when I got to
the bench and told me "never mind . . . we got a long way to go." He
didn't know how long. Then, in the fourth we got a break. The Cardinals were jittery too and, after Reese singled and Reiser was hit by
a pitched ball around Herman's infield out, Medwick hit to short.

It was a perfect double-play ball and Medwick was swearing in
disgust as he ran it out, but suddenly Marion fumbled and everybody
was safe. Then it was our turn to yell. We gave Marion a good going
over from the bench. We were still hollering when Lavagetto drove
out a fly that scored Reiser, and Camilli went up to hit. And he hit!
I pushed my way off the bench just in time to see the ball bounce on
the roof in right field and we were two runs in front. Did you ever feel
as though somebody had lifted an anvil off your back?

Funny thing, that home run cooled me off in a jiffy. I went out to
pitch again and as I picked up my glove I decided there was only one
thing for me to do . . . try and talk the Cards "out" the rest of the way.
I couldn't get any ball to break and they knew it. Fortunately my
control was all right . . . but they knew that, too, and they were ready
to swing. So I let 'em have it. I started to call 'em names and snarl and I

admit I meant it, too, because I never wanted to win a game like this one. If it had been my last, I would have been satisfied.

I started on Hopp in the fourth. I told him to get off his flat feet because the next pitch would be right under his chin. It was and he hit the dirt. The Card bench gave me a blast and I didn't blame 'em, but I'd made up my mind. I put another one so close that Hopp wound up with his pants in our dugout and then he let loose. The war was on. Up to then the game had gone along pretty well . . . just the usual "formalities" . . . but this was different. It was my fault . . . but there was no other way.

Padgett was next. I almost took his cap off and then got the next pitch over the inside corner for a called strike when he waited for another duster. "This is the one you were waiting for, you so-and-so," I yelled down to him and put No. 3 so close he could smell the horsehide. He looked a little surprised that I'd do such a thing on purpose and by then I was really taking a beating from both the crowd and the St. Louis bench. Even Billy Southworth was getting mad, but it worked. I got Padgett out.

Believe me, it was rough going. We had to hang onto that two-run lead because the way White was throwing it didn't look like we'd get any more. Johnny Mize came up in the fifth with one on and I warned him to be "loose" and he had to pull away from a couple. By this time both benches were in a turmoil. Everybody was raving and I was really getting hell. "So that blankety-blank Durocher is pitching for you, too," Mike Gonzales was hollering at me. "A fine guy you turn out to be after all these years." But by now I was so caught up in the game myself that I didn't care what anybody said . . . or did . . . just so I didn't get knocked outta there. I had to stay. If we could get by with me, it meant that the rest of the pitchers, who had been overworked because the race was so close, would have an extra day of rest. They needed it.

But things finally got so bad along about the seventh inning that Umpire Barlick finally took a hand. I'd been barkin' at him most of the game, because he knew my knuckler wasn't breaking and I was getting by on control and makin' the Cards mad—and I wanted every close decision I could get. I was still yelling at every hitter, fast as he came up, when Barlick finally walked over to our bench and told Durocher he'd put me out of the game if I didn't calm down. "He started it," said Barlick. "Those guys didn't say a thing to him."

Well, then Leo and Barlick had it out and you know Durocher. No umpire was going to put his pitcher out of any game and if the "so-and-so and such-and-such Cardinals couldn't take it, they could quit and Brooklyn would take the game." Al (Barlick) didn't want to put anybody out, but he knew I'd been giving those guys a tongue-lashing and he probably knew why, too; knew that I was "covering up." So the seventh got under way and maybe I was feeling the strain because I wound up hitting Brown in the leg.

Hopp forced Brown, but up came that big horse, Padgett, and he straightened one into right-center and Hopp went to third. This was a fine spot for me with Mize up and only one out, so I went to work on him once more. It was while I was dusting him off and calling him

Dolph Camilli

names that Barlick called time and walked halfway to the mound. "That's enough," he told me. "One more word and you're gone." He went back to the plate, but by the time he turned around in position to call 'em, I was right there, too, and I was sizzling.

"You're not putting me out of this game until it's over," I told him. "This is my game and I'm going to win it or lose it. This is a pennant game. I don't know whether you've got the guts to throw me out, but I'll tell you one thing: if you have, I've got the guts to kill you right where you stand ...and I WILL." I really yelled those last words at him and even now I know that I meant them. I don't know what I would have done if he'd given me the thumb... maybe I would have tried to kill him, because I was that mad. I'd a hit him, I guess.

But he didn't oust me. He must have realized how I felt ... maybe that I wasn't myself... and he didn't say anything except to "get back and pitch."

So I went back and made Mize hit to me ... a weak bounder. I fired to Reese for what could have been a double play... and he dropped the ball. Hopp scored. It was 4-3 in our favor. Then Estell Crabtree singled and Medwick made a great pickup and throw to the plate.

He had Padgett by five feet... but the ball got through Owen and the score was tied. I felt sick, I wasn't mad at Reese or Owen. Errors are part of a game and everybody makes them. But I'd gotten by so well up to then... and it meant so much to our team. When I got to the dugout as we went up to hit in the eighth, Durocher indicated he thought maybe a new pitcher would be in order. "I'm still pitching," I snapped at him.

Looking back at that 11th inning now, when we got two runs to win, 6-4, it seems like an anticlimax. We didn't even "jockey" any more; we were too tired. We just hung on and battled for the final "break" and we got it in that 11th when Medwick singled and Lavagetto walked ahead of Camilli who bunted; Mize fell fielding the ball.

It was an easy play and even if he'd made the out we still would have had men on third and second with one out, but the sight of "Big Jawn's" feet sliding out from under him at a critical moment did something to all of us. It made us laugh in spite of the fact that the winning run wasn't yet home. I can hear Durocher giving that victory bark of his to "Dixie" Walker who was marching to the plate with the bags loaded and NOBODY out:

"Rack it up, Dix....!"

That was Leo's war-cry... our war-cry... and it smote against Walker's ears as he eased into the batter's box. One ball... one strike ... then Dixie swung. It was "in there"... clean as a whistle and the needed runs came home.

I'd seen Hugh Casey warming up the last couple of innings and when I got up to start the last half of the inning, Durocher was standing near by and put a hand on my arm. "You've done enough, Fred," he said quietly. "Let Hugh put it away for you." I didn't argue. I was tired. I was all in. I was glad to sit down.

————

The next afternoon, as the Cards and Dodgers prepared to renew that battle Fitzsimmons was trudging past the batting cage when he ran into a covey of Redbirds . . . Brown, Marion, Mize, Hopp . . . who surrounded him. "Listen, Fitz," they said. "We want to apologize if anybody said anything to you yesterday, but damned if we know who was on you . . . we weren't. Geez, you were 'red' out there."

Fitzsimmons burst out into a loud guffaw.

"Nobody hollered at me," he said. "I just didn't have a thing and I decided I'd see if I could talk you out of the game. You don't have to apologize for anything. . . . I thought of it myself."

THE BOX SCORE
(Sept. 11, 1941)

BROOKLYN

	A.B.	R.	H.	P.	A.
Reese, ss.	6	1	1	5	4
Herman, 2b.	5	0	0	1	3
Reiser, cf.	4	1	2	4	0
Medwick, lf.	5	2	1	2	1
Lavagetto, 3b.	4	1	0	3	1
Camilli, 1b.	4	1	2	9	2
Walker, rf.	4	0	1	4	0
Owen, c.	4	0	0	4	1
Fitzsimmons, p.	4	0	0	1	4
Casey, p.	0	0	0	0	4
Galan	1	0	0	0	0
Totals	41	6	7	33	16

Galan batted for Fitzsimmons in 11th.

ST. LOUIS

	A.B.	R.	H.	P.	A.
Brown, 3b.	5	1	2	1	3
Hopp, cf.	3	2	1	3	0
Padgett, lf.	5	1	2	2	0
Mize, 1b.	4	0	1	13	1
Crabtree, rf.	5	0	1	3	0
Crespi, 2b.	5	0	2	1	3
Marion, ss.	5	0	0	0	4
Mancuso, c.	5	0	1	9	1
White, p.	4	0	0	1	1
Triplett	1	0	0	0	0
Totals	42	4	10	33	13

Triplett batted for White in 11th.

Errors—Reese (2), Medwick, Marion (2), Crespi, Owen, Mize. Runs batted in—Padgett, Crespi, Lavagetto, Camilli (3), Walker (2), Mize. Sacrifice hits—Owen. Three-base hit—Reiser. Home run—Camilli. Double plays—Lavagetto to Camilli. Left on bases—Brooklyn, 6; St. Louis, 8. Struck out—Fitzsimmons, 3; Casey, 1; White 8. Bases on balls—Fitzsimmons, 3; White, 2. Hits—Off Fitzsimmons, 10 in 10 innings; Casey, none in 1. Hit by pitcher—White (Reiser); Fitzsimmons (Brown).

MEL
OTT
as told to
JOHN P. CARMICHAEL

Mel Ott, playing manager of the Giants, has been, since 1928, one of the great sluggers and outfielders of the game. Since he joined the Giants as a boy of 16, he has averaged .310, led the league six times in home runs, twice in runs scored, and last season in his 34th year, hit 30 homers to run his lifetime total to 445, a league record and one only surpassed by Babe Ruth and Jimmy Foxx.

Can a fellow change his mind? You know for quite a few years I always remembered the day in 1926 that I reported to the Giants in Sarasota, when I was 16 years old, as my greatest thrill; when I first saw John McGraw and heard him say: "Go to the outfield, young man." I wondered afterward how I even had the courage to say a word...why didn't I just nod my head and run quick. Instead I heard myself: "But I'm a catcher, Mr. McGraw," and he didn't even seem to be looking at me when he came back:

"That's all right, Bresnahan always thought he was a pitcher, too!"

Can I change my mind again? Up to the night of August 7, 1940, in the Polo Grounds, whenever anybody asked me my greatest day it was that afternoon in Washington in 1933 when I hit the home run that gave us the World Series; when I saw ol' Dolph Luque break a curve off so sharp to Joe Kuhel for the strike which gave us the championship that Gus Mancuso had to dig it out of the dirt. But since August 7, 1940, I know what it means to have an outstanding day to remember. That was Mel Ott night with 53,000 fans in the stands.

All the things that I'd done in baseball for myself just seemed swallowed up in what the fans were doing for me that evening. Really, there was something unreal about it. I'll always be grateful to Mr. Stoneham for picking a regularly scheduled Brooklyn-Giant game for my night, because neither he nor myself wanted to use me to get people out . . . to swell the crowd. The Dodgers and Giants at night would draw anyhow, anytime, so nobody could say we were building up a gate.

I told my wife, before I left for the park, that she'd be lucky if I didn't fall down going after a ball or strike-out with the winning run on third and disgrace her, because I was as nervous as a cat. I've been knocked down and got up again and never thought a thing about it, but I knew there'd be speeches and gifts and I was as tense inside as could be. It's a little embarrassing at that, even though you know the fans mean it and you feel pretty proud. People had been contributing dimes and nickels and more to the committee and my wife knew in advance what I was going to get and she was tickled to death with the gifts. I didn't blame her after I saw 'em. In the clubhouse the boys were calling me the grand old man of the Giants. . . . I was 31 . . . and prophesying that Freddy Fitzsimmons, who was gonna pitch for Brooklyn, would fan me all night long. That's usually the way.

Well, finally we were around the plate and there were flowers all over and then came the gifts. You know what I got? Honestly, it was enough to make a guy choke up. I got a set of flat silver, 208 pieces, a coffee and tea set imported from England, a silver water pitcher, a complete set of golf clubs and bag (they were from the players) a couple of plaques and a gold card of membership in the Baseball Writers Association of America. Carl Hubbell presented the clubs, only it should have been the other way 'round. I ought to have been up there saying those things about him and the rest of the gang.

It was a relief to get the game started. Just as I walked to the plate the first time, a guy with a foghorn voice from upstairs bellowed: "You were a nice guy a little while ago, Ott, but you're a bum beginning now." He must have been a Dodger rooter and, after all, they were only five games behind the Reds at the time. Ol' Hub was pitching for us and you couldn't ask for a more perfect setup for the customers ... Hubbell against Fitzsimmons who used to be one of us. For Hub to win meant more to me than anything else, but I wasn't much help to him ... only one hit in five times up and I made the last out in the ninth after Brooklyn had won, 8-4, but even a homer then wouldn't have helped us.

They got five runs in the seventh and the only thing I did at all was in the fifth when Camilli hit one four country miles. I could see the ball going straight for the Giant bull pen and I just ran automatically and finally jumped at the last minute and it stuck in my glove. It made me feel good because at the time we were leading 4-3 and at least our fans got a chance to yell. Funny about a game like that; chances are most of the folks came out to see two great rivals play, but they'd sort of included me in the celebration.

While we were changing pitchers in the seventh I looked around those stands with fans yelling and laughing and I thought what an ungrateful guy a ballplayer could be who didn't just give everything he had all the time to people who only asked just that and were willing to even make a hero out of him. I never was what you'd call colorful, meaning I just tried to play hard and hit and give my best. You either have a flair for color or you don't and Bill Terry used to kid me lots and say:

"Why don't you do something ... go get drunk ... disappear for a few days ... roll over and catch a ball ... come into the plate on your hands?"

But that wouldn't have been me and he knew it, too. One time I got a job in a New Orleans clothing store. Didn't have to do a thing but hang around from about 11 A.M. until 3 in the afternoon and I was being overpaid. How could I earn it? Nobody came in to buy suits from the fellow . . . they just wanted to talk baseball. He didn't get any good out of it, so I quit.

Well, to get back to my biggest day, you'd think that I'd gotten everything a fellow could get in one night, but when the game was over and we were going home, there still was more to come. Way back when I first started to play ball, I went with a semipro club in Patterson, Miss. It was owned by a lumberman named Harry Williams, who wanted a camp team and it was Williams who sent me up to McGraw. They were old friends and so I've always had him to thank for my chance. Williams later married Marguerite Clark, the movie actress.

So I got home, with all my presents, and you can imagine how my wife acted over the silver and things and there was a special delivery letter for me. It was from Miss Clark. Williams had died about six or seven years before. The letter said:

"Do you mind if I add a little something to the gifts which all Giant fans are proud and happy to contribute? If Harry were alive, he would want me to do this I know. It would have made him very happy."

It arrived the next day . . . a salad set to match our silver. That just about made my greatest day complete and I don't think whatever comes now, even if I'm ever so fortunate as to win a pennant as a manager, will make me change my mind any more. To bring a Giant team into another World Series would be only returning a compliment.

BABE
ADAMS

as told to

HERBERT F. McDOUGAL

Charles Benjamin "Babe" Adams was one of the great names in baseball, pitching for the Pirates from 1909 to 1926. Born in 1888 at Tipton, Ind., Babe threw and batted right-handed. A Hoosier by birth, Adams is looked upon as a Missourian, spending most of his life in and around Mount Moriah. His winning record in the National League shows 204 victories against 104 losses. He boasted of blinding speed and a sharp curve and had the enviable earned run mark of 2.11 runs per game throughout his major league career.

About an hour and a half before the first game of the 1909 World Series at Pittsburgh, I was sitting on the bench with the other Pirate youngsters making jokes about how we'd handle the Detroit Tigers if we could get in the series. It was strictly fooling, for we all knew the team was full of stars and we were only kids. I was 21, and never was what you'd call high-strung—just a country boy who had been drawn to the game by all the interest around my home, Mount Moriah, Mo., and the near-by towns of Princeton, and the Shane-Hills from across the line in Kansas. Cy Young and his brother Lon were playing at Spickard. The woods were full of amateurs then.

A Missourian named Ham Hamilton, who was an umpire out on the Pacific Coast, came home the winter of 1904, I think it was, and was hired by the new Missouri Valley League to scout players. He watched me pitch for Mount Moriah and signed me to play with Parsons, Kansas. I did all right that 1905 season and had a trial with the St. Louis Cardinals in 1906 but didn't stick, and signed with Louisville where I lasted a couple of weeks and was shipped to Denver where a Pirate scout signed me in 1907. The Pirates tried me out then and gave me more seasoning at Louisville where I won 22 games in 1908 and was brought back up by the Pirates for the 1909 season.

Fred Clarke, the manager, used me in about 25 games or so, and I won about 12 and lost only three, but that was nothing to the big three on our club: Howard Camnitz, who won 25; Lefty Leifield, who won 19, and Vic Willis, who won 22. And Nick Maddox, with 13 wins was great in a tight game, and Deacon Phillipe, though getting along, was just the man for a World Series game. For relief we had old Sam Leever, as smart as they made them.

It was enough for me that I was on a team with those stars and Hans Wagner and Tommy Leach and George Gibson. Gibson had caught 133 consecutive games for us. I remember when he caught the 111th it broke the world's record.

We had a team that year, and had beaten out the Cubs and Giants by putting on a 16-game winning streak in August to clinch it. What helped us was the way Christy Mathewson beat the Cubs that season. As I remember it he hadn't beaten Mordecai Brown in a pitching duel in four or five years till that season when he turned the tables.

(The record book shows that on June 8, Mathewson beat Brown for the first time since 1903. Editor's note.)

It was Matty's greatest year, as I recall.

(Mathewson won 26 and lost 6 that year for an .806 average, his big league top. He was out several weeks with an injured finger or he might have reached his 1908 tops in games won, 37. Editor's note.)

Ty Cobb

Nobody ever had a more exciting freshman year I suppose. Playing a double-header against the Giants that summer I played to 35,000 people, which everybody said was the biggest crowd baseball had ever drawn. I remember we won the flag by taking 110 victories, but had to go like mad because the Cubs won 104.

Considering the opposition we had beaten that year we felt we could take the Tigers in the World Series, but the betting was in favor of Hughie Jennings' team. The experts figured that with Ty Cobb and Sam Crawford as the big batting punch, and with such pitchers as Mullin, a 29-game winner; Willett, a 22-game winner, and Summers, a 19-game winner, and Owen Bush, a whirlwind fielder at short, they'd chew us up.

To hear all the talk and read all the papers this Cobb was going to go this time. The Tigers had been licked by the Cubs in the 1907 World Series, four games to one, and again by the same dose in 1908. That meant they had won only two games in the last two World Series and they were raving.

I'd keep hearing how the Cub pitchers had stopped Cobb in the 1907 series, but how he'd broken out and hit them for a .368 average in the 1908 series, and how the Pirate pitchers weren't as good as the Cubs' Brown, Overall, Reulbach, Pfiester, and so on.

But we figured we were the National League champs, who had licked the American League in three of the last four World Series and that not even Cobb could stop us from making it four.

The newsapers had said I was to start the first game because Howard Camnitz was still weak from a throat operation he'd had, but we youngsters all thought that was Fred Clarke just working some pre-game tricks on the Tigers. I was enjoying myself kidding on the bench before the game, free as a bird, when suddenly we looked up and Clarke was standing there and he threw me the ball and said. "You're it."

I caught it and laughed, for he could be pretty funny. But he repeated, "You're it. Come on, kid."

I warmed up. I wasn't a bit excited, though I was sort of anxious about Ty Cobb. We had talked a lot about him, of course. He was in his fifth year with the Tigers and had burned that American League to a crisp. He had had a big year.

(Cobb had hit .377 that season, stolen 76 bases, driven in 115 runs and scored 110 times. He was only 22, although in his fifth season with the Tigers. Editor's note.)

Being too careful, I walked him that first time and Delehanty singled him home, but I got him out the rest of the game—and we won 4 to 1. I gave them 6 hits. The Tigers won the next game and we took the next and it see-sawed, turn about, that way up to the seventh. Clarke pitched me again in the fifth game and I won 8-4. Cobb got a single off me, but no more. They only got six hits, the same as the first game. But Wagner made some errors and Leach bumped into the fence on a long ball from Sam Crawford's bat and Sam got a homer to run the score up to four.

The Tigers won the sixth and we came to the deciding game in Detroit on October 16. I had had two days' rest, but I was young and wanted to pitch it. The weather was cold and raw, and held the crowd down to around 17,000. I remember this because I expected there'd be a sellout for the crucial game. Some friends of mine from northern Missouri had wired me to get them tickets and I didn't think I could, but when I tried I found there was plenty of room.

It wasn't the crowd, or anything much that happened that made this day the biggest I can remember in baseball. It was just that I shut the Tigers out in the big payoff game, and kept their big two, Cobb and Crawford, from getting hits. They were up four times apiece and down four times. I was really never in trouble, for Wild Bill Donovan for the Tigers was wild, walked six men in three innings, and Mullin who came in was about as wild as that and Hans Wagner tore them apart in the sixth inning with a triple that scored two and Fred Clarke stole two bases and we made altogether 11 hits and eight runs, while they were goose-egged and got six hits.

All three of my wins in that series were six-hitters. Eighteen hits, five runs they got in the three games and Cobb only got one hit in 11 times against me.

(Cobb hit only .231 for the series. Editor's note.)

THE BOX SCORE
(*October 16, 1909*)

DETROIT	A.B.	R.	H.	P.	A.	PITTSBURGH	A.B.	R.	H.	P.	A.
D. Jones, lf.	4	0	1	3	0	Bryne, 3b.	0	0	0	0	0
Bush, ss.	3	0	0	2	5	Hyatt, cf.	3	1	0	1	0
Cobb, rf.	4	0	0	1	0	Leach, cf.-3b.	3	2	2	5	2
Crawford, cf.	4	0	0	4	0	Clarke, lf.	1	2	0	4	0
Delehanty, 2b.	3	0	2	3	3	Wagner, ss.	3	1	1	3	2
Moriarty, 3b.	1	0	1	1	0	Miller, 2b.	5	0	2	3	0
O'Leary, 3b.	3	0	0	1	0	Abstein, 1b.	4	1	1	10	0
T. Jones, 1b.	4	0	1	9	0	Wilson, rf.	4	1	0	0	0
Schmidt, c.	3	0	1	3	2	Gibson, c.	5	0	2	1	1
Donovan, p.	0	0	0	0	2	Adams, p.	3	0	0	0	5
Mullin, p.	3	0	0	0	2						
Totals	32	0	6	27	14	Totals	31	8	8	27	10

```
DETROIT       0  0  0  0  0  0  0  0  0 — 0
PITTSBURGH    0  2  0  2  0  3  0  1  0 — 8
```

Errors—D. Jones, Crawford. Hits—Off Donovan, 2 in 3 innings; off Mullin, 6 in 6 innings. At bat—Against Donovan, 3; Mullin, 28. Two-base hits—Delehanty, Schmidt, Leach, Abstein, Gibson. Three-base hit—Wagner. Base on balls—Off Donovan, 6; off Mullin, 4; off Adams, 1. Hit by pitcher—By Donovan, Byrne; by Mullin, Bush. Errors—Pittsburgh, 1. Left on bases—Detroit, 7; Pittsburgh, 11. Struck out—By Mullin, 2; by Adams, 1. Double play—Bush to Schmidt to Delehanty. Time of game—2:00. Umpires—O'Loughlin and Johnstone. Attendance—17,565.

As the last man went out, we raced for hacks that were to take us down to our hotels, where we dressed. The crowd was rushing, too, and here came my friends from Missouri pushing roses at me, and screaming congratulations and saying I was the only man beside Mathewson ever to win three games in a World Series. There was a pin in the handle of the bouquet and it ran into the back of my hand deep. I guess I was thinking about that more than the game as the hack started downtown. I was wondering if it would keep me out of the barnstorming tour we were going to make. It didn't.

My share from the series was $1,745. I read last year that each of the winning Cardinals got around $6,200. That's all right. We lived in a different time, and I enjoyed myself in baseball, pitching, all told, 18 years for the Pirates.

JIMMY ARCHER

as told to
HAL TOTTEN

James P. (Jimmy) Archer, best remembered for his famous "squat" throw to second base, was born in Dublin, Ireland, broke into baseball with Pittsburgh in 1904, and rose to stardom as a catcher for the fabled Frank Chance's Cubs, with whom he played from 1909 through 1917. He is now promotion director for the Congress Recreation Center, one of Chicago's largest bowling establishments.

You're takin' me back a long way when you want to hear about my biggest baseball day—30 years ago, to be exact—and you can't expect me to remember much about that game, can you? But there's one thing I'll never forget—maybe that's why it's still my greatest day—and that's the fact that for once we were strangers in our own ball park.

Yes, sir, that's one day the old Cub rooters were pullin' for the Giants—and if you don't think that's somethin', you don't know much about the old Cubs and the old Giants—and those fans. But it's the truth—we were the only ones in the whole ball park who wanted the Cubs to win.

Frank Chance

Jimmie Lavender

It was a Monday in 1912—July 8 was the date. The old club was just starting to break up. From 1912 on it just dwindled off and dwindled off and new fellows came in—like Good and Pierce. But no matter how bad we were going, any time you showed us a Giant uniform we got tough. And this game was an extra special one, too. Rube Marquard, that big crooked-neck left-hander of the Giants, had won 19 straight games and this was the day he was going to make it 20—with us feedin' the kitty. But he didn't win—he didn't even finish the game—that was the tough part of it. That was the game—and here's the story of my biggest baseball day.

We came in from St. Louis that morning, where we'd won four out of five. But we'd been going terrible that year. The Giants were leading us by 15 games. The ball park was jammed that day—more than 25,000 fans were there. They were out to see Marquard win his 20th in a row.

When we walked into the park you could have knocked us over with a feather. Everybody in the park wanted that big crooked-neck to win. Even the ushers were pullin' for the Giants. I never saw anything like it. When we got in the clubhouse Frank Chance let out a roar. "What is this?" he hollered. "Where are we playing? Milwaukee? Brooklyn? Come on—let's go out there and get after this guy?"

We were starting a young pitcher named Jimmie Lavender. He was a peculiar little fella—one of those determined Southerners. His home was in Montezuma, Ga. And superstitious—my gosh! If he'd win a game, from then on he'd wear the same clothes; go to the ball park the same way; do the same things; eat the same food and drink the same stuff every day until he lost one.

He was a peculiar pitcher, too, and in his later days he was more peculiar than ever. By that I mean—he was one of the few pitchers in history who had both a spitball and a good curve. And he threw 'em both the same way. I'd take him through lots of games without a spitter, and other times I'd take him through without a curve. He was always pretty good against the Giants and he pitched even though he'd worked three innings the day before in St. Louis.

Well, all the time we were warming up that crowd was on us. Everything the Giants did was swell; everything we did was terrible. We weren't used to that sorta thing and I don't know just how the others felt, but for my part it made me mad—gave me more fight. You know what that old gang was—you'd tell 'em you could lick 'em and they'd tell you where you could go and then go out and prove you couldn't beat 'em.

The game itself isn't in my mind very much, but the atmosphere from the minute we stepped in the park impressed me and has stayed with me. We were a team on a foreign field. After we were through warming up and were sitting on the bench waiting to go out, I remember I said to Lavender: "Jim, if you ever pitched in your life, do it today. Don't let this big guy beat you."

The others felt the same way, too, especially Evers and Tinker, who didn't like Marquard very much anyway. Well, the game got going, and early in it Lavender was in a lot of critical spots. They had a lot of chances but got squeezed out of 'em. I remember one—they had men on first and third and they tried a double steal. We had a play set up for that and we pulled it on 'em. Evers would go over to cover second and Tinker would take a couple of steps straight in—not toward second. Then I'd fire the ball to Tinker and we'd have the runner off third right between us. And we cut 'im down.

We scored first—and after that they never had a chance. It was in the second inning and we really had 'em rattled. Heinie Zimmerman singled to center and Tommy Leach did the same thing, putting Zim on second. Vic Saier bounced to Heinie Groh, the second baseman, and he started for Leach to tag him and throw to first for a double play. But Tommy stopped and Heinie chased him a couple of steps and then threw to first. But he took so long that Vic got to first. Then Fred Merkle threw to second to try to get Leach and Zimmerman saw him throw so kept right on in to the plate.

He scored the first run of the game on that one. Then Evers beat out a bunt to fill the bases and the crowd groaned—and that was a Chicago crowd, remember. Then that big crooked-neck settled down and struck

Joe Tinker

me out and struck out Lavender. The crowd went wild. He got two strikes on Jimmy Sheckard. But then he put too much on one and it was a wild pitch and Leach scored the second run. Sheckard struck out on the next pitch.

Lavender was still in trouble in the third and they scored their first run. Fred Snodgrass was hit by a pitched ball and Beals Becker singled to right to put Snodgrass on third. Merkle smashed a hard one right back at Lavender and he threw to me and we caught Snodgrass going back to third. Red Murray singled to right and Becker scored. But Merkle tried to score too, and Frank Schulte made a perfect throw to the plate and we got him. Then Evers threw out Herzog.

Well, Lavender suddenly settled down after four innings and they couldn't do a thing with him. They made some errors behind Rube and finally Josh Devore batted for Marquard in the seventh and we had him out of there. We went on to win the game 7 to 2 and it snapped Marquard's winning streak at 19 straight.

Naturally, we were very much elated; tickled to death. To us it was the same thing as winning a world series. The Giants had challenged us; Marquard's record had challenged us; and even our own crowd challenged us. And we licked all three. But even though we won that game we were still strangers in our own ball park. As we walked off the field, our own fans were still on us. "Yeah," they yelled at us, "you guys would have to go and do a thing like that."

THE BOX SCORE
(*July 8, 1912*)

CUBS	A.B.	H.	P.	A.	GIANTS	A.B.	H.	P.	A.
Sh'ck'd, lf.	4	0	1	0	Snodgrass, lf.	2	1	0	0
Schulte, rf.	4	1	1	1	Becker, cf.	4	2	1	0
Tinker, ss.	4	0	3	3	Merkle, 1b.	4	1	8	1
Zimmerman, 3b.	3	1	2	1	Murray, rf.	4	1	1	0
Leach, cf.	3	1	1	0	Herzog, 3b.	3	0	1	3
Saier, 1b.	4	3	6	0	Myers, c.	3	0	6	1
Evers, 2b.	2	2	1	4	Wilson, c.	1	0	1	0
Archer, c.	3	1	12	2	Fletcher, ss.	3	0	2	2
Lavender, p.	4	1	0	1	Groh, 2b.	3	0	3	3
					Marquard, p.	2	0	0	1
					Tesreau, p.	0	0	1	0
					Devore	1	0	0	0
Totals	31	10	27	12	Totals	30	5	24	11

NEW YORK	0	0	1	0	1	0	0	0	0 — 2
CUBS	0	2	0	2	0	2	0	1	* — 7

Runs—Zimmerman, Leach (2), Saier (3), Archer, Snodgrass, Becker. Errors—Snodgrass (2), Fletcher, Groh. Devore batted for Marquard in 7th. Hits—Off Marquard, 8 in 6 innings. Three-base hit—Evers. Two-base hit—Saier. Struck out—By Lavender, 8; by Marquard, 5; by Tesreau, 1. Bases on balls—Off Lavender, 2; off Marquard, 3. Umpires—Klem and Bush.

LEFTY
O'DOUL
as told to
BILL LEISER

Frank "Lefty" O'Doul born in San Francisco, Calif., March 4, 1897. Broke into organized baseball with San Francisco in 1917. In 1932 he led the National League in hitting with .368 and had a lifetime batting average of .351.

PROLOGUE: On the walls of his low-ceilinged office, atop his prosperous bistro on San Francisco's busy Powell Street, are many framed reminders that Frank "Lefty" O'Doul was one of the greatest batters of his days as a major league outfielder. A native San Franciscan, "Lefty" spent seven seasons trying to be a winning pitcher and had two unsuccessful hitches with the Yankees.

Always a good hitter, he turned outfielder while playing with Salt Lake in the Pacific Coast league and then reached the National to star with the Giants, Phillies and Dodgers. One such reminder to quickly catch a visitor's eye is a clipping of Bob Ripley's "Believe It Or Not," depicting that: "In 1932, at Brooklyn, against Pittsburgh, Lefty O'Doul's first home run tied-up the first game of a double-header; that his second homer won that game and that his third home run of the day won the second game." Would that be "Lefty's Greatest Day"?

Yes that was an interesting day, admitted O'Doul as he paced his office, with an attentive ear tuned to the rapid ringing of the cash registers below. But let's go down the line, as they say. I certainly enjoyed that afternoon in the 1933 World Series when Washington was leading our Giants 1 to 0 in the sixth and Bill Terry sent me up to pinch hit. I got a single that started to break up the game and helped us win the series.

And since this story is for *The Chicago Daily News*, I shouldn't slight the Cubs in considering great days. You know the Cubs once owned me. They say I was the only ballplayer the late William Wrigley, Jr., ever bought strictly on his own. That was in 1925, the season I quit pitching for the outfield. I batted .375 for Salt Lake, and one day Mr. Wrigley was in town and came out to the game. He liked the way I batted and before he left, he bought me for $30,000. I reported to the Cubs the next spring but their new manager, Joe McCarthy, didn't go for me and shortly I was back with my old team, which Bill Lane had moved to Hollywood over the winter.

I didn't think much of McCarthy's judgment at that time and maybe I proved my point five years later, after I had landed with the Phillies. The Cubs came to Philly in mid-September, 1930, in first place and looked like repeaters for the championship they'd won the previous year. I was crippled at the time and couldn't play regularly but I got into three games of the series as a pinch hitter. In the second game, I hit a two-run homer off Pat Malone in the eighth that beat the Cubs and in the third game I hit one off Bud Teachout in the ninth that wrecked the Cubs 12 to 11. The Cubs left town in third place and St. Louis came up to win the pennant by two games. Those O'Douls have long memories.

But you want my Greatest Day. Well that was the one in which I put the O'Doul in the record books. It's still there and I hope it will remain awhile. That was October 6, 1929, in the final games of the season for the Phillies. It was a long day too, since we played a double-header against the Giants. But before I give you the details I'll have to backtrack a bit.

After the Cubs canned me, I played a season with Hollywood and then went back to San Francisco for my fourth hitch with the club that gave me my start. I hit .378 for the Seals and after the '27 season, John McGraw bought me for the Giants. I was glad to get back to the majors and particularly to the Big Town, where I had spent three seasons warming the Yankee bench. I played 114 games for the Giants in '28, hitting mostly against right-handed pitchers, and batted .319; which I thought was pretty fair. But the season wasn't much more than over when McGraw gave me and $20,000 cash to the Phillies for Fred Leach, another outfielder. So there was another guy who didn't think much of the O'Doul. Lefty certainly was seeing the country.

I got off to a good start with the Phillies, under Burt Shotton, and kept gaining through the season. As we swung down September I was batting around .400 while Leach was hitting less than .260 for McGraw. As we went on the field for the final games of the season, I had 247 hits. If I hadn't known it all too well, the fans wasted no time telling me that I needed only three hits to tie and four to break Rogers Hornsby's National League record for the most hits in one season.

Naturally you can guess how I felt. There was McGraw and Leach and the Giants. And there I was shooting for a new record. McGraw didn't make it easy. He started Carl Hubbell in the first game. That was Hub's second season with the Giants and he won 18 games. Hubbell didn't fool either. He gave me everything he had: that screw ball, which he really could throw, curves and hard ones.

Well, I got three singles in a row. That tied Hornsby's record. One more would bust it.

I got another chance, I guess maybe it was in the eighth The count didn't go down to three and two; nothing dramatic like that. In fact, I don't remember just what the count was. Maybe it was something like one and one.

Anyhow, I got one I liked. But I was so tense, so nervous and so scared that I knocked the ball out of the park. The hit that broke the record was a homer.

[*Editor's note: You may be able to detect a slight bit of sarcasm in that "tense, nervous and scared" quote from Mr. O'Doul.*]

McGraw started another left hander, Bill Walker, against us in the second game of the double-header. The first three times against him, I hit safely. That made seven straight for the day. I came up once more and hit a line drive to center that Chick Fullis brought down with a fine catch. But the seven for eight gave me a batting average of .398 and the championship. Incidentally Lew Fonseca (then with Cleveland) won the American League championship that year and so far as I know that's the only time two guys from the same town and same

THE BOX SCORE
(*October 6, 1929*)
(First Game)

GIANTS	A.B.	R.	H.	P.	A.	PHILS	A.B.	R.	H.	P.	A.
Fullis, lf.	3	1	0	2	0	Thompson, 2b.	3	1	0	3	4
Roush, cf.	2	0	0	1	0	O'Doul, lf.	4	2	4	3	0
Lindstrom, 3b.	4	1	1	0	1	Klein, rf.	4	1	1	1	1
Terry, 1b.	3	0	0	13	0	Hurst, 1b.	4	0	1	12	3
Ott, rf.	3	1	1	1	0	Whitney, 3b.	4	0	0	2	1
Jackson, ss.	3	1	1	2	1	Friberg, cf.	4	0	0	1	0
Hogan, c.	3	0	0	4	0	Thevenow, ss.	3	0	0	2	3
Marshall, 2b.	3	0	0	1	6	Lerain, c.	3	0	1	2	1
Hubbell, p.	2	0	1	0	4	Sweetland, p.	3	1	1	1	4
Fitzsimmons, p.	0	0	0	0	0	Koupall, p.	0	0	0	0	0
Totals	26	4	4	24	12	Totals	32	5	8	27	17

GIANTS	0	0	0	2	0	0	0	2	0 — 4
PHILS	0	0	3	0	2	0	0	0	* — 5

Runs batted in—Klein (2), Whitney (2), Jackson, Hogan, O'Doul, Lindstrom. Sacrifice hits —O'Doul, Klein. Hits—Off Hubbell 8 in 7 innings; Fitzsimmons, none in 1 inning; off Sweetland, 4 in 7 innings, none out in 8th; off Koupall, 1 in 2 innings. Strikeouts—Sweetland, 1; Hubbell, 2. Double plays—Thevenow to Thompson to Hurst (3). Home runs— O'Doul, Klein. Bases on balls—Off Sweetland, 6; off Hubbell, 1. Left on bases—New York, 4; Phillies, 4. Winning pitcher—Sweetland. Losing pitcher—Hubbell. Passed ball—Lerain. Umpires—Jorda, Klem and McLaughlin. Time—1:30.

sandlots ever won the big league batting titles the same season. Yeah, that was my biggest day. I didn't always get seven for eight with that much at stake."

EPILOGUE: Lefty's big league days long are past and now he is one of the most successful managers in the minors; the developer of Joe and Dominic Di Maggio and partially, of Ted Williams. He is an institution in San Francisco and the fans of that city gave him a Great Day every season. It's the O'Doul Day for Kids.

That event was started when Lefty was with the Seals in '27. More than 12,000 kids were guests of the Seals; Lefty rode into the park on a horse, wearing a sombrero and bandana. He helped give the kids 5,000 bats, 3,000 balls and 77,000 bags of peanuts. Although O'Doul then was an outfielder, the kids demanded he pitch. And pitch he did, allowing two hits and winning 3-2.

So when O'Doul came home for the last time from the big show, to manage San Francisco, his Kid Day became an annual festival.

JOE
TINKER
as told to
FRANCIS J. POWERS

My greatest day? You might know it was against the Giants. I think that goes for every Cub who· played for "Husk" Chance in those years on Chicago's West Side. I know it did for Johnny Evers and Miner Brown and I'm sure it would for Chance if he still was alive. All of us have bright memories of World's Series against the White Sox and Tigers and Athletics.

But the games you play over and over, even after more than 30 years, were against the Giants and John McGraw. Chance and McGraw were born to battle on baseball fields.

If you didn't honestly and furiously hate the Giants, you weren't a real Cub.

I was in the famous game when Fred Merkle failed to touch second and then the playoff for the 1908 pennant when Chance and McGraw never were far from blows. I was in the lineup when we beat the Tigers in eight out of ten games in two World's Series.

135

But the game which gave me the greatest thrill was on Aug. 7, 1911. That was the one in which I made four hits and stole home on Christy Mathewson which is something a man tells his grandchildren or writes down in a book.

The Cubs, with four pennants and two world's championships in five seasons still were on top of the National League on that August day but closer to a complete collapse than any of us knew. The old lineup was breaking. Young Vic Saier had taken "Husk's" job at first; Heinie Zimmerman was on third in place of Harry Steinfeldt and Jimmy Archer had replaced Johnny Kling back of the plate.

I guess my memory of the game is made keener by the fact that two days before I'd had a terrific argument with Chance and had been suspended. On Saturday—that'd be Aug. 5—we were playing Brooklyn and out in front 2-1 in the third. There was a strong wind blowing to left field and two were out and two on. The Dodger batter pumped one over my head. I went back and yelled to Jimmy Sheckard I'd take it. Well the wind blew the ball out and it dropped safe and two Dodgers scored.

By the seventh we were ahead again, 4-3, and once more the Dodgers had two on and two out. At that time the wind had changed and was coming in from left field. When the batter popped another one over my head, Sheck started in and I didn't move. The wind drove the ball back toward the infield but I thought Jimmy would get it and let it alone. Jimmy couldn't reach the ball and two more runs scored.

When I got back to the bench, Frank, his face red with fury, snarled: "I'm damn sick and tired of you letting those flies drop."

I was just as mad because the Dodgers had scored, so I screamed right back, "I'm damn sick and tired of you yelling at me."

"Husk" told me to turn in my uniform and fined me $150.

Well, there was no game on Sunday and Charlie Murphy, he owned the Cubs, sent for me to come to his office. He said he wanted Frank and me to straighten things out and I said it would be all right with me.

Now Monday also was an open day but the Giants were coming through and McGraw had agreed to stop off and play a postponed game. So "Husk" agreed to reinstate me for that game. Chance was a great guy and a square manager. And smart.

Only two games out of first place and going into August the game looked like the spot for New York to pick up some ground. And Mc-Graw had Matty ready to pitch. Chance countered with Brown, who always gave Matty a battle.

There was a good crowd at the old West Side Park to see Matty and Brownie. The game was in an uproar before it was one minute old. Brownie hit Josh Devore in the head with his first pitch and they had to carry the Giant left-fielder off the diamond.

McGraw sent Red Murray in to run for Devore and Brownie was nervous. He passed Larry Doyle, and Fred Snodgrass singled to fill the bases. It looked for a minute as if Brownie wasn't going to last. Then Sheck took Beals Becker's low liner so fast that Murray had to stay on third. Merkle slammed one hard at me and I could have forced Murray at the plate but I tossed the ball to Zim and he whipped it to Saier, and Snodgrass and Merkle were out by a mile.

Sheckard opened our half with a triple on Matty's first pitch. And then Matty guessed wrong when Schulte's bunt didn't roll foul. Archer hit to Matty, and Sheck was run down but Schulte went all the way to third and then was nailed at the plate, trying to score on Zim's roller. You ran the bases and took the chances for Chance. Zim and Archer tried a double steal but Meyers broke it up easily and we were all square.

I was up second in the next inning and hit a single to left and when Murray decided he'd throw to first, I went into second and scored on Saier's double to put us one run ahead.

We got all tangled up in the fourth when the Giants tied the score. Schulte fumbled Becker's liner and Beals went clear to third and scored on Herzog's single. Then Brownie threw over first and Buck reached second and we were shaky again. But Meyers hit to me and I started a double play with young Jack Doyle, who was subbing for Evers, on the pivot and we got clear.

Then we got two runs in the fourth, but I forget the details, for the big moments of my greatest day were coming.

In the sixth I hit off the left-field fence for a triple. It might have been a homer inside the park except that Zim got a slow start off first and I had to pull up at third. I guess maybe Matty thought I was winded and would rest awhile. But I broke on his next pitch and scored standing up.

Honestly, I believe that was one of the worst games Matty ever pitched. In the eighth, when Jack Doyle sacrificed Zim to third, Matty scooped the ball with his bare hand and when Bob Emslie called Heinie safe, Christy was so mad he almost stopped the game.

When I came up, Matty threw me one of those low, outside curves that almost sent me back to Kansas City before Frank made me change my batting style. I hit it for a long double to score Zim and Archer and that was the ball game. We won 8-6 and made 14 hits off Big Six.

And when we got back into the clubhouse, Chance came over to me with a big grin and said: "Damn it, I ought to suspend you every day."

THE BOX SCORE
(*August 7, 1911*)

CUBS	A.B.	R.	H.	P.	A.	GIANTS	A.B.	R.	H.	P.	A.
Sheckard, lf.	5	0	1	3	0	Devore, lf.	0	0	0	0	0
Schulte, rf.	4	0	1	3	0	Murray, lf.-rf.	4	1	1	2	0
Archer, c.	3	1	0	4	0	L. Doyle, 2b.	4	0	2	2	2
Zimmerman, 3b.	4	3	2	1	7	Snodgrass, cf.	5	2	3	2	0
J. Doyle, 2b.	3	1	0	1	2	Becker, rf.-lf.	4	2	2	1	0
Tinker, ss.	4	3	4	3	6	Merkle, 1b.	5	0	1	10	0
Saier, 1b.	4	0	1	12	0	Herzog, 3b.	5	0	2	1	2
Hoffman, cf.	4	0	1	0	0	Fletcher, ss.	4	1	2	0	4
Brown, p.	4	0	0	0	1	Myers, c.	3	0	1	6	2
						Mathewson, p.	4	0	0	0	7
Totals	35	8	10	27	16	Totals	38	6	14	24	17

Errors—Schulte, Brown, Murray, Merkle, Fletcher. Two-base hits—Saier, Tinker, Becker. Three-base hits—Sheckard, Zimmerman, Tinker, Murray. Sacrifice hits—J. Doyle. Stolen bases—Tinker. Double plays—Tinker to Zimmerman to Saier; Zimmerman to Tinker to Saier. Struck out—By Brown, 2; Mathewson, 3. Base on balls—Off Brown, 3; Mathewson, 1. Hit by pitched ball—By Brown (Devore).

GROVER CLEVELAND ALEXANDER

as told to
FRANCIS J. POWERS

Grover Cleveland Alexander, "Old Pete" to two genera-
tions of baseball fans, spent 20 years in the National
League with Philadelphia, St. Louis, and Chicago. He
was born at St. Paul, Neb., February 26, 1887, and was
one of the game's finest right-handed pitchers. He made
his big league debut with Philadelphia's Phillies in 1911
and wound up with 373 victories and 208 defeats while
pitching 686 games. He has been out of the majors since
1930 and now is employed as an airplane plant guard in
Cincinnati.

My greatest day in baseball has to be the seventh game of the
1926 World Series between the Cards and Yankees. If I picked
any other game the fans would think I was crazy. I guess just about
everyone knows the story of that game; it has been told often enough.
How I came in as a relief pitcher in the seventh inning, with two out
and the bases filled with Yankees, and fanned Tony Lazzeri to protect
the Cards' 3-2 lead. Actually, that was my greatest game, for it gave
me not one, but three, thrills. But if it wasn't I'm stuck with it like
George Washington with the hatchet.

There must be a hundred versions of what happened in the Yankee Stadium that dark, chilly afternoon. It used to be that everywhere I went, I'd hear a new one and some were pretty far-fetched. So much so that two-three years ago I ran across Lazzeri in San Francisco and said: "Tony, I'm getting tired of fanning you." And Tony answered: "Maybe you think I'm not." So I'd like to tell you my story of what took place in that game and the day before.

There are stories that I celebrated that night before and had a hang-over when Manager Rogers Hornsby called me from the bull pen to pitch to Lazzeri. That isn't the truth. On Saturday, I had beaten the Yankees 10-2 to make the series all even. To refresh your memory on the series, the Yankees won the opener and we took the next two. Then the Yanks won two straight and needed only one more for the world's championship and I beat 'em in the sixth.

In the clubhouse after that game, Hornsby came over to me and said: "Alex, if you want to celebrate tonight, I wouldn't blame you. But go easy for I may need you tomorrow."

I said: "Okay, Rog. I'll tell you what I'll do. I'll ride back to the hotel with you and I'll meet you tomorrow morning and ride out to the park with you." Hell—I wanted to win that series and get the big end of the money as much as anyone.

Jesse Haines started the seventh game for us, pitchin' against Waite Hoyt. We figured Jesse would give the Yanks all they could handle. He was a knuckle-baller and had shut 'em out in the third game. Early in the game Hornsby said to me: "Alex, go down into the bull pen and keep your eye on Sherdel [Willie] and Bell [Herman]. Keep 'em warmed up and if I need help I'll depend on you to tell me which one looks best."

The bull pen in the Yankee Stadium is under the bleachers and when you're down there you can't tell what's going on out on the field only for the yells of the fans overhead. When the bench wants to get in touch with the bull pen there's a telephone. It's the only real fancy, modern bull pen in baseball. Well, I was sitting around down there, not doing much throwing, when the phone rang and an excited voice said: "Send in Alexander."

I don't find out what happened until the game is over. Haines is breezing along with a 3-2 lead when he develops a blister on the knuckle of the first finger of his right hand. The blister breaks and the finger is so sore he can't hold the ball. Before Rog knows it the Yanks have the bases filled.

I take a few hurried throws and then start for the box. There's been a lot of stories about how long it took me to walk from the bull pen to the mound and how I looked, and all that. Well, as I said, I didn't know what had happened when I was called.

So when I come out from under the bleachers I see the bases filled and Lazzeri standing in the box. Tony is up there all alone, with everyone in that Sunday crowd watching him. So I just said to myself, "Take your time. Lazzeri isn't feeling any too good up there and let him stew." But I don't remember picking any four-leaf clovers, as some of the stories said.

I get to the box and Bob O'Farrell, our catcher, comes out to meet me. "Let's start right where we left off yesterday," Bob said. Yesterday [Saturday] Lazzeri was up four times against me without getting anything that looked like a hit. He got one off me in the second game of the series, but with one out of seven I wasn't much worried about him, although I knew that if he got all of a pitch he'd hit it a long piece.

I said okay to O'Farrell. We'll curve him. My first pitch was a curve and Tony missed. Holding the ball in his hand, O'Farrell came out to the box again. "Look, Alex," he began. "This guy

Tony Lazzeri

will be looking for that curve next time. We curved him all the time yesterday. Let's give him a fast one." I agreed and poured one in, right under his chin. There was a crack and I knew the ball was hit hard. A pitcher can tell pretty well from the sound. I spun around to watch the ball and all the Yankees on bases were on their way. But the drive had a tail-end fade and landed foul by eight-ten feet in the left-field bleachers.

So I said to myself, "No more of that for you, my lad." Bob signed for another curve and I gave him one. Lazzeri swung where that curve started but not where it finished. The ball got a hunk of the corner and then finished outside. Well we were out of that jam but there still were two innings to go.

I set the Yanks down in order in the eighth and got the first two in the ninth. And then Ruth came up. The Babe had scored the Yanks' first run of the game with a tremendous homer and he was dynamite to any pitcher. I didn't take any chances on him but worked the count to three and two, pitching for the corners all the time. Then Babe walked and I wasn't very sorry eith·r when I saw him perched on first. Of course Bob Meusel was the next hitter and he'd hit over 40 homers that season and would mean trouble.

If Meusel got hold of one it could mean two runs and the series, so I forgot all about Ruth and got ready to work on Meusel. I'll never know why the guy did it but on my first pitch to Meusel, the Babe broke for second. He (or Miller Huggins) probably figured that it would catch us by surprise. I caught the blur of Ruth starting for second as I pitched and then came the whistle of the ball as O'Farrell rifled it to second. I wheeled around and there was one of the grandest sights of my life. Hornsby, his foot anchored on the bag and his gloved hand outstretched was waiting for Ruth to come in. There was the series and my second big thrill of the day. The third came when Judge Landis mailed out the winners' checks for $5,584.51.

I guess, I had every thrill that could come to a pitcher except one. I never pitched a no-hit game. I pitched 16 one-hitters during my time in the National League and that's coming pretty close, pretty often.

You know you think of a lot of funny things that happened in baseball, sittin' around gabbing like this. I remember when I was with the Cubs, and I was with them longer than any other club, we were playing the Reds in a morning game on Decoration Day. The game was in the 11th when I went up to bat and I said: "If they give me a curve ball, I'll hit it in the bleachers. My wife's got fried chicken at home for me." They gave me a curve and I hit 'er in the bleachers.

THE BOX SCORE
(*October 10, 1926*)

ST. LOUIS	A.B.	R.	H.	P.	A.	NEW YORK	A.B.	R.	H.	P.	A.
Holm, cf.	5	0	0	2	0	Combs, cf.	5	0	2	2	0
Southworth, rf.	4	0	0	0	0	Koenig, ss.	4	0	0	2	3
Hornsby, 2b.	4	0	2	4	1	Ruth, rf.	1	1	1	2	0
Bottomley, 1b.	3	1	1	14	0	Meusel, lf.	4	0	1	3	0
Bell, 3b.	4	1	0	0	4	Gehrig, 1b.	2	0	0	11	0
Hafey, lf.	4	1	2	3	0	Lazzeri, 2b.	4	0	0	2	1
O'Farrell, c.	3	0	0	3	2	Dugan, 3b.	4	1	2	2	3
Thevenow, ss.	4	0	2	1	3	Severeid, c.	3	0	2	3	1
Haines, p.	2	0	1	0	4	Adams	0	0	0	0	0
Alexander, p.	1	0	0	0	0	Collins, c.	1	0	0	0	0
						Hoyt, p.	2	0	0	0	1
						Paschal	1	0	0	0	0
						Pennock, p.	1	0	0	0	1
Totals	34	3	8	27	14	Totals	32	2	8	27	10

Adams ran for Severeid in 6th.
Paschal batted for Hoyt in 6th.

ST. LOUIS	0	0	0	3	0	0	0	0	0 — 3
NEW YORK	0	0	1	0	0	1	0	0	0 — 2

Errors—Koenig, Meusel, Dugan. Runs batted in—O'Farrell, Thevenow (2), Ruth, Severeid. Two-base hit—Severeid. Home run—Ruth. Sacrifice hits—Haines, Koenig, Bottomley. Sacrifice fly—O'Farrell. Struck out—By Haines 2, by Alexander 1, by Hoyt 2. Bases on balls—Off Haines 5, off Alexander 1. Hits—Off Hoyt, 5 in 6 innings; off Pennock, 3 in 3 innings; off Haines, 8 in 6 2-3 innings; off Alexander, 0 in 2 1-3 innings. Winning pitcher—Haines. Losing pitcher—Hoyt.

JOHNNY
VANDER MEER
as told to
GABRIEL PAUL

(*Sketch by Hod Taylor*)

At 23 Johnny Vander Meer accomplished a feat un-likely to be repeated in big league baseball—he pitched two successive no-hit no-run games for Cincinnati in 1938. In 1943 Johnny won 18, with an earned run average of only 2.43, his best season in six years of major league pitching. Has won 60 and lost 50 during that stretch, all with the Reds.

It would seem natural for me to name the second successive no-hitter I pitched in 1938 as my biggest day in baseball, and I'll have to explain why it isn't.

Those games were as much a surprise to me as to the baseball world. I wasn't keyed up to their meaning then. Before the no-hitter against Boston on June 11 that year I was just a rookie that nobody but Bill McKechnie knew, and after the June 15 repeat of the performance against Brooklyn I was still just a novelty, a kid who had done a freakish thing.

144

To understand my feelings at the time you've got to understand that I came up to the Reds that year after an unsuccessful season at Syracuse in the International League. I had won only five and lost eleven for the Chiefs. Nobody thought I was good but Bill McKechnie, manager of the Reds, who told me, when I arrived at spring training in Florida, that he was counting on me to be a regular. He said he believed I could make it.

He gave me hope, and then on the way north that spring in an exhibition series with the Boston Red Sox Lefty Grove gave me some tips on what I was doing wrong. I'll never be able to thank Lefty for his friendliness and smartness in putting his finger on my errors. McKechnie kept giving me great advice, too, all spring.

I'll never forget the day that spring we were at Lynchburg, Va. I was pitching batting practice and after a little while McKechnie, on the bench, began to yell: "He's got it! He's got it! That boy is going to make it!"

That helped more than I can say, and I got off to a pretty good start in the season, pitching a shutout against the Giants at the Polo Grounds on May 20. I had my confidence. I felt I could do it. Then, all at once, came those consecutive no-hitters.

But they came too fast. I was more confused than thrilled. All the publicity, the attention, the interviews, the photographs, were too much for me. They swept me off my feet too far to let me have time to think about the games themselves. There were too many people around me.

As I look back at it now those days are the haziest period of my life—sort of like a dream.

I might have been dreaming then, but I awoke the next season, 1939, when I won five and lost nine. I was sick that spring and never did seem to regain my stride. My confidence went, too. I wasn't much better in the spring of 1940. Bill McKechnie and Warren Giles talked to me about going to Indianapolis of the American Association to regain my confidence. I thought it was a swell idea. I knew that was what I needed. At the same time it made me realize just how quickly a fellow can fall from the pedestal.

My going to Indianapolis was the best thing that ever happened to me. I got off on the right foot there, won six and lost four, had an earned-run average of 2.40 and struck out 109 in 105 innings. That satisfied Giles and McKechnie, for they brought me back for the last stages of the 1940 pennant race.

The Reds were in first place. They were on their way to the pennant, but they hadn't clinched it. I was given an opportunity to start a game and won it. Then we went to Philadelphia September 17, needing only two victories to clinch the pennant. We won on the 17th, then McKechnie gave me another chance to work, on September 18—the day that is my biggest.

I was up against Hugh Mulcahy, one of the smartest and most determined of pitchers and awfully tough when he was in form. We saw right off that he was in form when the game started. Joe Marty, whom the Phils had got from the Cubs, was on a rampage that day, too, getting three hits. And Mulcahy was leveling off with his bat, as well as with his arm. We could get hits, but we couldn't get runs. Mulcahy would turn us back.

The Phils got me for two runs in the second inning, and it was the fifth before we got one run. I began to wonder if I was going to let the team down on the one game it needed to clinch the flag. It was life-and-death in my mind. I had to hang on to my "comeback." I had to win.

We finally tied it in the seventh 2-2, but in the 10th we got one to give us what we thought was the game, but the Phils in their half got one off me to even it up again. It was true I had blanked them the seven innings between the second and the 10th, and the team was all the time telling me how good I was going, but there it was, we'd been ahead and I'd let the Phils tie us.

Was I really a comeback or not? Could I clinch the flag or couldn't I?

I gave everything I had straight through the 11th and 12th innings and blanked them. But we didn't score either and the scoreboard still showed 3-3.

I was up in the 13th at bat and I figured now was the time. All of Mulcahy's pitches were good, but I kept swinging and somehow all at once whistled one into left center and ran faster than I ever had before, I suppose. I got to second. They sacrificed me to third. Then Mike McCormick hit an infield ball and I was held at third, too risky to chance a run in. Mike beat it out.

Ival Goodman was up. Twice he cracked the ball and I tore for home, only to be called back because the drive went foul. Then he got one fair, a short fly to the outfield and I tagged up and when McKechnie on the coasting line said, "Run, Johnny, run!" to give me the exact moment the ball settled into the fielder's glove, I sure ran. I took off in the hardest slide I ever made and looked up through the dust. The umpire was motioning "safe."

We were ahead.

McKechnie, cool always, looked at me and figured how much running I'd done that inning, and told me to sit it out, he'd send in Joe Beggs to pitch the last half. Joe got them 1-2-3 and the flag was ours.

LEROY SATCHEL PAIGE

as told to
EARNEST MEHL

(*Sketch by Hod Taylor*)

For 15 years Leroy "Satchel" Paige has been a fabulous figure in Negro baseball, barnstorming here in the summer and in the Latin-American countries during the winter. Named by many baseball men as the greatest pitcher of modern times.

In some ways it seems the best day I ever had pitchin' was in the 4th and final game of the colored World Series in 1942 when the Kansas City Monarchs beat the Philadelphia Homestead Grays. I was in all four of those games and they didn't get a hit offa me in the last game. Lessee, that was for seven innings, I remember.

I was driving to that last game in Philadelphia and must have been goin' pretty fast because a traffic cop stopped me. By the time I got to the ball park it was the first of the third inning and the Monarchs is behind 0 to 5, and the Grays has got the bases filled with none out.

I ain't got no time to warm up 'cept to throw a few while I'm walking to the mound, but I strike out the first two batters and makes the last one hit up a pop fly. We finally win out, 6 to 5, and I don't give no hits.

Maybe that's my best day, although when a fellow has pitched about some 2,000 or more games there's lots of them seems his best day. I guess maybe that time down in San Domingo you might say was my biggest day, although I only win the game—that is, my team—by a 6-to-5 score and I had to bear down all the way to get that. But I bet no pitcher ever had more reason to bear down than I did that day.

Sometimes I wonder where ol' Satchel would be if the other team had won that game. All I know is that we were told we better win if we knew what was good for us. "What do you mean we better win?" I asked the manager. He says, "I mean just that. Take my advice and win."

Funny thing, too, we knew we had the umpires on our side in that game and it was a cinch we'd get all the close ones. But then the strain we were playing under was so great sometimes I think we looked like a bunch of scrub-lotters. We knew all we had to do was get the ball over to first somewheres around the time the batter got there and he was out. Them umpires wasn't no fools.

But maybe I better start from the beginning because I guess nothing like it ever happened before and you bet I ain't never going back there and so far as I am concerned President Trujillo and me is gonna stay as far apart as possible.

Down there they don't know much about baseball rules, anyway.

Satchel's hobby is photography

They get a baseball guide, only maybe it's a 1907 guide or something like that, and then they read part of the rules, them they can understand, and the rest they make up themselves. But do they like to win! Once when I was pitching in Puerto Rico I win 25 games in a row and then lost one and do you know nobody would speak to me.

However, I got to tell you about this game we played in Ciudad Trujillo, which is a town named after President Di Rafael L. Trujillo. Boy, I never did see a president like him. Power! He's got it. If that man don't like you some day you wake up and you're movin'. And from what I seen it don't take much for him not to like you. For instance, if he wants his team to win a ball game to save his honor and you pitch and don't win—see what I'm up against that day?

That was back in 1937 and I was pitching for the Pittsburgh Crawfords and at the end of the season several of us gets a proposition from a fellow by the name of Dr. Jose Enrique Aybar, who is the manager of the Ciudad Trujillo team, to go down there to play some games. He comes to this country with the cash, too, and puts it in the bank. I don't know for sure, but the papers says it was about $30,000. I know I done all right. That is, financially.

You see this President Trujillo, who runs the whole show down in San Domingo, wants a team so good it will win the championship, which is a feather in his cap. He's got troops of soldiers around him all the time and he's got power. I never seen a man with such power. He flies us down to Ciudad Trujillo on a big plane and we ain't put out no place to let other passengers on. No, sir. We got right of way. And what's more, we don't even have passports.

Not having passports kinda made me uneasy anyway but that president he fixes it up someways. But I wasn't down there very long until I wished I wasn't. Just to show you, the president he give an order that none of the American ballplayers could be sold any whisky. And we wasn't, either. The guy that done it would have been shot, I guess. We was kept at a hotel and had to be in bed early. No matter what we done—like if we went in swimming—there was soldiers around and nobody could speak to us. The president he didn't want any of his people following us and starting up a conversation.

It was almost like we was in jail. But we was being paid good money. We was President Trujillo's ball club and we got to win that championship because if we don't win maybe the people won't re-elect him again. It's that important.

That's why the manager of the team, Dr. Aybar, says there was only one piece of advice he would give us. We better win. He don't know nothing about baseball hisself but he does know what the winning of this championship game means to President Trujillo.

We was down there to play 15 games and when we come to the championship game we had win seven and lose seven and in some of them we played like we never seen a baseball before. That's because of the strain we was under. Some of them guys the president had watching us sent shivers up and down your spine. They was that tough looking. They packed guns and long knives and I know they could use 'em. We didn't want to give them a chance. I think that's what the manager meant when he said we better win if we know what's good for us. When he said that he looked at them guys carrying them guns. If you think it ain't tough to field a grounder in a situation like that.

It was tough enough, anyway, because the diamond was in a place that looked something like a bull ring only there ain't no bull fights down there. And when we come up to that championship game with Estrellas de Oriente there must have been about 7,000 people in the stands. And all of them had guns, too, and we wondered what would happen if one of them umpires made a decision they didn't like and they started shooting. Boy, my mouth was dry that day!

You see this Estrellas de Oriente team was sponsored by the fellow who was President Trujillo's political rival, only the president was in power and he had the army and so the fans that come to see the game from Estrellas de Oriente didn't dast say too much. You know how it is: they was outnumbered.

But if we lose that game then the Estrellas de Oriente team is champion and that's a political blow to President Trujillo and maybe when there is an election again the votes go against him. We find that out. "Satchel, old boy," I say to myself, "if you ever pitched, it's now."

But it ain't no cakewalk because that Estrellas de Oriente team is tough because, you see, they loaded up with important stars, too. We got a flock of colored Americans on our team but they got as many on theirs. How them babies could hit that ball! I don't think I ever throwed harder but I wouldn't say I was relaxed: That was one day Paige was not free and easy.

All we could hear from them fans was warnings about we better win. The more they yelled the harder I threw and I bet I never did have a better fast ball only I never see any better hitters than them guys. But in the seventh inning we score two runs and then I manage to shut them out the last two frames and we win, 6 to 5.

No sooner was the game over than we was hustled back to our hotel and the next morning when we got up there was a United States ship in the harbor. Sister ship to one which was blowed up at Pearl Harbor.

There was a plane waiting for us, too, and were we glad to get on board. We never did see President Trujillo again, although that night after the game we were taken to a picnic and showed a nice time.

I read in a newspaper that Dr. Aybar, our manager, says "baseball in Trujillo City is not commercial. Money makes no difference. Baseball is spiritual in every respect, as indulged in by Latin races."

I am saving the clipping of that paper because I am thinking that if he is right and baseball is spiritual as it is played there ol' Satchel could be a spirit right now if we didn't win that big game. Yep, I guess so far as I'm concerned that was the biggest day of my baseball life although it's one I never want to live over again.

Di Rafael L. Trujillo,
president of San Domingo

PEPPER MARTIN

as told to
JOHN P. CARMICHAEL

Pepper Martin managed the San Diego club in the Pacific Coast League in 1945. Previously he was a successful pilot of the Sacramento club in the same league and also of Rochester in the Cardinal farm chain. During the off season, Martin is a rancher in Oklahoma.

("'Pepper' Martin always could run," said Roy Moore, a Houston (Tex.) teammate back in 1929. "He used to scoot alongside a bunch of rabbits and every so often he'd reach for one and heft it for size. If it scaled a little thin, Martin'd put it down again; if it felt nice and fat, he'd drop it in his bag.")

I'm not a dignified man myself (said Martin) but when I look back over the World Series between the Cardinals and Athletics of 1931, I always remember how the fans booed President Herbert Hoover in the first game at Philadelphia.

They cheered me; me, a rookie from Oklahoma who could run a little, and booed the President of the United States.

It just didn't seem right and I sure felt sorry for Mr. Hoover and I was kinda put out with the fans because, after.all, being President of the United States is a pretty big job and should command respect.

My biggest day, of course, was right in this series but I ain't sure whether it was October 2, when "Wild Bill" Hallahan beat the A's 2-0 or when I spoiled George Earnshaw's no-hit game or even when I batted in four runs . . . and got a homer to boot . . . in the fifth game.

You know I was a pretty lucky fellow that year. I don't think the Cardinals were gonna play me regular at all in '31, even though I'd hit .363 at Rochester, so finally one day I got hold of Branch Rickey and I said:

"Look, Mr. Rickey, I'm a little tired chasin' up and down these minor leagues and if you can't use me here, why don't you trade me so I can play every day?"

Well, ol' Uncle Branch looked at me through those glasses and chewed on his cigar and finally said that he'd see. So I did all right, but I sure never looked for no series hero role and, anyway, my stealing five bases wasn't because I wanted to show off or anything.

No, we decided to run whenever we could against Catcher "Mickey" Cochrane because he wouldn't be looking for it and "Gabby" Street (Cardinal Manager) told both George Watkins and I to "limber up" right from taw.

"I don't know how much hittin' we'll get off Grove and Earnshaw," said Gabby, "so we better not waste time on the bases. Let's run everything out."

We lost the first game to Grove, but Hallahan gave up only three hits in the next game and we won, 2-0. I scored both runs. I came up in the second inning and hit a single in front of Al Simmons in left. Now Al could throw pretty good but I figured he wouldn't expect me to try for second, so I kept right on going. As I hit second in a cloud of dust I turned my head around to look at Simmons and he was standin' there lookin' at me as much as to say: "Oh, a smart busher, huh."

I took a quick glance at our bench and Street looked sort of happy, so just as Earnshaw threw the next pitch to Jim Wilson, I lit out for third.

Cochrane almost threw the ball into left field tryin' to get me and I was safe again. Wilson flied and I scored easily. Then in the seventh I singled again and Wilson was up once more and I stole on the first pitch. I took third when Wilson grounded out.

Street decided to put the squeeze-play on, figuring Earnshaw was pretty apt to "get" Charley, so he told Charley to lay one down. I was all set and slid under Cochrane while Earnshaw was trying to field the bunt.

It's a good thing we did a little runnin' that day, because we weren't hitting. I bet Earnshaw got good and mad at me before the series was over, 'cause four days later he'd a had a no-hitter in the fourth game if I hadn't got both blows off him.

But I guess I'll have to take the fifth game as my biggest day. I got two singles and a home run and drove in four men. That made it 12 hits for me in five games and if I'd only got one more I'd a broken a series mark, but they horse-collared me in the last two games. It's probably just as well things didn't go on because my sombrero mightn't a fit me after all the luck I had.

The day we beat 'em 5-1 we started out with a run in the first inning. Sparky Adams singled past third to open the game, but he pulled a leg muscle turning first base and Andy High replaced him. This turned out to be a good move because, after Watkins flied, Frankie Frisch singled and High went to third. Adams wouldn't have been able to make it. I got a long fly and High scored.

In the fourth inning both Jim Bottomley and I singled, but Wilson lined into a double play. We were still in front, but only by one run, so we didn't feel too safe and ol' Sarge (Street) kept tellin' us on the bench: "Let's get some power at the plate. This ain't Earnshaw or Grove today."

We finally sewed up the game in the sixth. Frisch doubled to left with one gone and I was up again. I think Hoyt got a little careless with me . . . or maybe he figured I'd try to get Frisch to third by laying one down . . . because he put a pitch right down the middle and took a couple of steps as if to field the ball.

It looked so good I couldn't help swinging and the ball went into the left-field stands for a homer . . . my first in my first World Series.

Frisch waited for me at the plate and held out his hand. "If you'd a bunted that ball and made me run, I'd a died between third and home," he said. "That's the way to hit . . . so old man Frisch can walk home."

Well, that's about all. I got a single in the ninth to score Watkins and then I tried to steal another base, but this time Cochrane nailed me easy. But we'd won the game . . . that was the main thing.

You remember, of course, my vaudeville engagement after the series ended. Hell, I couldn't stand that. I'm a ballplayer, not an actor so I just quit after a couple of weeks.

I couldn't go on takin' a man's money under false pretenses.

THE BOX SCORE
(*October 7, 1931*)

ST. LOUIS	A.B.	R.	H.	P.	A.	PHILADELPHIA	A.B.	R.	H.	P.	A.
Adams, 3b.	1	0	1	0	0	Bishop, 2b.	2	0	0	3	2
High, 3b.	4	1	0	2	3	McNair, 2b.	2	0	0	1	1
Watkins, rf.	3	1	0	3	0	Haas, cf.	2	0	0	2	0
Frisch, 2b.	4	1	2	6	1	Moore, lf.	2	0	1	1	0
Martin, cf.	4	1	3	0	0	Cochrane, c.	4	0	1	3	2
Hafey, lf.	4	0	1	1	0	Simmons, lf-cf.	4	1	3	5	0
Bottomley, 1b.	4	1	2	7	1	Foxx, 1b.	3	0	0	8	1
Wilson, c.	4	0	2	7	0	Miller, rf.	4	0	1	2	0
Gelbert, ss.	4	0	1	1	2	Dykes, 3b.	4	0	1	0	1
Hallahan, p.	4	0	0	0	0	Williams, ss.	4	0	1	2	5
						Hoyt, p.	2	0	0	0	0
						Walberg, p.	0	0	0	0	0
						Heving	1	0	0	0	0
						Rommel, p.	0	0	0	0	0
						Boley	1	0	0	0	0
Totals	36	5	12	27	7	Totals	35	1	9	27	12

Heving batted for Walberg in 8th.
Boley batted for Rommel in 9th.

ST. LOUIS	1	0	0	0	0	2	0	1	1 — 5
PHILADELPHIA	0	0	0	0	0	0	1	0	0 — 1

Runs batted in—Martin (4), Gelbert, Miller. Two-base hits—Frisch, Simmons. Home run—Martin. Left on bases—St. Louis 6, Philadelphia 8. Double plays—Bishop to Foxx, Gelbert to Bottomley to Wilson. Stolen base—Watkins. Struck out—By Hallahan 4, Hoyt 1, Walberg 2. Bases on balls—Off Hallahan 1, Walberg 1. Hits—Off Hoyt, 7 in 6 innings; Walberg, 2 in 2; Rommel, 3 in 1. Losing pitcher—Hoyt. Umpires—Klem (N.), Nallin (A.), Stark (N.) and McGowan (A.). Time—1:56.

GEORGE SISLER

as told to

LYALL SMITH

George Harold Sisler is famed as one of baseball's greatest first basemen. His .420 batting average in 1922 is still tops for American League batters. Starred for the Browns from 1915 to 1927 and finished major league career with the Braves in 1930.

Every American kid has a baseball idol. Mine was Walter Johnson, the "Big Train." Come to think about it, Walter still is my idea of the real baseball player. He was graceful. He had rhythm and when he heaved that ball in to the plate he threw with his whole body just so easy-like that you'd think the ball was flowing off his arm and hand.

157

I was just a husky kid in Akron (Ohio) High School back around 1910-11 when Johnson began making a name for himself with the Senators and I was so crazy about the man that I'd read every line and keep every picture of him I could get my hands on.

Naturally, admiring Johnson as I did, I decided to be a pitcher and even though I wound up as a first baseman my biggest day in baseball was a hot muggy afternoon in St. Louis when I pitched against him and beat him. Never knew that, did you? Most fans don't. But it's right. Me, a kid just out of the University of Michigan beat the great Walter Johnson. It was on August 29, 1915, my first year as a baseball player, the first time I ever was in a game against the man who I thought was the greatest pitcher in the world.

I guess I was a pretty fair pitcher myself at Central High in Akron. I had a strong left arm and I could throw them in there all day long and never have an ache or pain. Anyway, I got a lot of publicity in my last year in high school and when I was still a student I signed up one day to play with Akron.

I didn't know at the time I signed that contract I was stepping into a rumpus that went on and on until it finally involved the National Baseball Commission, the owners of two big league clubs and Judge Landis.

I was only 17 years old when I wrote my name on the slip of paper that made me property of Akron, a club in the Ohio-Pennsylvania League and a farm club of Columbus in the Association. After I signed it I got scared and didn't even tell my dad or anybody 'cause I knew my folks wanted me to go on to college and I figured they'd be sore if they knew I wanted to be a ballplayer.

In a way, that's what saved me, I guess. For by not telling my dad he never had a chance to okay my signature and in that way the contract didn't hold. The way it worked out Akron sold me to Columbus and Columbus sold me to Pittsburgh and all the time I was still in high school and hadn't even reported to the team I signed with! Wasn't even legally signed the way it turned out.

They wanted me to join the club when I graduated from high school

but I was all set to go to Michigan
so I said "no" and went up to Ann
Arbor. Well, to make a long story
short the story came out in the open
there and when the whole thing was
over I had been made a free agent
by the old National Commission and
signed up with Branch Rickey who
at that time was manager of the St.
Louis Browns.

I pitched three years of varsity ball
up at Michigan and when I graduated on June 10, 1915, Rickey wired
me to join the Browns in Chicago.
Now, all this time I was up at school
I still had my sights set on Walter
Johnson. When he pitched his 56 consecutive scoreless innings in 1912 I

Walter Johnson

was as proud as though I'd done it myself. After all, I felt as though
I had adopted him. He was my hero. He won 36 games and lost only
seven in 1913 and he came back the next season to win 28 more and
lose 18. He was really getting the headlines in those days and I was
keeping all of them in my scrapbook.

Well, then I left Michigan in 1915 and came down to Chicago where
I officially became a professional ballplayer. I hit town one morning
and that same day we were getting beat pretty bad so Rickey called
me over to the dugout.

"George," he said, "I know you just got in town and that you don't
know any of the players and you're probably tired and nervous. But
I want to see what you have in that left arm of yours. Let's see what
you can do in these last three innings."

I gulped hard a couple of times, muttered something that sounded
like "thanks" and went out and pitched those last three innings. Did

pretty good, too. I gave up one hit but the Sox didn't get any runs so I figured that I was all right.

Next day, though, I was out warming up and meeting more of the Browns when Rickey came over to me. He was carrying a first base-man's glove. "Here," he said. "Put this on and get over there on first base."

Well, nothing much happened between the time I joined the club in June until long about the last part of August. Rickey would pitch me one day, stick me in the outfield the next and then put me over on first the next three or four. I was hitting pretty good and by the time we got back to St. Louis the sports writers were saying some nice things about me.

They were saying it chiefly because of my hitting. I'd only won two-three games up to then. I still remember the first one. I beat Cleveland and struck out nine men. Some clothing store gave me a pair of white flannels for winning and I was right proud of them. Didn't even wear them for a long time, figured they were too fancy.

As I was saying, we got back to St. Louis late in August. Early one week I picked up a paper and saw that a St. Louis writer, Billy Murphy, had written a story about Washington coming to town the following Sunday and that Walter Johnson was going to pitch.

I was still a Johnson fan and I guess Murphy knew it, for when I got about halfway through the story I found out that he had me pitching against Johnson on the big day, Sunday, August 29.

That the the first I knew about it and I figured it was the first Manager Rickey knew about it, for here it was only Tuesday and Murphy had the pitchers all lined up for the following Sunday.

Well, he knew what he was talking about, because after the Saturday game Rickey stuck his head in the locker room and told me I was going to pitch against Johnson the next day. I went back to my hotel that night but I couldn't eat. I was really nervous. I went to bed but I couldn't sleep. At 4:00 A.M. I was tossing and rolling around and finally got up and just sat there, waiting for daylight and the big game.

I managed to stick it out, got some breakfast in me and was out at

Sportsman's Park before the gates opened. It was one of those typical August days in St. Louis and when game time finally rolled around it was so hot that the sweat ran down your face even when you were standing in the shadow of the stands.

All the time I was warming up I'd steal a look over at Johnson in the Washington bull pen. When he'd

Branch Rickey (left)
and Sam Breadon

stretch 'way out and throw in a fast ball I'd try to do the same thing. Even when I went over to the dugout just before the game started I was still watching him as he signed autographs and laughed with the photographers and writers.

Well, the game finally started and I tried to be calm. First man to face me was Moeller, Washington's left fielder. I didn't waste any time and stuck three fast ones in there to strike him out. Eddie Foster was up next and he singled to right field. Charley Milan singled to right center and I was really scared. I could see Mr. Rickey leaning out of the dugout watching me real close so I kept them high to Shanks and got him to fly out to Walker in center field. He hit it back pretty far though and Foster, a fast man, started out for third base. Walker made a perfect peg into the infield but Johnny Lavan, our shortstop, fumbled the relay and Foster kept right on going to score. That was all they got in that inning, but I wasn't feeling too sure when I came in to the bench. I figured we weren't going to get many runs off Johnson and I knew I couldn't be giving up many runs myself.

Then Johnson went out to face us and I really got a thrill out of watching him pitch. He struck out the first two Brownies and made Del Pratt fly to short center. Then I had to go out again and I got by all right. In the second inning, Walker led off with a single to center field and Baby Doll Jacobson dumped a bunt in front of the plate. Otto Williams, Washington catcher, scooped it up and threw it 10 feet over the first baseman's head. Walker already was around second and he came in and scored while the Baby Doll reached third.

I think I actually felt sorry for Johnson. I knew just how he felt because after all, the same thing had happened to me in the first inning. Del Howard was next up for us and he singled Jacobson home to give us two runs and give me a 2-1 lead.

Well, that was all the scoring for the day, although I gave up five more hits over the route. Johnson got one in the first of the fifth, a blooper over second. I was up in the last of the same inning and I'll be darned if I didn't get the same kind. So he and I were even up anyway. We each hit one man, too.

There wasn't much more to the game. Only one man reached third on me after the first inning and only two got that far on Johnson.

When I got the last man out in the first of the ninth and went off the field I looked down at the Washington bench hoping to get another look at Johnson. But he already had ducked down to the locker room.

I don't know what I expected to do if I had seen him. For a minute I thought maybe I'd go over and shake his hand and tell him that I was sorry I beat him but I guess that was just the silly idea of a young kid who had just come face to face with his idol and beaten him.

THE BOX SCORE
(August 29, 1915)

WASHINGTON	R.	H.	P.	A.	ST. LOUIS	R.	H.	P.	A.
Moeller, lf.	0	0	2	0	Shotton, lf.	0	0	0	0
Foster, 2b.	1	2	3	3	Austin, 3b.	0	2	2	1
C. Milan, cf.	0	1	0	0	Pratt, 2b.	0	0	4	3
Shanks, 3b.-rf.	0	1	0	2	Walker, cf.	1	1	4	0
Gandil, 1b.	0	1	6	3	Jacobson, rf.	1	1	1	0
Johnson, p.	0	1	1	1	Howard, 1b.	0	1	9	1
Williams, c.	0	0	6	3	Lavan, ss.	0	0	3	5
McBride, ss.	0	0	5	1	Severeid, c.	0	1	4	1
Acosta, rf.	0	0	1	0	Sisler, p.	0	1	0	1
Morgan, 3b.	0	0	0	0					
H. Milan, rf.	0	0	0	0					
Totals	1	6	24	13	Totals	2	7	27	12

WASHINGTON	1	0	0	0	0	0	0	0	0—1
ST. LOUIS	0	2	0	0	0	0	0	0	*—2

Errors—Williams, Lavan (2). Sacrifice hits—Williams, Pratt, Lavan, Johnson, Moeller. Double plays—Lavan to Howard (2); Severeid to Austin. Bases on balls—Off Sisler, 2. Hit by pitched ball—Acosta by Sisler; Sisler by Johnson. Struck out—By Johnson, 6; Sisler, 3.

JIMMIE DYKES

as told to
HAL TOTTEN

James Joseph "Jimmie" Dykes, manager of the White Sox, has long been called the ideal ball players' player, although he hasn't been on active duty since 1939. Dykes broke in with the Athletics in 1917, moved to the White Sox with Al Simmons and Mule Haas in 1932 and became manager May 9, 1934, succeeding Lew Fonseca. To prove his versatility in those days, Jimmie played every position on the Athletics at one time or another, even taking a fling at pitching and catching in addition to his duties as regular third baseman.

I'll never forget the day I made five hits in five times at bat against the Yankees—and each on the first ball pitched. The first four were off Garland Braxton. Herb Pennock was on the mound the last time. Apparently Benny Bengough, who was catching Herb, wanted him to "hook" me, but he kept shaking off the sign.

Finally Ben let out a wild yell, "For Pete's sake, Herb, he's made four hits already." And all Herb did was grin and say: "All right; let him get another."

Then there was the time right here in Chicago when—officially—I made three errors. The official scorer was pretty lenient, because it could have been five or six easily. And I kicked in six runs. But I got four for five that day and I remember, I drove in just one more run for the Athletics than I booted across—seven. And some woman sitting behind our bench hollered: "It's easy to see why the Old Man keeps you in there. You can't catch anything. But you sure can hit everything." Funny thing was—usually I could catch everything and couldn't hit a thing.

Then there was the fourth game of the 1929 World Series, when we went into the seventh inning losing 8 to 0, and came out in front 10 to 8. A lot of things happened in that inning. But the thing I remember most is the double I clouted off Pat Malone with the bases full.

We were licked—well licked—when we came to bat in that seventh inning. They had us 8-0, and Charlie Root was pitching like a machine. We hadn't been able to do a thing with him, and it didn't look as if we were going to.

As a matter of fact it looked so hopeless that I found out later that Connie Mack had made up his mind to let the regulars take their turns at bat in the seventh and then put in all the youngsters who hadn't ever been in a World Series, and probably never would be. But they never got to play.

We were so completely resigned to losing that game that when Al Simmons opened the big inning with a home run, the only comment anybody made on the bench was: "Well, we won't be shut out, anyway." And it wasn't as though the game didn't mean a lot, either, because, if the Cubs had won, it would have tied up the series at two games apiece. Guy Bush had beaten us the day before 3 to 1.

Nobody got very excited even when Jimmy Foxx and Bing Miller singled and I shut my eyes and got one, too. That scored Foxx. But we were still six runs behind. Then Joe Boley scored Miller with another one-base shot. But five runs are a lot of runs to overcome—especially in a World Series game. And when George Burns, batting for Eddie Rommel, popped to English, it looked as though our fun was over.

But Max Bishop belted one and I scored. That cut the big lead in half and I think we all began to feel that we might do something now. I guess Joe McCarthy thought so, too, because he took Charlie Root out and put in crafty old Art Nehf to pitch to Mule Haas, who batted left-handed.

Then came the blow that really turned the tide in our favor. The "Donk" (Mule Haas) hit a line drive over second base. Hack Wilson started for it and then seemed blinded by the sun. Anyway, he hesitated, and the ball shot past him into deep center. Every one of us jumped to our feet and started to shout at the top of our lungs. Boley crossed the plate! Bishop scored!

The ball was coming in now. I was standing in front of the dugout yelling: "He's gonna make it! He's gonna make it! There he goes!" And as Mule slid across the plate with a home run inside the park, I clouted the player next to me across the back and yelled: "We're back in the game, boys."

Only it wasn't a player I hit. It was Connie Mack. I'd never seen him leave his seat during a game before. But here he was, standing up there leaning out of the dugout, watching Haas race to the plate. And when I smacked him, I knocked him clear out over the bats.

I was horrified and grabbed Mr. Mack and helped him to his feet. "I'm sorry," I told him—and I must have had a funny look on my face, because he smiled, reached out, patted me on the arm, and said in that quiet way of his: "That's all right Jimmy. Everything's all right. Anything you do right now is all right. Wasn't it wonderful?" So that's one time I socked the manager and got away with it.

But it wasn't over yet. Nehf gave Mickey Cochrane a pass. That brought Fred Blake into the game. And Al Simmons, up for the second time, slammed one to left for his second hit—a single. Foxx then got his second hit of the inning—a one-baser—and Cochrane scored the tying run. Only, believe it or not, I didn't know the score was tied. No, sir!

McCarthy called in big Pat Malone. And he hit Miller with a pitched ball. And when I stepped up to the plate, I had the impression that we were still one run behind, with only one out. And with the bases full, I had only one thought

Pat Malone

in mind—to hit one far enough to let that tying run score. All I wanted was a long fly.

Lefty Grove

Malone threw one past me and it was a strike. I knew right then that the next one would be a fast ball, too. So I got set for it and swung. I pulled it to left and was sure it was far enough to score Simmons—and, as I thought, tie it up. So I lit out for first. I didn't see what happened, but they tell me that Stephenson jumped up against the wall; that the ball hit his glove and dropped to the ground. All I know is that when I rounded first, I saw him stooping over to pick it up, so I headed for second.

Well, as it turned out, it drove in both Simmons and Foxx and those were the two runs we won by, 10 to 8. Malone struck out the last two men. But we weren't worried any more. Why? Because Mr. Mack put in Lefty Grove, and when Lefty went into a ball game, it was all over. We knew he'd set 'em down, and he did—six in a row—and struck out four of 'em. And that ended not only my biggest and most important day, but just about the biggest one in World Series history.

THE BOX SCORE
(*October 12, 1929*)

ATHLETICS	A.B.	R.	H.	P.	A.	CUBS	A.B.	R.	H.	P.	A.
Bishop, 2b.	5	1	2	2	3	McMillan, 3b.	4	0	0	1	3
Haas, cf.	4	1	1	2	0	English, ss.	4	0	0	2	1
Cochrane, c.	4	1	2	9	0	Hornsby, 2b.	5	2	2	1	1
Simmons, lf.	5	2	2	0	0	Wilson, cf.	3	1	2	3	0
Foxx, 1b.	4	2	2	10	0	Cuyler, rf.	4	2	3	0	0
Miller, rf.	3	1	2	3	0	Stephenson, lf.	4	1	1	2	1
Dykes, 3b.	4	1	3	0	2	Grimm, 1b.	4	2	2	7	0
Boley, ss.	3	1	1	1	5	Taylor, c.	3	0	0	8	1
Quinn, p.	2	0	0	0	0	Root, p.	3	0	0	0	0
Walberg, p.	0	0	0	0	0	Nehf, p.	0	0	0	0	0
Rommel, p.	0	0	0	0	0	Blake, p.	0	0	0	0	0
Burns	2	0	0	0	0	Malone, p.	0	0	0	0	0
Grove, p.	0	0	0	0	0	Hartnett	1	0	0	0	0
						Carlson, p.	0	0	0	0	1
Totals	36	10	15	27	10	Totals	35	8	10	24	8

Burns batted for Rommel in 7th.   Hartnett batted for Malone in 8th.

CUBS	0	0	0	2	0	5	1	0	0— 8
ATHLETICS	0	0	0	0	0	0	0	10	*—10

Errors—Miller, Walberg, Wilson, Cuyler. Two-base hits—Cochrane, Dykes. Three-base hit—Hornsby. Home runs—Grimm, Simmons, Haas. Sacrifice hits—Taylor, Haas, Boley. Runs batted in—Cuyler (2), Stephenson, Grimm (2), Taylor, Haas (3), Simmons, Foxx, Dykes (3) Boley. Left on bases—Chicago, 4; Philadelphia, 6. Double play—Dykes to Bishop to Foxx. Bases on balls—Off Quinn, 2; Rommel, 1; Nehf, 1. Struck out—By Quinn, 2; Walberg, 2; Grove, 4; Root, 3; Malone, 2; Carlson, 1. Hits—Off Quinn, 7 in 5 innings; Walberg, 1 in 1; Rommel, 2 in 1; Grove, 0 in 2; Root, 9 in 6 1-3; Nehf, 1 in 0; Blake, 2 in 0; Malone, 1 in 2-3; Carlson, 2 in 1. Hit by pitcher—Malone (Miller). Winning pitcher—Rommel. Losing pitcher—Blake. Umpires—Van Grafian, Klem, Dineen and Moran. Time—2:12.

MARTIN MARION

as told to

LYALL SMITH

It was a cocky bunch of Cardinals that went into that big barn of a Yankee Stadium on October 7 in the 1942 World Series. We'd found out by this time that we could whip the Yanks. We were on the long end of a 3-1 score in series games by now, but we wanted to do one thing. And that was to beat big Red Ruffing.

We knew we could lick him even though he'd won the opener down in St. Louis. He had us nibbling out of his hands for eight innings before we finally got over our chills and teed off on him to knock him out in the last of the ninth. But even though we chased him, Red won that game 7 to 4 and we still wanted to whip him all the way.

We knew he was going to face us in the fifth game when we went out to the park and even though we were anxious to pick on him we still had a few misgivings. For the day was one of those dark, dreary ones in New York with low misty clouds sailing in off the ocean.

Captain Terry Moore was standing at the window when I went into the locker room under the stands to dress for the game. He was staring out at the dull skies. "That Ruffing will be hard to hit today," he murmured. "If that fast one is working he'll be tough."

There's no fooling about our being chesty when we went out that day.

None of us was superstitious except Moore and he was really worried. I remember I walked into the dugout with Kurowski and we started talking about what we were going to do with the $6,000 that went to the winners.

"Holy smokes," moaned Terry. "Don't talk like that, you guys. We haven't won it yet." He really was fretting.

Well, we started the game. Jimmy Brown opened with a walk but Ruffing fooled Moore on a third strike and Slaughter banged into a double play. That was the first one we had hit into all through the series and Enos was really talking to himself when he went into the outfield.

It didn't take the Yanks long to score, for Phil Rizzuto, their little shortstop, slammed one of Johnny's fast balls into the stands the first time up and boom . . . just like that we were behind 1 to 0.

We pecked away at Ruffing in the second when Walker Cooper got a single, and then picked up another hit in the third on a liner by Jimmy Brown.

Came the fourth and Slaughter put us back in the game with a homer off Ruffing that tied it up. We felt better but didn't have long to feel that way for Rolfe opened up the last half of the same inning with a bunt down to Beazley.

Johnny was too anxious and after fielding the ball badly he threw wild to first and Red went on down to second. He got around to third on a long fly by Roy Cullenbine and Joe Di Maggio then socked a single to left on the first pitch to put the Yanks in front again 2-1. It looked bad for awhile when powerful Charlie Keller, toughest looking player I ever saw at the plate, hit another one of Beazley's slow curves for another single to put Di Mag on third. But Gordon fanned and I threw out Bill Dickey.

We got our fourth hit in the fifth when Beazley broke his bat on a single but nothing came of it and we still trailed as the Yanks came up in their half. Gerry Priddy opened with a smash through the box but I was playing him in the right spot and threw him out on a close play. But Ruffing beat out a tap to Beazley and when Johnny Hopp made a low throw to me on a grounder by Rizzuto I couldn't hold the ball and they had men on second and first with one out. We got jittery for a minute and Jimmy Brown kicked Rolfe's roller to load the bases.

Then Beazley really bore down. He made Cullenbine pop out to me and Kurowski came up with Di Maggio's hot grounder to step on third for the out.

Up we came again. Moore hit Ruffing's first pitch for a single and Slaughter, who really was hungry that day, got another hit on the first pitch. We started whooping it up then and Ruffing looked a little rattled. He got Musial on an infield pop but Walker Cooper socked a fly down the foul line and although Cullenbine caught it, Terry came ripping in from third to score and tie it all up again.

That made it 2-2 and it stayed that way through the next two innings. Up came the ninth inning. Cooper was the first batter and he brought us off the bench when he reached out those long arms of his and poked a slow curve into right-center. Southworth gave Johnny Hopp the bunt sign and he laid down a beauty to put Walker on second. That brought up Kurowski.

Ruffing stood out there for a few short seconds that seemed like ages while he looked down at Whitey in the batter's box. He'd fanned him three times in that first game of the series, probably was trying to figure what he threw him those times. He got one strike and one ball on Kurowski and then served him another one. Whitey swung and he really hit it.

"There it goes," screamed Moore. "There it goes." Right into the stands and we had two more runs. We nearly killed Whitey when he crossed the plate. I remember tackling him and we mobbed him until he begged for us to let him go.

Then we sobered down in a hurry for we still knew the Yanks had a punch in those bats of theirs. And they proved it. Joe Gordon led off with a single and we started to worry. Dickey up. He hit a bouncer down to Brown at second, the kind that Jimmy had gobbled up all year easy-like. But he muffed this one and Bill was safe at first and Gordon was on second. We stopped to talk things over again with Cooper walking slowly out to the mound to talk to us.

He talked to Beazley for a while and then looked at me. "Watch it, Marty," he said. "We might try something."

That's all he said but I nodded. I knew. Priddy was at bat and we knew he was going to try to bunt those runners along. Walker called for a high fast one and Beazley sent one down a mile a minute that was right across Priddy's eyes. Quick as I could I cut behind Gordon who had about a 10-foot lead off second base. I dove for the bag and just as I hit it the ball got there too.

Cooper had reared back and thrown it with all the power he had in his big wide shoulders. And that was plenty. It came to me waist high just as I hit the bag. Gordon was on his way back to second and crashed into me. But I held the ball. He rolled over and I went at Umpire George Barr.

I just about jumped out of my shoes. "You're out," he bellowed. We'd picked him off!

THE BOX SCORE
(October 5, 1942)

ST. LOUIS (N. L.)	A.B.	R.	H.	P.	A.
Brown, 2b.	3	0	2	3	4
T. Moore, cf.	3	1	1	3	0
Slaughter, rf.	4	1	2	2	0
Musial, lf.	4	0	0	2	0
W. Cooper, c.	4	1	2	2	1
Hopp, 1b.	3	0	0	9	2
Kurowski, 3b.	4	1	1	1	1
Marion, ss.	4	0	0	3	5
Beazley, p.	4	0	1	2	0
Totals	33	4	9	27	13

NEW YORK (A. L.)	A.B.	R.	H.	P.	A.
Rizzuto, ss.	4	1	2	7	1
Rolfe, 3b.	4	1	1	1	0
Cullenbine, rf.	4	0	0	3	0
Di Maggio, cf.	4	0	1	3	0
Keller, lf.	4	0	1	1	0
Gordon, 2b.	4	0	1	3	3
Dickey, c.	4	0	0	4	0
Stainback	0	0	0	0	0
Priddy, 1b.	3	0	0	5	1
Ruffing, p.	3	0	1	0	1
Selkirk	1	0	0	0	0
Totals	35	2	7	27	6

Stainback ran for Dickey in 9th.
Selkirk batted for Ruffing in 9th.

CARDINALS	0	0	0	1	0	1	0	0	2 — 4
YANKEES	1	0	0	1	0	0	0	0	0 — 2

Errors—Brown (2), Hopp, Beazley, Priddy. Home runs—Rizzuto, Slaughter, Kurowski. Runs batted in—Rizzuto, Slaughter, Di Maggio, W. Cooper, Kurowski (2). Sacrifice hits—T. Moore, Hopp. Double plays—Gordon to Rizzuto to Priddy, Hopp to Marion to Brown. Bases on balls—Off Ruffing 1 (Brown), off Beazley 1 (Priddy). Struck out—By Beazley 2 (Gordon, Ruffing), by Ruffing 3 (Beazley (2), T. Moore). Earned runs—St. Louis 4, New York 2. Left on bases—St. Louis 5, New York 7. Umpires—Magerkurth (N. L.) at plate; Summers (A. L.) first base; Barr (N. L.) second base; Hubbard (A. L.) third base. Time of game—1:58.

Priddy popped out to Brown and Jimmy came right back to make up his his earlier boots by throwing out George Selkirk who hit for Ruffing.

That gave us the World Series. We beat Red Ruffing. We smashed a Yankee hold on the world championship. And my day was complete. I was in the right spot at the right time for a throw.

A throw that I knew was coming just because Walker Cooper, best catcher I ever saw, told me we might try something.

MORDECAI
BROWN
as told to
JACK RYAN

Mordecai Brown lost half of the index finger of his right hand when a farm boy, but became one of the great pitchers, winning 20 to 29 a season for Frank Chance's Cubs.

When Manager Frank Chance led the Chicago Cub team into New York the morning of October 8, 1908, to meet the Giants that afternoon to settle a tie for the National League pennant, I had a half-dozen "black hand" letters in my coat pocket. "We'll kill you," these letters said, "if you pitch and beat the Giants."

Those letters and other threats had been reaching me ever since we had closed our regular season two days before in Pittsburgh. We'd beaten the Pirates in that final game for our 98th win of the year and we had waited around for two days to see what the Giants would do in their last two games with Boston. They had to win 'em to tie us for the National League championship.

Well, the Giants did win those two to match our record of 98 wins and 55 losses so a playoff was in order. I always thought that John

McGraw used his great influence in National League affairs to dictate that the playoff must be held on the Giants' home field, the Polo Grounds.

I'd shown the "black hand" letters to Manager Chance and to the Cub owner, Charley Murphy. "Let me pitch," I'd asked 'em, "just to show those so-and-sos they can't win with threats."

Chance picked Jack Pfeister instead. Two weeks before, Pfeister had tangled with Christy Mathewson, McGraw's great pitcher, and had beaten him on the play where young Fred Merkle, in failing to touch second on a hit, had made himself immortal for the "boner" play. Since Mathewson had been rested through the series with Boston and would go against us in the playoff, Chance decided to follow the Pfeister-Mathewson pitching pattern of the "boner" game. I had pitched just two days before as we won our final game of the schedule from Pittsburgh.

Matter of fact, I had started or relieved in 11 of our last 14 games. Beyond that I'd been in 14 of the last 19 games as we came roaring down the stretch hot after the championship.

In our clubhouse meeting before the game, when Chance announced that Pfeister would pitch, we each picked out a New York player to work on. "Call 'em everything in the book," Chance told us. We didn't need much encouragement, either.

My pet target, you might say, was McGraw. I'd been clouding up on him ever since I had come across his sly trick of taking rival pitchers aside and sort of softening them up by hinting that he had cooked up a deal to get that fellow with the Giants. He'd taken me aside for a little chat to that effect one time, hoping, I suppose, that in a tight spot against the Giants I'd figure I might as well go easy since I'd soon be over on McGraw's side.

Sure, it was a cunning trick he had and I didn't like it. So, the day after he'd given me that line of talk I walked up to him and said: "Skipper, I'm pitching for the Cubs this afternoon and I'm going to show you just what a helluva pitcher you're trying to make a deal for." I beat his Giants good that afternoon.

But that was early in the season and I want to tell you about this playoff game. It was played before what everybody said was the biggest crowd that had ever seen a baseball game. The whole city of New York, it seemed to us, was clear crazy with disappointment because we had taken that "Merkle boner" game from the Giants. The Polo Grounds quit selling tickets about 1 o'clock, and thousands who held tickets couldn't force their way through the street mobs to the entrances. The umpires were an hour getting into the park. By game time there were thousands on the field in front of the bleachers, the stands were jammed with people standing and sitting in aisles, and there were always little fights going on as ticket-holders tried to get their seats. The bluffs overhanging the Polo Grounds were black with people, as were the housetops and the telegraph poles. The elevated lines couldn't run for people who had climbed up and were sitting on the tracks.

The police couldn't move them, and so the fire department came and tried driving them off with the hose, but they'd come back. Then the fire department had other work to do, for the mob outside the park set fire to the left-field fence and was all set to come bursting through as soon as the flames weakened the boards enough.

Just before the game started the crowd did break down another part of the fence and the mounted police had to quit trampling the mob out in front of the park and come riding in to turn back this new drive. The crowds fought the police all the time, it seemed to us as we sat in our dugout. From the stands there was a steady roar of abuse. I never heard anybody or any set of men called as many foul names as the Giant fans called us that day from the time we showed up till it was over.

We had just come out onto the field and were getting settled when Tom Needham, one of our utility men, came running up with the news that, back in the clubhouse he'd overheard Muggsy McGraw laying a plot to beat us. He said the plot was for McGraw to cut our batting practice to about four minutes instead of the regular 10, and then, if we protested to send his three toughest players, Turkey Mike Donlin, Iron

Man McGinnity and Cy Seymour charging out to pick a fight. The wild-eyed fans would riot and the blame would be put on us for starting it and the game would be forfeited to the Giants.

Chance said to us "Cross 'em up. No matter when the bell rings to end practice, come right off the field. Don't give any excuse to quarrel."

We followed orders, but McGinnity tried to pick a fight with Chance anyway, and made a pass at him, but Husk stepped back, grinned and wouldn't fall for their little game.

I can still see Christy Mathewson making his lordly entrance. He'd always wait until about 10 minutes before game time, then he'd come from the clubhouse across the field in a long linen duster like auto drivers wore in those days, and at every step the crowd would yell louder and louder. This day they split the air. I watched him enter as I went out to the bull pen, where I was to keep ready. Chance still insisted on starting Pfiester.

Mathewson put us down quick in our first time at bat, but when the Giants came up with the sky splitting as the crowd screamed, Pfiester hit Fred Tenney, walked Buck Herzog, fanned Bresnahan, but Kling dropped the third strike and when Herzog broke for second, nailed him. Then Turkey Mike Donlin doubled, scoring Tenney and out beyond center field a fireman fell off a telegraph pole and broke his neck. Pfiester walked Cy Seymour and then Chance motioned me to come in. Two on base, two out. Our warmup pen was out in right center field so I had to push and shove my way through the crowd on the outfield grass.

"Get the hell out of the way," I bawled at 'em as I plowed through. "Here's where you 'black hand' guys get your chance. If I'm going to get killed I sure know that I'll die before a capacity crowd."

Arthur Devlin was up—a low-average hitter, great fielder but tough in the pinches. But I fanned him, and then you should have heard the names that flew around me as I walked to the bench.

I was about as good that day as I ever was in my life. That year I had won 29 and, what with relief work, had been in 43 winning ball games.

But in a way it was Husk Chance's day.

That Chance had a stout heart in him. His first time at bat, it was in the second, the fans met him with a storm of hisses—not "boos" like you hear in modern baseball—but the old, vicious hiss that comes from real hatred.

Chance choked the hisses back down New York's throat by singling with a loud crack of the bat. The ball came back to Mathewson. He looked at Bresnahan behind the bat, then wheeled and threw to first, catching Chance off guard. Chance slid. Tenney came down with the ball. Umpire Bill Klem threw up his arm. Husk was out!

Chance ripped and raved around, protesting. Most of us Cubs rushed out of the dugout. Solly Hofman called Klem so many names that Bill threw him out of the game.

The stands behind us went into panic, they were so tickled and the roar was the wildest I ever heard when Matty went on to strike out Steinfeldt and Del Howard.

Chance was grim when he came up again in the third. Tinker had led off the inning by tripling over Cy Seymour's head. We heard afterward that McGraw had warned Seymour that Tinker was apt to hit Mathewson hard, and to play away back. Seymour didn't. Kling singled Tinker home. I sacrificed Johnny to second. Sheckard flied out, Evers walked. Schulte doubled. We had Matty wabbling and then up came Chance, with the crowd howling. He answered them again with a double, and made it to second with a great slide that beat a great throw by Mike Donlin.

Four runs.

The Giants made their bid in the seventh. Art Devlin singled off me, so did Moose McCormick. I tried to pitch too carefully to Bidwell and walked him. There was sure bedlam in the air as McGraw took out Mathewson and sent up the kid, Larry Doyle, to hit. Doyle hit a high foul close to the stand and as Kling went to catch it, the fans sailed derby hats to confuse him—and bottles, papers, everything. But Kling had nerve and he caught it.

Every play, as I look back on it, was crucial. In the seventh after

Tenney's fly had scored Devlin, Buck Herzog rifled one on the ground to left but Joe Tinker got one hand and one shin in front of it, blocked it, picked it up and just by a flash caught Herzog who made a wicked slide into first.

In the ninth a big fight broke out in the stands and the game was held up until the police could throw in a cordon of bluecoats and stop it. It was as near a lunatic asylum as I ever saw. As a matter of fact the newspapers next day said seven men had been carted away, raving mad, from the park during the day. This was maybe exaggerated, but it doesn't sound impossible to anyone who was there that day.

As the ninth ended with the Giants going out, one-two-three, we all ran for our lives, straight for the clubhouse with the pack at our heels. Some of our boys got caught by the mob and beaten up some. Tinker, Howard and Sheckard were struck. Chance was hurt most of all. A Giant fan hit him in the throat and Husk's voice was gone for a day or two of the World Series that followed. Pfiester got slashed on the shoulder by a knife.

We made it to the dressing room and barricaded the door. Outside

THE BOX SCORE
(October 8, 1908)

CHICAGO	A.B.	H.	P.	A.		NEW YORK	A.B.	H.	P.	A.
Sheckard, lf.	4	0	4	0		Tenney, 1b.	2	1	9	0
Evers, 2b.	3	1	0	3		Herzog, 2b.	3	0	1	2
Schulte, rf.	4	1	4	0		Bresnahan, c.	4	1	10	2
Chance, 1b.	4	3	13	0		Donlin, rf.	4	1	0	0
Steinfeldt, 3b.	4	1	0	3		Seymour, cf.	3	0	2	0
Hofman, cf.	0	0	0	0		Devlin, 3b.	4	1	2	0
Howard, cf.	4	0	1	0		McCormick, lf.	4	1	3	1
Tinker, ss.	4	1	1	4		Bridwell, ss.	3	0	0	1
Kling, c.	3	1	4	1		Mathewson, p.	2	0	0	3
Pfeister, p.	0	0	0	0		Doyle	1	0	0	0
Brown, p.	2	0	0	1		Wiltse, p.	0	0	0	0
Totals	32	8	27	12		Totals	30	5	27	9

Doyle batted for Mathewson in 7th.

CHICAGO	0	0	4	0	0	0	0	0	0 — 4
NEW YORK	1	0	0	0	0	0	1	0	0 — 2

Error—Tenney. Runs—Tenney, Tinker, Kling, Evers, Schulte, Devlin. Runs batted in—Donlin, Kling, Schulte, Chance (2), Tenney. Two-base hits—Donlin, Schulte, Chance, Evers. Three-base hit—Tinker. Double plays—Kling to Chance; McCormick to Bresnahan. Bases on balls—Off Pfeister, 2; off Brown, 1; off Mathewson, 1. Hit by pitcher—By Pfeister, 1. Struck out—By Mathewson, 7; by Wiltse, 1; by Pfeister, 1; by Brown, 1. Hits—Off Pfeister, 1 in 2-3 inning; off Mathewson, 7 in 7 innings. Umpires—Johnstone and Klem.

wild men were yelling for our blood—really. As the mob got bigger, the police came up and formed a line across the door. We read next day that the cops had to pull their revolvers to hold them back. I couldn't say as to that. We weren't sticking our heads out to see.

As we changed clothes, too excited yet to put on one of those wild clubhouse pennant celebrations, the word came in that the Giants over in their dressing room were pretty low. We heard that old Cy Seymour was lying on the floor, in there, bawling like a baby about Tinker's triple.

When it was safe we rode to our hotel in a patrol wagon, with two cops on the inside and four riding the running boards and the rear step. That night when we left for Detroit and the World Series we slipped out the back door and were escorted down the alley in back of our hotel by a swarm of policemen.

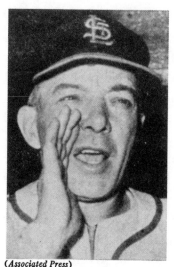

(*Associated Press*)

Billy Southworth

William Southworth was born in Harvard, Neb., March 9, 1894. Broke into organized ball with Portsmouth in 1912 and began his major league career in 1913 with Cleveland. He also played with the Pirates, Braves, Giants and Cardinals.

BILLY SOUTHWORTH

as told to

BOB HOOEY

On June 14, 1926, New York traded me to the St. Louis Cardinals for Heinie Mueller, another outfielder. I wasn't very happy about the deal on that spring day for few ballplayers ever wanted to leave John McGraw's Giants. There was a glamour to being a Giant in his days unmatched anywhere in baseball. But baseball luck is a strange thing. If McGraw hadn't traded me to the Cardinals, I might never have become a major league manager and managed a world championship team.

I achieved a boyhood ambition when McGraw bought me from the Braves in 1924. I was a Giant. But working for McGraw a player ceased to be an individual. He was a cog in a machine and the fact was clearly impressed on him that his success with the Giants depended entirely upon how good a cog he could make himself. I was a veteran

180

when I came to the Giants and by temperament and experience I was unable to subordinate myself to McGraw's rigid system. So when he decided in 1926 that I was, from his viewpoint, hopeless he traded me and with no personal feeling one way or the other.

So I went off to join the Cardinals and Rogers Hornsby, who that spring had succéeded Branch Rickey as manager. The Cardinals started the year with a great dash and in the first series against them we Giants knew they would be hard to beat. Then the Cardinals slumped and in May Hornsby saw his team floundering instead of making headway. I don't suppose the fans took them too seriously for no St. Louis team had won a pennant since the original Browns in the American Association back in 1888. Pittsburgh, defending champion and world's champion, was one of the favorites and the other was Cincinnati. Then the Cards began to pickup and when I joined them in mid-June they were in third place, only two and one-half games behind the leading Reds.

Hornsby had rounded up a good, solid team; a pretty hard bitten bunch that was the foundation for the famous Gas House Gangs of later years. You remember the '26 Cards: Jim Bottomley at first, Hornsby on second, Tommy Thevenow at short, Lester Bell at third, Bob O'Farrell for catcher and Chick Hafey and Taylor Douthit with me in the outfield. And for pitchers there were old Alex, Flint Rhem, Jesse Haines, Bill Sherdel and Bill Hallahan. We got good pitching and good hitting and Hornsby flogged the team at a furious pace. We headed into September in front and finally came to the Polo Grounds on Sept. 24, needing just one more victory to cinch the pennant. That was the day of my greatest thrill in baseball since the day I played my first game before the home folks in Columbus, Ohio, back in 1913.

I couldn't have asked for a better setting, in the Polo Grounds, against the Giants who had traded me and who were settling for a fifth place finish. And there was an added thrill to being with the Cardinals for of the squad only three of us, Alexander, Bill Killifer, one of our coaches, and myself, ever had been in a World Series.

Hornsby sent Flint Rhem to the box for the Cards while McGraw countered with Hughie McQuillan, who always was pretty tough for St. Louis. Before the first inning was finished it looked to most of us as if we'd have to wait another day to clinch the pennant and when the season is that far gone you can't afford to waste any time.

Mueller led off with a single but O'Farrell figured the hit and run was on, so he called for a pitch-out and threw Heinie out at second. Then Freddie Lindstrom cracked a terrific liner to left center that was tagged for two or three but was cut off when Douthit made one of the greatest running catches you ever saw. That was the tipoff it wasn't Rhem's day. There were two out but trouble was just starting. Frankie Frisch and George Kelly hit safely and that brought Bill Terry, playing right field, to the plate. Bill knocked one into the right field stands and we were three runs behind.

Hornsby poured acid on us as we came back to the bench. He told us we hadn't been taking our full cuts at the ball for several games and to get out there and swing. We went out and proved he was wrong and in a hurry.

Lester Bell led off for us in that second inning and drove a double down the left-field line; where he loved to hit a ball. Bell went to third when McQuillan made a wild pitch and scored when O'Farrell singled to center. That left us two runs behind. Then Thevenow doubled and so did George Torporcer, who batted for Rhem, and the score was tied. Douthit flied out and that brought me to the plate.

Our bench was yelling for me to get a hit and break the tie. McQuillan's first pitch was outside. The next one looked in there. I started to swing but checked myself. Then Hornsby was yelling from where he stood waiting to bat and I still can hear his rasping voice. "Have your cut Bill. Have your cut. We need that run. It can be the pennant."

I dug my spikes in a little deeper. I wanted that hit more than any of our gang. The pitch was coming and just where I liked it. I swung and hard. The ball took off and so did I. As I neared first base Otto Williams, our coach, was jumping up and down like a madman, jibbering and pointing to the right-field stands. The ball was bouncing around the upper tier and Torporcer was rounding third.

That was the timeliest home run I ever hit and to have hit it against the Giants, with McGraw snarling his defiance from the bench, made it doubly thrilling and satisfying. We never gave up our lead and backed Sherdel, who replaced Rhem, with some of the greatest defensive play you ever saw. McGraw kept on playing the hit and run but O'Farrell was a sheer genius that afternoon and three more times he called the play and flagged Giant runners at second.

Of course you know how the Cardinals went on to beat the Yankees in the World's Series and how Old Pete Alexander fanned Lazzeri to clinch the series in the seventh game. The Cardinals of '26 were a great team and until my own Redbirds of 1942 won the National League championship and beat the Yankees for the world's championship I always pointed back to that home run against the Giants as the high spot of my baseball career. Even today it remains the greatest thrill of my playing days.

THE BOX SCORE
(September 24, 1926)

ST. LOUIS

	A.B.	R.	H.	P.	A.
Douthit, cf.	4	0	0	2	0
Southworth, rf.	5	1	2	4	0
Hornsby, 2b.	5	0	1	2	4
Bottomley, 1b.	4	1	1	6	0
L. Bell, 3b.	4	1	1	1	1
Hafey, lf.	4	0	1	3	0
O'Farrell, c.	4	1	2	3	3
Thevenow, ss.	4	1	3	5	4
Rhem, p.	0	0	0	0	0
Torporcer	1	1	1	0	0
Sherdel	2	0	0	1	0
	—	—	—	—	—
Totals	37	6	12	27	12

Torporcer batted for Rhem in 2nd.

NEW YORK

	A.B.	R.	H.	P.	A.
Mueller, lf.	1	0	1	1	0
Moore, lf.	3	0	0	2	1
Lindstrom, 3b.	4	0	2	3	2
Frisch, 2b.	4	1	1	4	5
Kelly, 1b.	4	2	2	9	1
Terry, rf.	4	1	1	3	0
Tyson, cf.	4	0	3	2	0
Jackson, ss.	4	0	2	0	3
Florence, c.	4	0	1	2	0
McQuillan, p.	0	0	0	0	0
Carter	1	0	0	0	0
Barnes, p.	1	0	0	1	1
Farrell	1	0	0	0	0
Greenfield, p.	0	0	0	0	1
Scott	1	0	0	0	0
	—	—	—	—	—
Totals	36	4	13	27	14

Carter batted for Greenfield in 9th.
Farrell batted for McQuillan in 2nd.
Scott batted for Barnes in 7th.

ST. LOUIS	0 5 0 0 0 0 1 0 0	— 6
NEW YORK	3 0 0 0 0 0 0 1 0	— 4

Two base hits—L. Bell, Thevenow (2), Hafey, Kelly. Three-base hit—Bottomley. Home runs—Terry, Southworth. Stolen bases—Southworth, Douthit. Sacrifices—Moore, Sherdel. Double plays—Jackson to Frisch to Kelly. Bases on balls—Off Barnes, 2; off Greenfield, 1. Struck out—by McQuillan, 1; by Barnes, 1; by Sherdel, 1. Hits—Off Rhem, 6 in 1 inning; off Sherdel, 7 in 8; off McQuillan, 6 in 2; off Barnes, 5 in 5; off Greenfield, 1 in 2. Wild pitch—McQuillan. Winning pitcher—Sherdel. Losing pitcher—McQuillan.

(*Associated Press*)

RAY SCHALK

as told to

LLOYD LEWIS

Ray Schalk, now proprietor of a large bowling estab-lishment in Chicago, was born in Litchfield, Ill., July 10, 1892. First played with Taylorville in 1911, going to Milwaukee that season where he stayed until 1912. Joined White Sox in 1913. Caught in 1,721 games for the Sox and although small was famed for his enthusiasm and scrappy play on the diamond.

If you've caught baseball across 22 years you have a lot of big days, and it's hard, years later, to pick out the biggest. For a long time I thought the day I caught Charley Robertson when he pitched his no-hit, no-man-on-base game for the White Sox was the biggest. Part of the time I thought it was the day—I can't now recall the year—when I made a putout at second base and became what they told me was the first big-league catcher to have made a putout at every base.

But, all in all, as time went on I settled on Oct. 18, 1912, as my biggest day in the game.

I had come to the White Sox in August that year, had caught 50 or

60 innings—a little shaver looking up to Jimmy Callahan, the manager; to Billy Sullivan, the Sox catcher, and to Ed Walsh and Doc White, the heroes of the pitching staff. But I didn't expect to get into the City Series which was coming up that October.

The City Series was young and hot. It had started with a 7-7 game tie in 1903, had got to civil war proportions in 1906 when—it was also a World Series—the Sox, "The Hitless Wonders," had amazed everybody by licking Frank Chance's famous Cubs 4 to 2 games. The Cubs had come back to win 4 games to 1 in 1909 and the Sox had taken the rubber in 1911 four games to none.

This 1912 series was the one the Cub fans said was going to put the upstart White Sox in their place, and to tell the truth we did have only a mediocre club compared to those Cubs, who had great stars like Sheckard in left, Tinker on short, Evers on second (hitting .341 that year), Schulte in right, Heine Zimmerman (the league's heaviest swatter) on third, Jimmy Archer behind the bat, and on the mound Cheney, a 26-game winner; Richie, a 16-game winner, and Lavender, a 16-game winner. Big Ed Ruelbach hadn't had a good year, but he could do a lot of damage to your bats in spot games. Frank Chance was managing from the bench, having put Vic Saier on first.

The Cubs had finished third after one of their annual hot battles with the Giants and Pirates, with a winning average of .607, 11 games out of first place. We had finished fourth with a .506 average, 28 games out of first place.

We wanted to win bad, but didn't see how we could. Ed Walsh was our pitching staff; he'd gone 393 innings that summer, winning 27 and losing 17. Eddie Cicotte had won 10 and lost 10. Doc White had only won 8 while losing 10 for us. Our best regular hitter was Ping Bodie, who was always problematical up there at the plate.

The first day, Oct. 8, it rained and the next day came a game I could put down as one of the greatest I ever saw—0-0 in nine innings. Jimmy Lavender against Big Ed Walsh—Walsh giving the Cubs one hit, Lavender giving the Sox six, and the fans about half and half as to noise, in the Cubs' old park out on the West Side.

The next day rain again. Then Cheney and Cicotte went 12 innings for another tie. Ed Walsh went in the last three innings. The third game of the series Jimmy Lavender beat Doc White 5-4. The fourth game Walsh was beaten by Reulbach 4-2 and in the fifth the Cubs got 8 off our Cicotte and Bill Lange.

Three straight lickings for us and everybody in Chicago thought it was all over. We packed our bags before we got into our uniforms for the taxi ride over to the Cubs Park. Most of our players were figuring on catching trains for home that night. So were the Cubs.

Big Ed Walsh warmed up for us. He was all that was left. Jimmy Lavender was to work for the Cubs.

I was out in center shagging flies when Callahan wigwagged me to come in. "You're going to catch today," he said. "I grabbed the mitt. I couldn't believe it. Easterly had been up nine times in the series and had got eight hits. Why were they switching to me, the rookie? Nobody ever told me why. We hit Lavender for five runs, getting the last in the 11th inning to win. Still we didn't see how we could take three more and packed our bags again the next morning. Callahan sent me in again to catch Doc White, who gave up three runs the first two innings, and in came Butcher Boy Joe Benz, another spitballer, who went all the way while we were hitting Ruelbach and Cheney for enough to win—7-5.

Three games to two now against us, but we still packed our bags, so did the Cubs. I caught the next—and eighth game—too—got three hits. We got Cheney off the mound and came from behind to make four in the ninth and win 8-5.

And now came the big game—the payoff game. Series tied and everything depending on this, the ninth game we had played. Big Ed Walsh again. He had pitched nine innings on Oct. 9, three innings on Oct. 11, nine more on Oct. 13, 11 more on Oct. 15, one more on Oct. 17 and was now to go nine more on Oct. 18—42 innings in 10 days, giving up 24 hits and eight runs.

The game was in the Cubs Park and we got to Jimmy Lavender in the first inning for one run. I knew when the Cubs batted in the first inning we would win, for "the Big Moose" burned his fast one and broke his spitter off like vengeance. He wasn't going to be beaten.

In the second, when we got two more runs off Jimmy Lavender, we knew we were in. We knew it and so did the Cubs. In the third we hit Smith and Ruelbach for eight runs, and Frank Chance, "the Peerless Leader," got up at the end of the inning, called Jimmy Archer out of the game and the two of them left the park. After that we got two in the fourth and three in the fifth and had hammered Lefty out, too, and felt we could hit Fred Toney, the fifth Cub pitcher, if we had had to.

But the great thrill to me was Ed Walsh standing out there, refusing to let up or to coast with a three-run or an 11-run or 16-run lead. Sixteen runs ahead and overworked, but he wouldn't let Callahan take him out for a rest that he deserved, if ever a man did.

No, indeed. He not only stayed out there, but he kept pouring it through harder and harder the further he went. He was out to get even with the Cubs. He was out to humiliate them, rub their noses to the dust. He wanted a shutout.

I'll always see him—a great, handsome figure of a man, with shoulders like a schoolhouse, dark face, sharp eyes, smashing that spitter in there, snapping his arm to make it sink past the bat, pitching harder and harder as we got near the end of the long game in what had been the longest drawn-out postseason series.

Five hits were all they had, none after the fifth, and when the last batter rolled out Big Ed came down off the mound. We couldn't get near him. The Sox fans had him.

It was Big Ed's finish. He was through. Next year he pitched in only 16 games and the year after that nine, and by the end of 1914 was gone from Comiskey Park—a 10-year man and gone.

So, really I got to catch him only a few games, but I was there when he burned himself—and the Cubs—out. The Cubs lost the next five City Series in a row. It always seemed to me they couldn't ever get out from under the shame of 1912. To have it 3-0 and then lose four straight, the last 16-0, was too much.

JIMMY FOXX

as told to
LYALL SMITH

It looks like my slugging days are over now. I was afraid of it last spring when I reported to the Cubs down at French Lick. It's my eyes. I'd stand up there at the plate and feel great. I still have the power in my arms and my wrists. My legs are all right. But my eyes!

Well, for example, I'd be standing up there ready to lean on a pitch but when the ball came in to the plate I'd only see about half of it. And when I'd swing I'd somehow always hit that half that wasn't there.

There was a time though when I'd see the whole ball and all this last season when I was with the Cubs as a player and then as a coach, even when I went out to Portsmouth as manager, I still could sit there in the dugout and remember some of my good days.

I guess I've hit just about as many home runs as anyone still wearing a baseball uniform but for just one good solid punch I'd have to take the afternoon in the fifth game of the 1930 World Series when I smacked one into the stands as a personal tribute to Mr. Mack (Manager Connie Mack of the A's).

But there were other afternoons, too, that I'll never forget. Some were before that day in '30, some after but most were wound up in one way or another with Mr. Mack.

I met him the first year I ever played. That was in 1925 when the A's bought me as a kid of 17 with nothing but a bunch of muscles and a big desperate lunge at the ball.

That previous fall I'd received one of those penny post cards from Frank "Homerun" Baker who was managing a team in the Eastern League and that was a thrill, too. I was just 16 when I got this card. Baker had scribbled on the back: "Would you be interested in being a professional ballplayer? If you are contact me." Naturally I wrote him and he signed me up. That next summer he sold me to the Athletics who shipped me out for seasoning.

I was hitting pretty good then and kept right on till the A's brought me up again to help out Cy Perkins, one of the best catchers I ever saw. I didn't have much to do until 1927 when Mr. Mack stuck me over at third base. I played there a while and then Ossie Orwoll, our first baseman, got into a slump and one day after I had been warming up a pitcher in the bullpen Mr. Mack walked over to me.

"Ever play first base, Jimmy?" he asked. I told him no. "You are today," he said, and tossed me a first baseman's mitt.

That '29 season was a big one for me. I was still pretty young but I didn't have to do very much on a team that was as murderous as any I ever saw.

We had Bishop and Haas, Cochrane and Simmons, Miller and Dykes, and pitchers like Earnshaw, Ehmke, Walberg, Grove and Quinn. That was the year we breezed to an American League pennant and faced the Cubs in the Series.

In the first game I smacked a homer off Charlie Root to break a scoreless tie in the 7th inning and help us win 3-1. I hit another one in the second game when we slapped them around 9-3 and had a lot of fun in the fourth game when we made those 10 runs in the 7th inning after trailing 8-0. I didn't hit any long ones in that game but poked out a couple of singles to take part in the big spree.

But that was nothing like the buzz I got the next year when we went into the series again. The Cards had won the National title and were giving us a stiff battle. In that first game we were up against

Burleigh Grimes and his spitter. He was tough to hit when he gave that ball a working-over and was really putting the stuff on it that day.

In the second inning I came up after Al Simmons had bounced out to Grimes and I stepped in to one of Burleigh's spitters and slapped it off the right field wall over Ray Blades' head for a triple. Bing Miller was up next. He hit a long fly that time out to Blades again and I came in with the first run after the catch.

I felt pretty good about that but old Burleigh wasn't through with me yet. In the fourth I was up again right after Simmons had poked out a home run to tie the score, but Burleigh fooled me on a low spitter and I struck out. In the sixth we went ahead when Maxie Bishop worked Grimes for a walk and scored when Jimmy Dykes doubled. With two out Burleigh walked Simmons on purpose to get at me.

I fell right into his plans and was easy for him. I was expecting him to throw me a spitter if the count was close. And it was for I worked him up to a 3-2 with two runners on base and two out.

Burleigh stood out there and went through his motions. He put the glove up to his mouth, looked out at Dykes on second, glanced over at Simmons on first. Then stepped off the mound and turned around for another look at the scoreboard. Then he took his stance again and pitched. I was sure it'd be a spitter, a low one around the knees like the one he had fanned me on in the second inning. But it was a curve, a fast hopper that came in waist high and caught me way off balance.

Everybody was surprised for Burleigh didn't throw a curve very often. But they weren't nearly as surprised as I was. I stood there at the plate for a minute still trying to figure out what had happened, but I was out.

We won that game anyway and took the second one before moving down to St. Louis feeling pretty good. Then Wild Bill Hallahan shut us out 5-0 before Jess Haines set us down on four hits to beat Lefty Grove 3-1 and even up the series at two games apiece.

Well, we're in St. Louis for the fifth game and all of us are keyed up pretty high. We wanted to win that one, for any baseball man will tell you that the fifth game is the big one. If you win it you're over the hump and coasting. If you lose it—well, that's not good at all.

It's Grimes' turn again and Mr. Mack picks out big George Earnshaw to go for us. Mr. Mack took me to one side of the dugout just before the game started. "Jimmy," he said, "you watch out for that pitcher out there. He figures he has your number and I think he'll try to get to you if he gets in a pinch. And watch for that curve ball. Don't let him fool you with that spitter motion. Just because he goes through like he's going to throw it is no sign he will."

The game starts and right away you can tell it's going to be a honey. Both Grimes and Earnshaw are really tough, although Mike Cochrane gets a single for us in the first inning and Adams pokes one off Ehmke.

I come up in the second and hit the first pitch, a fast ball, out to Chick Hafey in deep left for just another out and then come up again in the fifth. I swing on the first pitch again and poke a single into center field for our second single and the third hit of the game, but it doesn't do any good and nobody scores.

I bat again in the seventh and Burleigh gets me in a 2-1 hole. I'm still thinking about a curve ball when he throws a fast one past me and all I hit was a big hunk of air.

They scared us in their half when Jimmy Wilson doubled down the line, but there were two outs and Mr. Mack waved his score card for George to walk Gelbert to get at Grimes. Burleigh hit one hard, but Mule Haas ran it down and we were out of the jam.

In the eighth we had a good chance to score when two singles and an error by Frankie Frisch loaded the bases with only one out. But Burleigh reached down into his bag of tricks to make Bishop ground to Bottomley, who forced Haas at the plate, and make Dykes hit one to Gelbert at short, who flipped to Frisch in time to force Bishop to end the inning.

Earnshaw had been lifted for a pinch hitter in that frame and Mr. Mack put in Lefty Grove, who got by the Card half, although he was nicked for a single, the third Redbird hit, by Frisch.

Then came the ninth. There still was no score. Each team had made

only three hits and Grimes was bearing down. But he pitched too carefully to Cochrane and Mickey jogged down to first base on a pass.
Al Simmons came up, but he undercut a spitter and lifted a high pop
fly to Gelbert for the first out. That brought me up again.

I was nervous. But Grimes was cool as ice. He was deliberately slow
in getting ready to pitch, so I stepped out of the box. I got some dirt
on my hands and stepped in again. He raised his hand to his mouth in
his spitter motion. Then he threw the first pitch. I knew in that flash
second it wasn't a spitter, for it was coming in close. It was a curve and
I swung!

Well, that was it. The big thrill. I heard the Athletic bench yell all
at once and there it went. Some fan reached up and pulled it down
when it hit in the left-field bleachers for a home run.

THE BOX SCORE
(October 6, 1930)

ATHLETICS	A.B.	R.	H.	P.	A.	CARDINALS	A.B.	R.	H.	P.	A.
Bishop, 2b.	4	0	0	1	0	Douthit, cf.	4	0	0	2	0
Dykes, 3b.	3	0	0	0	1	Adams, 3b.	4	0	1	0	1
Cochrane, c.	3	1	1	7	1	Frisch, 2b.	4	0	1	3	3
Simmons, lf.	4	0	0	3	0	Bottomley, 1b.	4	0	0	9	1
Foxx, 1b.	4	1	2	12	0	Hafey, lf.	3	0	0	1	0
Miller, rf.	4	0	0	0	0	Watkins, rf.	3	0	0	1	0
Haas, cf.	4	0	1	2	0	Wilson, c.	4	0	1	9	0
Boley, ss.	3	0	1	2	1	Gelbert, ss.	2	0	0	2	8
Earnshaw, p.	2	0	0	0	4	Grimes, p.	2	0	0	0	0
Moore	0	0	0	0	0	Blades	0	0	0	0	0
Grove, p.	0	0	0	0	1						
Totals	31	2	5	27	8	Totals	30	0	3	27	13

Moore batted for Earnshaw in 8th.   Blades batter for Watkins in 9th.

ATHLETICS	0	0	0	0	0	0	0	0	2 — 2	
CARDINALS	0	0	0	0	0	0	0	0	0 — 0	

Error—Frisch. Hoeh run—Foxx. Sacrifice hit—Grimes. Double play—Adams to Frisch
to Bottomley. Left on bases—St. Louis 8, Philadelphia 5. Bases on balls—Off Grimes 3
(Dykes, Moore, Cochrane); off Earnshaw 3 (Gelbert 2, Hafey); off Grove 1 (Blades). Struck
out—By Grimes 7 (Bishop 2, Boley, Cochrane, Earnshaw, Foxx, Miller); by Earnshaw 5
(Watkins, Bottomley 2, Adams, Hafey); by Grove 2 (Bottomley, Gelbert). Hits—Off Earnshaw 2 in 7 innings, off Grove 1 in 2 innings. Winning pitcher—Grove. Umpires—Moriarty,
plate; Rigler, first; Geisel, second; Reardon, third. Time—1:53.

HIPPO VAUGHN
as told to
HAL TOTTEN

(*Sketch by Hod Taylor*)

Big Jim Vaughn, star southpaw hurler for the Chicago Cubs from 1913 to 1921, won more than 20 games every year but one, until he was side-tracked by a sore arm. Came from Kansas City after trials with Yankees and Senators.

I don't believe there has been another game in the history of base-ball like the one I'm going to talk about. It was between the Cubs and the Cincinnati Reds at Weeghman Park on May 2, 1917—it wasn't until two years later that it became known as Wrigley Field.

The attendance that day was only about 3,500, but since then at least 10,000 people and maybe more have told me they saw that game. In fact, a couple of years ago a young lad rushed up and told me about it—said he was there. I asked him how old he was, and he said 23. Now—that game had been played 22 years before, so I said:

"How did you go, in your mother's arms?"

"Naw," he said, "my dad took me—but," and he grinned a bit sheep-ishly—"I was pretty young."

Art Wilson   *Fred Toney*

Well—to get back to that game—it was the one where neither Fred Toney nor I allowed a hit for nine innings, but I lost out in the 10th. There didn't seem to be very much unusual about the game as it went along. I was just taking care of each batter as he came up there, that was all. And I didn't even notice what Toney was doing.

As a matter of fact, I never even spoke to Toney in the entire game— but I'll have to go back a little to explain that. When I broke into the big leagues with the Yankees in 1908, it was with such hard-boiled old-timers as Willie Keeler, Jack Chesbro, Al Orth, Jack Newton—a bunch of old heads. I learned my baseball from them.

We never spoke to a player on another team on the field—there was none of this glad-handing and hello business. Why, if anyone on the other club ever spoke pleasantly to me, I thought he was framing on me. I didn't want 'em to speak to me at all.

I'd always given Toney's team, Cincinnati, a fit, so this day they laid for me. One feature that seldom has been mentioned is the fact that there wasn't a left-handed hitter in the Red's lineup that day. They even took Ed Rousch out of there to give 'em another right-handed hitter and an all-right-handed lineup.

Another feature is this—after I'd got the first two men out in the first inning, Greasy Neale came up and hit a little looping fly just back of second base. The second baseman could have gotten it easy, but Cy Williams came in from center and made the catch. That was the only ball hit out of the infield off me until the 10th inning.

Well, while we were having our "outs" in the eighth inning, I was sitting on the bench. Remember how that old dugout was—with a partition in the middle cutting the bench in two? I was sitting in the end nearest the clubhouse. One of the fellows at the other end said: "Come on, let's get a run off this guy." Another one chimed in: "Run, hell; we haven't even got a hit off 'im!" "Well," another chap chimed in, "they haven't

Indian Jim Thorpe

got a hit off Vaughn, either."

Well, I figured: "If this is a no-hitter and only one more inning to go, I'm going to give it everything I've got to get through that inning." And with the last three men in the batting order coming up, I really intended to get past them. I got Cueto on a line fly to Charley Deal at third and I got a third strike past Kuhn. Then that big Toney came to bat.

Remember how he used to hit—with that powerful, stiff-armed swing? Well, I gave him everything I had on that first pitch—and was careful to keep it inside. He took that big swing and missed. It looked like he might have hit it a mile, but he missed it with the handle of his bat.

He missed the second one. And I

Hal Chase

made up my mind to give him everything I had on the next one. I pitched—he missed—and I'll never forget the great cheer that went up. But Toney went out and set us down too, and we went into the 10th inning. I knew I was tired, but I felt that I still had my stuff.

Getz, the first man up, hit a pop fly which our catcher, Art Wilson, got in front of the plate. Then came the first hit of the game. Larry Kopf hit one into right center for a single. But Neale hit an easy fly to Williams in center and Hal Chase also hit a fly out that way. It was a hard hit ball, but not a line drive, and it was right at Williams. He got both hands on it—and dropped it. Any outfielder ordinarily would catch it easy. It was just a plain muff. Kopf got to third on that one, and Chase stole second.

There's been a lot of discussion about the play that came up next— the one that lost the ball game. Indian Jim Thorpe, the famous old football player who was trying to make good in baseball, was at bat and he sent a swinging bunt toward third. I knew the minute it was hit that I couldn't get Thorpe at first. He was fast as a race horse. So I went over to the line, fielded the ball, and scooped it toward the plate. Kopf, running in, was right behind me and he stopped when he saw me make the play to the plate. I didn't see him, or I could have just turned around and tagged him out.

Now, some of the writers said that Wilson didn't expect the play. The truth is that Art just went paralyzed—just stood there with his hands at his sides staring at me. The ball hit him square on the chest protector—I'll never forget—it seemed to roll around there for a moment—and then dropped to the ground. The instant Kopf saw it drop, he streaked for the plate. But Wilson still stood there, paralyzed. I looked over my shoulder and saw Chase round third and start in, too. So I said to Art:

"Are you going to let him score, too?"

He woke up, grabbed the ball and tagged Chase out easily. But it was too late, the one big deciding run was in. Wilson cried like a baby after the game. He grabbed my hand and said: "I just went out on you, Jim—I just went tight."

In the clubhouse afterward everybody was pretty sore. Charley Weeghman, the boss, stuck his head in the door and yelled:

"You're all a bunch of — — —s."

But I wasn't sore. I'd just lost another ball game, that's all.

I do remember this about it, though. After the game I told Fred Toney: "You've got to pitch the kind of ball you did against me today to beat me from now on, Old Man." He shook hands, but he looked at me kind of funny when I said that. He must have taken it as a bad omen. Anyway, he never did pitch that well against me again—and I don't believe he ever beat me again. We met a lot of times, and most of the games were close, but he'd licked me for the last time.

THE BOX SCORE
(*May 2, 1917*)

CINCINNATI	A.B.	H.	P.	A.	CUBS	A.B.	H.	P.	A.
Groh, 3b.	1	0	2	3	Zeider, ss.	4	0	1	0
Getz, 3b.	1	0	1	2	Wolter, rf.	4	0	0	0
Kopf, ss.	4	1	1	4	Doyle, 2b.	4	0	5	4
Neale, cf.	4	0	1	0	Merkle, 1b.	4	0	7	1
Chase, 1b.	4	0	12	0	Williams, cf.	2	0	2	0
Thorpe, rf.	4	1	1	0	Mann, lf.	3	0	0	0
Shean, 2b.	3	0	3	1	Wilson, c.	3	0	14	1
Cueto, lf.	3	0	5	0	Deal, 3b.	4	0	1	0
Kuhn, c.	3	0	4	0	Vaughn, p.	3	0	0	4
Toney, p.	3	0	0	1					
Totals	30	2	30	11	Totals	31	0	30	10

CINCINNATI	0	0	0	0	0	0	0	0	0	1—1	
CUBS	0	0	0	0	0	0	0	0	0	0—0	

Run—Kopf. Errors—Zeider, Williams. Strikeouts—By Vaughan, 10; Toney, 3. Bases on balls—Off Vaughan, 2; Toney, 2. Double plays—Doyle to Merkle to Zeider; Vaughan to Doyle to Merkle. Left on bases—Cubs, 2; Cincinnati, 1. Umpires—Orth and Rigler. Time —1:45.

CASEY
STENGEL
as told to
JOHN P. CARMICHAEL

*Casey Stengel, manager of the Braves from 1938 until
he resigned last winter, was an outfielder with Dodgers,
Pirates, Phillies, Giants and Braves from 1910 to 1925.
Few know him by his given name—Charles Dillon
Stengel. Once attended Western Dental College in
Kansas City, but decided baseball was more of a career.
Now manager of Milwaukee Brewers.*

Two ballplayers lolled on a bench one day in Kankakee, Ill., in 1910
watching the antics of a teammate in the outfield. The object of their gaze
would haul down a fly ball, throw it into the infield, then sail his glove ahead
of him on the grass, take a run and slide into the mitt. "He won't be with us
long," observed one onlooker. "You mean he's going up?" asked the other.
"No," replied the first, "there's an institution here to take care of guys like
that. . . .!"

I was only practicing three things at once (said Stengel) like running, throwing and sliding. And I fooled them, because two years
later, in September, I got off a train in New York, a brand new suitcase

in one hand and $95 in my pocket. The next day was my greatest in baseball. I was reporting to Brooklyn. Is that 30 years ago? I must be getting old.

The bag was Kid Eberfield's idea. He was back from the majors and playing with us at Montgomery, Ala., in the Southern League when Manager Johnny Dobbs gave me the offer to join the Dodgers. The Kid and Mrs. Eberfield came over to say good-by and good luck while I was packing. I had one of those cardboard valises . . . they'd last about 1,000 miles if you got good weather, but if you ever got caught in the rain with one, you'd suddenly find yourself walking along with just a handle in your hand.

Well, they told me I couldn't go to the big leagues with a thing like that and made me lay out $18 for a good one. I'd gone two and a half years to dental school and I was trying to save up enough tuition dough for another year. It cost about $150 plus more for instruments and everything and I was short enough without buying a bag. "You won't come back," said Eberfield. "Never mind the money. Forget about being a dentist."

So I got to New York. It was in the evening and no use going to the park then, so I asked a cab-driver for a place to stay and he drove me to the Longacre Hotel at 47th st. I checked in and went down and sat in the lobby. I was afraid to go out, it was so dark, but finally I walked down to 46th st. and then hustled back, for fear I'd get lost. About 20 minutes later I went as far as 45th and back. I kept adding another block each trip and had been clear to 42d st. and returned by midnight when I decided to turn in. Next morning I started for the park. Brooklyn played then at the old Washington st. grounds at 5th av. and 3d and with the help of an elevated and a streetcar I made it. The gateman found out what I wanted and waved toward the clubhouse. "Go on down there," he said . . . and, as I walked away, he called after me: "You better be good."

I'll never forget walking into the locker room. There was a crap game going on in one corner. The only fellow who paid any attention to me was Zack Wheat. He introduced me around. Nobody shook

Zack Wheat

hands. Some grunted. A few said hello. I walked over to the game and decided maybe I ought to get in good with the boys by participating in their sport, so I fished out $20 and asked if I could shoot. Somebody said: "Sure," and handed me the dice. I rolled 'em out. A hand reached for my 20 and a voice said: "Craps, busher," and I never even got the bones back. I was about to reach for more money when I felt a tap on my shoulder and there was Manager Bill Dahlen.

"Are you a crapshooter or a ball-player, kid?" he asked. I told him I was a player and he said: "Well, get into a suit and on that field while you still have carfare." I hustled, believe me, and I've never touched dice since, either. I got to the bench and just sat there. I knew better than to pick up a bat and go to the plate. Eberfield told me what happened to rookies who tried that. Finally Dahlen came over and said: "Let's see you chase a few" and I ran like hell for the outfield. Behind the fence was a big building with fire escapes all down one side and guys in shirt sleeves were parked on the steps, passing around pails of beer and getting set for the game.

I never expected to play, but just as the umpires came out Dahlen told me to "get in center." Hub Northern, the regular center fielder, had been sick, and I guess they decided they might as well get me over with quick. My first time at bat we had a man on first and Dahlen gave me the bunt sign. The pitch wasn't good and I let it go by. Claude Hendrix, the league's leading pitcher was working for Pittsburgh and George Gibson catching. Hendrix threw another and I singled to right-center. When I got to the bench after the inning Dahlen stopped me. "Didn't you see the bunt sign?" he asked. I told him yes, but that down South we had the privilege of switching on the next pitch if we wanted to. "I don't want you to carry too much responsibility, kid," he said, "so I'll run the team and that way all you'll have to worry about is fielding and hitting." My ears were red when I got to center field.

Up on the fire escape the boys were having drinks on my hit and I could hear them speaking real favorably of me. I heard somebody holler and it was Wheat telling me to move back. Hans Wagner was at the plate. He larruped one and I went way back and grabbed it. In the dugout Wheat said: "Better play deeper for him." I thought of the catch I'd made and said to myself: "I can grab anything he can hit." Two innings later he came up again and Wheat waved me back, but I wouldn't go and wham! old Hans peeled one off. The ball went by me like a bee bee shot and he was roosting on third when I caught up with it.

I got three more hits right in a row. The first time Hendrix had fed me a fast ball, figuring why waste his best pitch, a spitter on a busher. He was pretty mad by the time I combed two blows off his spitter and another off his hook. Once when I was on first Dahlen gave me the steal sign and away I went. I beat Gibson's throw and Wagner just stood there, looking down at me. Never said a word. I stole two bases and when I came up the fifth time we'd knocked Hendrix out and a left-hander was pitching for the Bucs. Manager Fred Clark hollered at me: "All-right, phenom, let's see you cross over." I was feeling cocky enough to do it.... I stepped across the plate and stood hitting right-handed and damned if I didn't get a base on balls.

The Dodgers were playing the Cubs two days later when Stengel came to bat the first time with nobody on. Cub Catcher Jimmy Archer looked up at him and said: "So you're the new Brooklyn star, huh? A base-stealer, too, huh? Well, I hope you get on and go down." Stengel got on and, with two out, Dahlen gave him the green light. "I was 20 feet from the bag when I saw Johnny Evers with the ball," said Casey. "I tried to slide around him, but no use. He really crowned me. As I lay there, he pulled up one pant leg. 'Oh, tryin' to spike me,' he growled, although I hadn't even touched him. "I'll stick this ball down your throat if you ever try it again, busher!"

Stengel's greatest day was over. His education had begun!

JIMMY
WILSON
as told to
JOHN P. CARMICHAEL

Jimmy Wilson, ex-manager of the Cubs, and now Cincinnati coach, started career in 1920. Managed Phils and played with Cards and Reds before coming to Chicago. Caught in four World Series.

All we have to do is go back almost 12 years when I was with the Cards and you'll remember the day the minute I tell you it was the second game of the 1931 World Series with the Athletics. We beat 'em 2-0 . . . and that was the famous afternoon I threw out Jimmy Foxx at third in the ninth. Oh, yes . . . he was out. I pulled a boner. Granted. I never denied I did. But if Bill Klem hadn't booted the play . . . well, anyway, that's the story . . . a day I'll never forget!

"Pepper" Martin hit the front pages one day. He stole two bases, scored both our runs. I'll always think it was one of the best games I ever caught. Not that I was doing anything specially good . . . everything seemed to be going smoothly right from the start and old "Wild Bill" Hallahan was pitching like clockwork. But before the fifth inning was over, I damn near had the dunce's cap on the first time, never mind the ninth. I remember Gabby Street shakin' his finger at me after the game and saying: "You were pretty lucky out there today, boy." Maybe I was, but he didn't make me feel any better.

Hallahan hadn't allowed a hit into the fifth, but he'd been a little off the plate and Foxx, first up, walked. Then "Bing" Miller singled for the first Athletic blow. Jimmie Dykes bunted and up came Dibs Williams. I walked out to the mound and called in Frank Frisch, who was team captain. I wanted to put Williams on first and pitch to George Earnshaw. "Wild Bill" said no. "I can get that Williams out," he said. "He's just a punk." Frisch chimed in with: "If you walk Williams, they'll send up a pinch-hitter for Earnshaw."

"All right," I told him, "so much the better. We'll have him outta here then. He's a better pitcher than any pinch-hitter they got. Williams might hit a long fly and get a run home. He don't hit for me." Well, we argued a while and finally I had my way. We walked Williams. Instead of sending up a hitter, Connie Mack let Earnshaw bat. Boy, he hit one! That ball went off his bat like a bullet and I don't think Frisch knew he had the ball as it took one fast hop and bounced against his stomach. He turned it onto a double play and we were out of the inning, but if that thing had been six inches either way it'd have been a cinch double.

So we go into the ninth, leading 2-0 and Foxx walked again. Miller went out but Dykes walked. Williams was so anxious to hit one in the clutch that he fell all over himself missing a third strike and this time Mack yanked Earnshaw and sent up Jim Moore. We had two strikes on him . . . one away from the last out. Just as I took my eye off Foxx, down at second, to follow Hallahan's pitch, I saw Jim head for third. Instinctively I fired down there . . . I mean, I just did it, sort of automatically, but the second I let go of the ball, it dawned on me what I'd done. Moore had fanned, but the pitch was in the dirt. It was a pickup . . . and I should have either tagged him or tossed to first.

At the instant I let the ball go, I swear there were only two people in the park who knew what had happened. One was myself. The other was Umpire Dick Nallin at home. He didn't walk away. He stood right there. But instead of walking away myself . . . and some of the A's were already trotting past me en route from their bench to the clubhouse, thinking that was all . . . I reached out after the ball . . . you know, trying to pull it back. If I only could have! Eddie Collins, coaching at third, saw me do that and tumbled instantly to what had happened. I had tipped him off. He hollered to Moore to run and, eventually, Jim did. When I saw him go, I turned to look at first and nobody was on the bag. Jim Bottomley had gone. Even if I'd had the ball, there was nobody to take it down there. That isn't an alibi for my mistake . . . just to keep the story straight.

I never threw more on a dime to a base in my life. It was the wrong play, of course, but Jake Flowers had the ball with Foxx still 20 feet from the bag. He couldn't have helped tagging him if he even kept the glove where the ball hit it. Foxx was really out. No runner ever was "outer" but Klem hasn't called the play either way to this very day. Honestly, he hasn't. He never gave a decision . . . just stood there. I

Wild Bill Hallahan

finally got the ball, but Moore was on first so there was nothing to do but go on with the game.

When I got back to the plate, Umpire Nallin said to me: "There was nothing I could do, Jim" and I told him: "I don't blame you, Dick . . . it was my own fault . . ." which it was. But Klem and I were at swords' point long before that game and we didn't exactly hit it off for a while afterward either. Foxx was out at third and Bill never made a move. Anyway, I went out to see Hallahan and it's a good thing those 35,000 customers didn't have guns with 'em that day or I'd a been a dead catcher. I told Bill:

"Including these 35,000 customers and the Cardinal ball club, I think you're the only guy in the place who ain't down on me." Hallahan grinned . . . he was quite a guy . . . and said, "You've played pretty good ball behind me, Jim . . . we'll get the next guy . . . who was it?" I told him Max Bishop. "He couldn't hit me with six bats," rumbled Bill and we went back to work.

Bishop hit Bill's first pitch for a high foul back of first which Bottomley caught over the box-seat rail and the game was over. Believe me when I tell you the sweat was pretty cold on my forehead. We got in the clubhouse and the first thing I did was go over to Frisch. I was pretty sore at him about not going after Klem on the play at third. I couldn't argue, because I'd pulled a skuller and it'd look like I was trying to cover up. I asked Frank: "Did you think Foxx was out at third?" He said yes. "Well, why didn't you go over and howl?" I wanted to know. "You're team captain. I suppose because you didn't figure in the play, to hell with it, huh?"

We jawed back and forth and suddenly the door opened and Bozeman Bulger, the writer, came in. John McGraw was in the stands and Bulger was ghosting the series for him. He asked me: "Was Foxx out at third?" I told him I didn't know. . . . I wasn't close enough to see. "You're a so-and-so liar," snapped Bulger. "You know he was out. You know what happened down there. So do I." I knew, of course, that "Bose" wanted me to put the finger on Klem so McGraw, who was always fighting with Bill, could blast him in his next day's article. But I just told Bulger again that I couldn't say and by that time all the other newspapermen were inside. You know a funny thing . . . I didn't get much of a riding for what I'd done. The first game in Philly, two days later, I didn't even hear any boos. I just told the writers I'd pulled one for the books and let it go at that. So did they. Besides, Martin was more of a hero than I was a bum.

But when Mrs. Wilson and I got to our apartment I took one look at a stack of telephone calls and said to her: "Come on, let's get out of here and have dinner some place else." We did, but before we could get away I heard steps in the corridor and recognized them as belonging to a Cardinal pitcher's wife who lived in our building. I knew she was coming down to find out what had happened and I walked into the bedroom where our daughter Jane was lying on the bed. She was nine weeks old at the time and when I heard this lady talking to my wife, I began talking to Jane in a voice loud enough to be heard in the next room.

"I'll tell you what happened, Jane," I said, "because you can't answer me back, and when you're a big girl I'll buy you all kinds of pretty things for being so nice and not asking me what went on. I don't want to hear any more about it, but if you insist, why here goes . . .!"

About then I heard the door slam and Mrs. Wilson said: "It's all right now, Jim, you can come out. . . ." So we went to dinner.

THE BOX SCORE

(October 2, 1931)

PHILADELPHIA	A.B.	R.	H.	P.	A.	ST. LOUIS	A.B.	R.	H.	P.	A.
Bishop, 2b.	5	0	0	1	5	Flowers, 3b.	4	0	0	2	1
Haas, cf.	4	0	1	5	0	Watkins, rf.	4	0	2	1	0
Cochrane, c.	2	0	0	5	0	Frisch, 2b.	4	0	1	4	4
Simmons, lf.	4	0	0	1	0	Bottomley, 1b.	3	0	0	7	0
Foxx, 1b.	2	0	1	11	1	Hafey, lf.	4	0	0	4	0
Miller, rf.	4	0	1	0	0	Martin, cf.	3	2	2	0	0
Dykes, 3b.	2	0	0	0	2	Wilson, c.	3	0	0	7	0
Williams, ss.	2	0	0	1	2	Gelbert, ss.	2	0	1	2	3
Earnshaw, p.	3	0	0	0	2	Hallahan, p.	2	0	0	0	0
Moore	1	0	0	0	0						
Totals	29	0	3	24	12	Totals	29	2	6	27	8

Moore batted for Earnshaw in 9th.

PHILADELPHIA	0	0	0	0	0	0	0	0	0 — 0
ST. LOUIS	0	1	0	0	0	0	0	1	* — 2

Error—Wilson. Two-base hits—Watkins, Frisch, Martin. Runs batted in—Wilson, Gelbert. Left on bases—St. Louis 6, Philadelphia 10. Double play—Frisch to Gelbert to Bottomley. Sacrifice hits—Gelbert, Hallahan, Dykes. Stolen bases—Martin (2). Bases on balls—Hallahan 7, Earnshaw 1. Struck out—Hallahan 8, Earnshaw 5. Wild pitch—Hallahan. Umpires—Nallin (A.), Stark (N.), McGowan (A.), Klem (N.). Time—1:49.

CHRISTY MATHEWSON

By LLOYD LEWIS

(Noted author and former sports editor of
the *Chicago Daily News*)

(*Associated Press*)

Christy Mathewson

When the bleacher gates at Shibe Park in Philadelphia were thrown open on the morning of October 24, 1911, I was in the mob that went whooping toward the front seats. I got one, partly because the right-field crowd was smaller than the one in left. Most Philadelphians wanted to sit close to their worshiped Athletics, for the World Series at that moment stood two games to one for Connie Mack against John McGraw, and Philadelphia was loud and passionate in the confidence that now they would get revenge for the bitter dose—4 games to 1—three shutouts the Giants had given them six years before.

Me, I wanted to get as close to the Giants as possible, and found a place at the rail close to the empty chairs which would that afternoon become the Giants' bull pen. My whole adolescence had been devoted, so far as baseball went—and it went a long way to an Indiana farm boy—to the Giants and to their kingly pitcher, the great, the incomparable Christy Mathewson. I hadn't had the courage to cut classes in the nearby college and go to the first game of the series at Shibe

Park. But today I had. Things were desperate. Up in New York's Polo Grounds to start this, the World Series, Mathewson had won—2 to 1— giving but five hits and demonstrating that with 12 years of herculean toil behind him he was practically as invincible as when in 1905 he had shut out these same Athletics three times.

It had looked like 1905 over again; then in the second game, the A's long, lean yokel third baseman J. Franklin Baker had suddenly and incredibly knocked a home run off Rube Marquard, the Giants' amazing young pitcher. Baker, who had hit only 9 homers all season, had tagged the 22-year-old Giant and two runs had come in—and the final had stood 3-1.

The papers which I read, as the morning wore on, were still full of that home run and its aftermath.

From the start of the series the newspapers had been publishing syndicated articles signed by Giant and Athletic stars—the real start of the "ghost writers" whose spurious trade flourished so long but which the better papers in time eliminated. And in the article signed by Mathewson the day after Marquard's disaster it had been said that Rube had lost the game by failing to obey orders. The article rebuked the boy for throwing Baker the high outside pitch he liked, instead of the low fast one he didn't like and which McGraw had ordered.

The rebuke had been a sensation which grew in the third game when Baker had hit another homer off Mathewson himself, and had been the main wrecker of the great man's long sway over the A's. Up to the ninth inning of that third game Matty had kept command. Always when the Athletics had got men on bases he had turned on his magic. As he went to the bench at the end of the eighth, New York had risen and given him a tremendous ovation, for in 44 innings of World Series play, 1905 and 1911, he had allowed the Mackmen exactly one run— and the A's were hitters, indeed. Their season's average for 1911 had been .297.

Then in the ninth, Eddie Collins had gone out, and only two men had stood between Matty and his fifth series victory over his victims. Up had come Baker with the American League fans begging him to do to

Matty what he had done to Marquard—and, incredible as it seemed, he did.

As home runs go, it hadn't been much more than a long fly that sailed into the convenient right-field stand at the Polo Grounds, but it went far enough to tie the score and give Baker a nickname for life—"Home Run" Baker.

Snodgrass, the Giants center fielder, one of the smartest and greatest of base runners, had ripped Baker's trousers almost off him, sliding into third in the first of the 10th inning. With McGraw snarling, railing, jeering from the coaching line, the Giants made no secret of their hatred of Baker. To them he was merely a lucky lout, a greenhorn who had by sheer accident homered off the two top pitchers of the season.

But Baker had hit again, a scratch single in the eleventh which had been part of the making of the run which had won, and Marquard in his "ghosted" article had quipped at Mathewson's advice.

All that was in everybody's mind—and mine, as on October 24 the fourth game came up. The papers had had time to chew the sensation over and over, for it had rained for a week after the third game and now, with seven days' rest, Mathewson was to try again—this time in Shibe Park.

The long delay hadn't cooled excitement. The press box was still as crowded as at the opening game. This was the first World Series to be handled in the modern publicity fashion—the first to have as many as 50 telegraphers on the job—the first to wire the game play-by-play to points as distant as Havana, Cuba—the first to which newspapers in the Far West and South sent their own writers. And though the A's now had a lead of two games to one, the threat of the Giants was still great enough to keep fever high.

It was a little after 1 o'clock when my long vigil ended. Onto the field came the Giants with their immemorial swagger, chips still on their shoulders—the cocky, ornery, defiant men of Muggsy McGraw—the rip-roaring demons who had that season of 1911 set a record of 347 stolen bases—a record which would stand for another 31 years

without any other club ever coming nearer to it than the Senators'
288 in 1913.

And here at long last they were. I knew them from their pictures as,
clad in dangerous black, they came strutting across toward their dugout.
McGraw had dressed his men in black, back in 1905 when he had
humbled the Athletics, and he was playing hunches now.

Muggsy was first—stocky, hard-eyed. Behind him came slim, handsome Snodgrass, the great base-stealer who was a genius at getting
hit by pitched balls and in scaring infielders with his flashing spikes.
Then came swart, ominous Larry Doyle; lantern-jawed Art Fletcher;
Buck Herzog, whose nose curved like a scimitar; lithe little Josh Devore; burly Otis Crandall; flat-faced mahogany-colored Chief Meyers,
the full-blooded Indian; Fred Merkle, all muscles even in his jaws, a
lion-heart living down the most awful bonehead blunder ever made
in baseball.

There came Marquard, 6 feet 3, his sharp face wreathed in a
smile—his head tilting to the left at the top of a long wry neck—
Marquard the meteoric. At 19 years of age he had been bought at a
record price from Indianapolis and had immediately flopped two
straight years for McGraw, becoming the nationally goatish "$11,000
lemon." Then this 1911, he had flamed out, won 24 games and become
the "$11,000 beauty."

As the Giants began to toss the ball around, I couldn't see my hero,
the Mathewson whom I had come to see, the great one who from the
time I was 9 I had pretended I was, playing ball in the Indiana cow
pasture, throwing his famous "fadeaway" which, for me, never came
off. Then, suddenly, there he was, warming up and growling "Who
am I working for, the Giants or the photographers," as the cameramen,
not 20 feet from my popeyed head, begged him for poses.

I was let down for a minute. He didn't speak like a demi-god, but
as I stared, he looked it, all the same. He held his head high, and his
eye with slow, lordly contempt swept the Athletics as they warmed
up across the field. He was 31, all bone and muscle and princely poise.
Surely he would get those Athletics today and put the Giants back in

the running. Surely his unique "fadeaway," the curve that broke backward, his speed, his snapping curve, his fabulous brain couldn't be stopped. It had been luck that had beaten him in the last game. Now he'd get them.

My eye never left him till the bell rang and he strode, hard but easy, with the swing of the aristocrat, into the dugout and little Josh Devore went up to hit.

Josh singled, Doyle tripled, Snodgrass scored Larry with a long fly. Black figures were flying everywhere. The big copper-colored Chief Bender on Mack's mound was wobbling, and when the side was finally out he practically ran for the dugout. Later, we learned, he had run in to cut out bandages from his ribs, from an old injury. After that he was to be unworkable.

Up came the Athletics. Matty, as though in princely disdain, fanned the first two men. The third man, Eddie Collins, singled. Here came Baker, his sun-tanned face tense, his bat flailing—the air thick with one word from 25,000 throats, "Homer! Homer!"

Matty studied him as a scientist contemplates a beetle, then struck him out! What I yelled, I don't know. All I remember is standing there bellowing and paying no heed to the wadded newspapers the Athletic fans around me threw. It was wonderful.

On the fourth, Baker came up to start it and doubled. Dannie Murphy doubled, Harry Davis doubled. Ira Thomas hit a sacrifice fly—three runs. It couldn't be. Up came Baker again in the fifth with Collins on first and another double boomed across the diamond. I saw Snodgrass eventually stop it, but he didn't really have it in his glove at all. It had stuck in my gullet.

Right in front of me an unthinkable thing happened. Hooks Wiltse, the southpaw, began warming up for the Giants. Was Matty knocked out? Another figure rose from the bull pen. Rube Marquard. He didn't warm up, he only strolled up and down, a great sardonic grin on his face. The fans around me were screaming at him, "You're even with Matty now, Rube! He won't tell you what to pitch anymore!" etc., etc. Rube smirked at them.

Matty got by without more scores, but in the seventh with a man on third Christy walked Baker and Shibe Park's walls waved in a cyclone of "boos." I wished I was dead.

The eighth. A pinch hitter went up for Mathewson. I was sorry I hadn't died in the seventh. Finally it was all over.

I walked out through 25,000 of the most loathsome individuals ever created—all jeering at Mathewson, all howling Baker's virtues. I dragged my feet this way and that trying to escape the currents of fans. At the end of a dolorous mile I stopped at a saloon. I had never had a drink. Now was the time.

"Beer," I said, in the voice of Poe's raven.

"You ain't 21," the bartender rasped. Then he took a second look, saw that I was 100 years old, and splashed a great stein in front of me.

I took one swallow. It was bitter, just as bitter as everything else in the world. I laid down a nickel and walked out. Every step of the way downtown I kept telling myself that in my coffin, some day, there'd be only room for one thing besides myself—my hatred of the Athletics.

But what I started out to tell was about my greatest day in baseball. That came three years later, October 9, 1914, when the lowly despised Boston Braves wallowed, humbled, trampled, laughed at the lofty Athletics to the tune of 7 to 1. I came out of Shibe Park, spent hours hunting that same saloon, but I couldn't find it. It had to be that one. What I wanted to do was to walk in all alone—find nobody else in there—order two beers and when the bartender looked inquiringly at the extra one, say to him in a condescending voice, "Oh, that? That's for Mathewson."

ENOS
SLAUGHTER
as told to
LYALL SMITH

Enos Slaughter, St. Louis Cardinals' right fielder, broke into organized baseball in 1935, joining the Cards in 1938. Won American Association batting title in 1937 with a mark of .382. Born at Roxboro, N. C., on July 26, 1920.

Maybe it doesn't sound just right to say it, but we Cards never were scared of the Yankees. After all, we beat them in the '42 spring series in Florida six games out of nine and showed them we were just as tough as they were. Maybe even tougher.

We'd lost the first two spring games and I remember that third one real well. Somebody hit a home run for us. I think it was Mort Cooper, and Marv Breuer, pitching for the Yanks, was real mad. Jimmy Brown was up and Marv threw right at his head once. Jimmy got up, brushed himself off and then went down again in a hurry as Marv threw for his head again. He would have beaned him if Jimmy's bat hadn't turned it away from his temple. We really went after them then, got into a big fight and beat them the next six out of seven.

Before the World Series started last fall we figured we could lick 'em again, even after that 7-4 score in the first game when they beat us to the punch. After that ninth inning when we got going for four runs we knew we had them and the day of the second game in the clubhouse we all said: "We can handle these fellows. We can score on them." So we went out and did it.

Remember how we jumped off to a two-run lead in the first inning and then got another in the seventh? All this time Johnny Beazley was bearing down hard and never had a lot of trouble. In the fourth though, Keller just about took off Beazley's head with a single over the mound. Joe Gordon slammed a liner at Kurowski, who stuck up a glove, grabbed it and almost doubled Keller off first. Dickey was up next and he swung on one of Johnny's curve balls for a single to me on the ground.

As I raced over to get it I figured Keller would go for third sure. Anybody would go from first on a single that was taking more than one bounce into far right. I hoped to get the ball clean and be able to fire it across to Kurowski on third for a close play, anyway.

This throw to third was one I'd practiced ever since I came up to the Cards in 1938. My arm was wild in those days and the word had gone around the league: "Run on Slaughter. Take an extra base on him." So I'd practiced mornings and off days, anytime I could get somebody to hit fungoes to me and a bat boy to stand on third for a target.

I had improved, but I wondered as I grabbed up the ball off the grass if I could deliver now, when the chips were down. I didn't see anything but Kurowski waiting on the bag as I threw, but as the ball left my hand I saw Keller's back, about 15 to 20 feet past second, splitting himself going for third. I looked back and saw the ball going right to Kurowski on the bag. It was going to be a strike!

Then I saw Art Fletcher, the Yank coach, right behind the bag wave his arms and jump and waggle that long jaw of his, and I saw Keller stop, turn and hustle back to second. At that, he didn't much more than make it for Kurowski fired the ball to second fast.

I was still thinking about having made the play right, when Hassett flied out to me, deep, to end the inning.

That Keller, though, homered in the eighth to tie the score at 3-3. When we batted in the last half of the inning I was up with two outs and nobody on. Ernie Bonham was pitching for the Yanks and he was tough on me so far. I hadn't hit the whole game and was as mad as one of them Carolina fighting roosters.

Ernie got the first one in for a strike and then wasted two low out-side ones trying to make me bite. I waited though and on his next pitch I slapped a liner down over Hassett's head and it rolled clear down the right-field line for a double. I slid into second ahead of Cullenbine's peg

Red Ruffing

but got up when I saw Rizzuto muff the throw in. I went down to third and slid again but it wasn't necessary. Musial was up next and he got one of those poky singles of his out over second and I came in with the run that eventually won for us.

But my big thrill came in the first of the ninth on that throw I made on Hassett's single which caught Stainback sliding into third with what could a' been the tying run.

That big Dickey started out the Yanks' ninth with a smash that was too hot for Jimmy Brown to hold and then McCarthy sent out Tucker Stainback to run for Bill. Buddy Hassett came up. He let a couple of Beazley's streakers go by and then swung on one that they told me afterwards was outside. It was a grounder that went down toward Johnny Hopp at first. Johnny went over fast as he could, but when he got to the spot the ball already was through and rolling out toward me.

Now I kinda had a hunch Hassett was going to hit one out my way and I was coming in just about as soon as he swung. We out-fielders don't have any way to know what our pitchers are throwing some special batter, but I recalled how before the game we were talk-ing about keeping them outside to Buddy. Anyway, I was charging in as fast as I could run when I saw that roller get through between Hopp and Brown. Here was lightning hitting twice at me in the same place. Could I do it again? Could I throw another strike to third?

I picked the ball up on the run and without ever knowing where Stainback was by now—I knew he must be well on his way to third though—I let one go. Well, you know what happened. They told me afterwards and the newspaper fellows had it in their stories that the throw was my greatest one. I saw it go across that infield and get to Kurowski while Stainback, a fast man, was still five feet away.

Guess it was a pippin at that for the ball came in to Kurowski right at his knees and he was waiting there when Stainback came charging into the bag. Umpire Magerkurth was right there on the play and Stainback was out. That made it two out for the Yanks and that big run, the tying one, had been cut down. The next fellow up was Ruffing, who came in to hit for Bonham and he boosted one out to me that went about as high as a Georgia pine and I got under easy. That was the ball game and we were all even with the champs.

Some fellows like to say that throw of mine was one that cut the

Bill Dickey

hearts out of the Yankees. Said it made them more cautious when they were running the bases after that but I don't know. That throw was my best though and I guess it meant the biggest baseball thrill in my life.

I got another big one though in the last game of the series in New York when we put the clincher on the title and beat the Yanks 4-2. I was first man up in the fourth and got a homer off Ruffing that tied the game. I can remember just as plain as I'm sitting here how I hit his first pitch for a homer. It's funny, too, because I generally wait a pitcher out for a while to see what he's going to try on me. But that first one was too good to pass up. Old Red wound up and tried to fog one right past me about waist high. I got a good toe hold and belted it with all I had. It came down in the bleachers.

Looking back a little more though, I guess I'd have to take one day in Philly as my best hitting day. About 18 fellows came up from my home town of Roxboro, N. C., to see me play. It was in 1939 and none of them had ever seen me in the big time before. I used to play second base with those fellows down in the tobacco country and boy, I was really hoping to go some.

Well, I ended up with a good day. It was a double-header and when it was all over I had five hits out of eight times up, including two doubles, a triple, a single and a home run with the bases loaded.

THE BOX SCORE
(October 1, 1942)

NEW YORK	A.B.	R.	H.	P.	A.	ST. LOUIS	A.B.	R.	H.	P.	A.
Rizzuto, ss.	4	0	1	0	3	Brown, 2b.	3	1	0	0	3
Rolfe, 3b.	4	0	1	0	2	T. Moore, cf.	3	1	0	2	0
Cullenbine, rf.	4	1	1	2	0	Slaughter, rf.	4	1	1	2	1
Di Maggio, cf.	4	1	1	7	0	Musial, lf.	4	0	1	5	0
Keller, lf.	4	1	2	1	0	W. Cooper, c.	4	0	1	4	0
Gordon, 2b.	4	0	1	0	3	Hopp, 1b.	3	1	2	11	0
Dickey, c.	4	0	2	5	0	Kurowski, 3b.	3	0	1	2	1
Hassett, 1b.	4	0	1	9	0	Marion, ss.	3	0	0	1	4
Bonham, p.	2	0	0	0	0	Beazley, p.	3	0	0	0	0
Stainback	0	0	0	0	0						
Ruffing	1	0	0	0	0						
Totals	35	3	10	24	8	Totals	30	4	6	27	9

Stainback ran for Dickey in 9th.
Ruffing batted for Bonham in 9th.

NEW YORK	0	0	0	0	0	0	0	3	0 — 3
ST. LOUIS	2	0	0	0	0	0	1	1	* — 4

Errors—Rizzuto, Hassett. Runs batted in—W. Cooper (2), Kurowski, Di Maggio, Keller (2) Musial. Two-base hits—W. Cooper, Gordon, Rolfe, Slaughter. Three-base hit—Kurowski. Home run—Keller. Sacrifice hit—T. Moore. Stolen bases—Rizzuto, Cullenbine. Double play—Brown to Marion to Hopp. Struck out—By Bonham 3, Beazley 4. Bases on balls—Off Bonham 1, Beazley 2. Winning pitcher—Beazley. Losing pitcher—Bonham. Umpires—Summers, Barr, Hubbard and Magerkurth. Time—1:57. Attendance—34,255.

(Wide World)

Connie Mack

Born Cornelius McGillicuddy on December 23, 1862, at Brookfield Mass., Connie Mack is unquestionably "Mr. Baseball" today. He holds all records for longevity as a baseball manager, piloting major league clubs for 50 years—starting as pilot of the Pittsburgh Nationals in 1894. Started his major league career as a catcher for Washington in 1886 and was an active player through 1896. Personally discovered such greats as Eddie Plank, Chief Bender, Jack Coombs, Eddie Collins, Frank Baker, Stuffy McInnis and many others. Joined Athletics as manager in 1901 and has been there ever since. In the 664 games he caught he had 842 assists.

I've been fortunate enough to have seen some great baseball in my days. It is wonderful to remember pitchers like Matty and Walsh and Waddell and Johnson and Dean and Grove for more than 40 years. But to me the most thrilling World Series ever played was between the Cubs and Athletics in 1929 and I'll never forget the performance of Howard Ehmke. You see, Howard and I sort of put a fast one over on everybody and an old man likes to enjoy a chuckle at the expense of a younger generation. Only the two of us knew, two weeks ahead of time, that he was going to pitch the opening game, October 8.

We were leaving on the final western trip of the regular season when I called Howard up to my office in Philadelphia. We had the pennant pretty well in hand by then and so did the Cubs, so we could make plans. Ehmke came in and sat down and I watched him for a few minutes while we just chatted and finally I said: "Howard, there comes a time in everybody's life when he has to make a change. It looks like you and I finally must part."

Well, he didn't say a word for the longest time, it seemed, just twiddled his hat and then he looked right at me and said: "All right, Mr. Mack, if that's the way it has to be. You've been fine to me and I haven't been much help to you this year. Lucky you haven't needed me. But I've been up a long time and I've always had an ambition to pitch in a World Series ... anywhere, even for only an inning. Honestly, I believe there's one more good game left in this arm ..." and he held it up to me like a prize fighter showing his muscle.

I couldn't help smiling. Howard of course, had no way of knowing what I thought of him. Really he was one of the most artistic pitchers of all time. He was bothered with a sore arm most of his major league career, but he had a great head on him and studied hitters. He might have been a fine pitcher. So I asked him: "You mean you think you could work a World Series game?" He told me: "Yes, Mr. Mack. I feel it." Then I explained what I had in mind. "So do I," I said. "I only wanted to see how you felt about it. Now you stay home this trip. The Cubs are coming in. Sit up in the stands and watch them. Make your own notes on how they hit. You're pitching the first game but don't tell anybody. I don't want it known."

After he'd gone I sat thinking about Howard. Maybe he never realized how close he came to not pitching at all. If he hadn't talked the way he did ... if he'd said, for instance: "I realize I'm all through ... my arm is gone" and accepted what he thought was dismissal, I wouldn't have worked him even though I had no intention of letting him go anyway.

Finally the big day came around in Wrigley Field. Funny part of it was that none of my players nor even the newspapermen, bothered to ask me who'd start. They all took it for granted it would be Grove, or maybe Earnshaw. Since then people have asked me why I didn't start Grove, but that's a secret. I can't tell, but there was a reason. Anyway we were in the clubhouse before the game and somebody asked Grove if he was working and I heard him say: "The old man didn't say nothin' to me." Mose probably figured it was Earnshaw. When we got outside, they all threw the ball around. Ehmke must have had a sudden doubt that his dream was coming true because he came up to me on the bench and whispered. "Is it still me, Mr. Mack?" I said. "It's still you . . ." and he was smiling as he walked away.

When it came time for the rival pitcher to warm up, Ehmke, naturally, took off his jacket and started to throw. I made sure I was where I could look along our bench and you could see mouths pop open. Grove was looking at Earnshaw and George was looking at Mose. Al Simmons was sitting next to me and he couldn't stop himself in time. "Are you gonna pitch him?" he asked in disbelief. I kept a straight face and looked very severely at him and said: "Yes, I am Al. Is that all right with you?" You could sense him pulling himself out of his surprised state and he replied quickly: "If you say so, it's all right with me, Mr. Mack."

Voices were muttering down the dugout. Phrases like "the old man must be nuts" and "hell, the guy's only finished two games all year" trailed off for fear I'd hear 'em. But I heard. I've often wondered what they'd thought of me if we'd been beaten with Grove and Earnshaw and Walberg on the bench. Bob Quinn, who was president of the Red Sox then, was in a box behind our dugout and he said he almost swooned when he saw Ehmke peel off his coat. I suppose the fans and you gentlemen of the press thought old Connie was in his dotage at last. But I was certain about Howard, although if he'd had any trouble early I would have had Grove in the bull pen. We didn't want to lose.

It was beautiful to watch. I don't suppose these old eyes ever strained themselves over any game as much as that one. Ehmke was smart. He was just fast enough to be sneaky, just slow enough to get hitters like Wilson and Hornsby and Cuyler, who like to take their cuts, off stride. If you recall, he pitched off his right hip, real close to his shirt. He kept the ball hidden until just before he let it go. The Cubs never got a good look at it and, when they did, it was coming out of those shirts in the old bleachers. Charley Root was fast himself and by the end of the sixth inning neither team had scored. Then Jimmy Foxx hit over Wilson's head, into the stands, and we led 1-0.

Jimmy touched home plate and came back to the bench and Ehmke said: "Thanks, Jim" and I knew he'd made up his mind maybe that was all the runs he'd get and it would have to do. Only in the third had Howard been in a jam when McMillan singled and English doubled with one out and Hornsby and Wilson were up. Some of my players looked at me as if to say: "Better get somebody warmed up . . . here's where Ehmke goes," but he stood there calm and unhurried and struck out the two men on seven pitches. You could tell the crowd had caught the melodrama of what was going on; I don't believe I ever felt as happy in my life as when he fanned Hornsby and Wilson. Very few pitchers would have done as well in such a tense situation. He justified my faith in him right there.

Hack Wilson

Howard Ehmke

In the seventh, after Foxx's hit, Cuyler and Stephenson each singled and Grimm sacrificed. Joe McCarthy decided on pinch hitters. He had Cliff Heathcote hit for Zach Taylor and Simmons took care of a short fly for the second out. Then Gabby Hartnett batted for Root and I was tempted to have Howard put him on and take a chance on the next man, but I said to myself:

"No. This is his game. He asked for it and I gave it to him."

He struck out Hartnett and we got two runs in the ninth on fumbles by English. I relaxed a little then, but we weren't quite out of the woods. The Cubs got the tying runs on bases in the ninth, with two out and Charlie Tolson up to pinch-hit.

If Ehmke fanned him, he'd break the strikeout record for world series play set by Ed Walsh against the Cubs in 1906 when he fanned 12. Howard already had struck out Hornsby, Wilson, Cuyler and Root twice each. It happened. Tolson went down swinging, too, for Howard's 13th strikeout and the battle was over. He has lived on that game ever since. So have I.

THE BOX SCORE
(October 8, 1929)

ATHLETICS	A.B.	R.	H.	P.	A.	CUBS	A.B.	R.	H.	P.	A.
Bishop, 2b.	4	0	0	1	1	McMillan, 3b.	4	0	1	1	2
Haas, cf.	3	0	0	1	0	English, ss.	4	0	2	1	3
Cochrane, c.	3	1	1	14	1	Hornsby, 2b.	4	0	0	1	3
Simmons, lf.	4	1	0	2	0	Wilson, cf.	4	0	0	3	0
Foxx, 1b.	4	1	2	4	0	Cuyler, rf.	4	1	1	1	0
Miller, rf.	4	0	1	3	0	Stephenson, lf.	4	0	2	4	0
Dykes, 3b.	4	0	1	1	1	Grimm, 1b.	2	0	2	8	0
Boley, ss.	4	0	0	1	0	Taylor, c.	2	0	0	6	0
Ehmke, p.	4	0	1	0	2	Gonzales, c.	0	0	0	2	0
						Root, p.	2	0	0	0	0
						Bush, p.	0	0	0	0	2
						Heathcote	1	0	0	0	0
						Hartnett	1	0	0	0	0
						Blair	1	0	0	0	0
						Tolson	1	0	0	0	0
Totals	34	3	6	27	5	Totals	34	1	8	27	10

Heathcote batted for Taylor in 7th.
Hartnett batted for Root in 7th.
Blair batted for Gonzales in 9th.
Tolson batted for Bush in 9th.

ATHLETICS	0	0	0	0	0	0	1	0	2—3
CUBS	0	0	0	0	0	0	0	0	1—1

Errors—Dykes, English (2). Home run—Foxx. Two-base hit—English. Sacrifice hit—Grimm. Struck out—By Ehmke 13, Root 5. Bases on balls—Off Ehmke 1, Root 2.

WALTER
JOHNSON
as told to
JOHN P. CARMICHAEL

Walter Johnson, still the subject for debate wherever fast ball pitchers are discussed, owns and operates a farm near Germantown, Md.

("As the hitter sees Johnson's arm descending, just swing," said Outfielder "Birdie" Cree years ago. "The bat will then cross the plate at about the same time the ball reaches it and, if you're lucky, you hit the ball. A fellow does not have to judge the height of the pitch... or if it was a curve.")

This won't be very original, I'm afraid (said Johnson) because there couldn't be a bigger day for me than the one everybody knows about... October 10, 1924, in the last game of my first World Series. It was Weiser, Idaho, and Detroit and Washington put together; I guess you'd call it a piece of every day for 18 years and it didn't look like I'd ever see it come around. After all, I was 36 years old and that's pretty far gone to be walking into the last game of a series... especially when you couldn't blame people for remembering I'd lost two starts already.

You see I didn't have much besides a fast ball in my life and there comes a time when speed alone won't stop a batter. If a boy hasn't got real, natural speed it isn't worth his while to try and force a fast ball, because a slow pitch and a curve can fool a hitter better than unnatural speed. Besides, the arm may suffer. A free, loose motion and control are the main assets for a pitcher. That's all I ever had to amount to anything.

Why, when I started out at 18 years of age I couldn't even land a job on the Pacific Coast. I went to Weiser, Idaho, because it had a semipro team and the players worked in the mines. I won my first game 4-0 on two hits. I won the next 2-1 in 15 innings and then fanned 15 to make my string three straight.

Weiser people began calling me "pardner" instead of "sonny." I still was at Weiser in 1907 and had won 13 and lost 2 when Cliff Blankenship, a Washington scout, arrived. He'd really come out to look at Clyde Milan; I was just a by-product of his trip.

Well, he never saw me pitch at all, but he knew my record and offered me a job. I wouldn't take it until he'd promised me a return ticket to California in case I failed. I joined Washington at Detroit August 2, 1907, despite the pleas of Weiser folk who offered to buy me a cigar stand and set me up in business if I'd stay there. But you know how you are at 18 . . . you want to see things.

I saw something my first start. I got beat 3-2 and Ty Cobb and Sam Crawford bunted me all over the infield. I fell all over myself . . . and the 1,000 people in the stands laughed themselves sick. I was so confused I even missed the bus back to the hotel . . . and was walking there in my uniform when some fans gave me a lift.

Seventeen years later I was in a series, but I wasn't happy about it. I'd been beaten in New York for the second time by the Giants and I'll admit when I got on the train to Washington, where we were to play the seventh game, there were tears in my eyes. I was carrying my youngest boy on my shoulder and trying not to speak to people when Clark Griffith put a hand on my arm. "Don't think about it anymore, Walter," he told me. "You're a great pitcher. We all know it.

"Now tonight when we get home don't stand around the box offices buying seats for friends or shaking hands with people who feel sorry for you. I've seen many a fast ball shaken right out of a pitcher's hand.

Go home and get to bed early ... we may need you tomorrow." I told him I would, but as far as needing me further ... I didn't think Manager "Bucky" Harris would call on me again. But I got my family off the train and we went straight home.

You can imagine how "red hot" Washington was next day ... the last game of its first World Series coming up. Thirty-five thousand people were crammed into our park. President Coolidge was there. I made myself as inconspicuous as possible on the bench, because I didn't want any sympathy ... and I didn't even want Harris to think of me in a jam. Well, "Bucky" started Curley Ogden but pretty soon George Mogridge was in there and then "Firpo" Marberry, our big relief ace.

We were all tied up in the ninth when I came in. I'll always believe that Harris gambled on me because of sentiment, but he said no. He just told me: "You're the best we got, Walter ... we've got to win or lose with you." So I walked out there and it seemed to me the smoke from the stands was so thick on the field that nobody could see me clearly anyway. I remember thinking: "I'll need the breaks" and if I didn't actually pray, I sort of was thinking along those lines.

I was in trouble every inning. After getting Fred Lindstrom in the ninth, Frank Frisch hit a fast ball to right center for three bases. We decided to pass Ross Young and then I struck out George Kelly and "Irish" Meusel grounded to third. In the 10th I walked "Hack" Wilson and then, after striking out Travis Jackson, I was lucky enough to grab a drive by ol' Hank Gowdy and turn it into a double play.

Heinie Groh batted for Hugh McQuillan, the Giant pitcher, in the 11th and singled. Lindstrom bunted him along. I fanned Frisch, this time, on an outside pitch and once more passed Young. Kelly struck out again.

They kept after me, though. Meusel singled in the 12th, but I'd settled down to believe, by then, that maybe this was my day and I got the next three hitters. I'd tried to win my own game in the 10th with a long ball to the wall, but Wilson pulled it down. So I was up again in the 12th when it was getting pretty dark. "Muddy" Ruel had lifted a pop foul to Gowdy, who lost it, and on the next pitch Ruel hit past third for two bases. Then I sent an easy grounder to short . . . and Jackson fumbled. We all sat there staring at Earl McNeely as he hit an easy grounder to Lindstrom.

The ball never touched Fred. It hit a pebble and arched over his head into safe territory. I could feel tears smarting in my eyes as Ruel came home with the winning run. I'd won. We'd won. I felt so happy that it didn't seem real. They told me in the clubhouse that President Coolidge kept watching me all the way into the clubhouse and I remember somebody yelling: "I bet Cal'd like to change places with you right now, Walter."

A long time later Mrs. Johnson and I slipped away to a quiet little restaurant where I used to eat on Vermont Avenue, in Washington,

THE BOX SCORE
(October 10, 1924)

NEW YORK	A.B.	R.	H.	P.	A.	WASHINGTON	A.B.	R.	H.	P.	A.
Lindstrom, 3b.	5	0	1	0	3	McNeely, cf.	6	0	1	0	0
Frisch, 2b.	5	0	2	3	4	Harris, 2b.	5	1	3	4	1
Young, rf.-lf.	2	1	0	2	0	Rice, cf.	5	0	0	2	0
Kelly, cf.-1b.	6	1	1	8	1	Goslin, lf.	5	0	2	3	0
Terry, 1b.	2	0	0	6	1	Judge, 1b.	4	0	1	11	1
Meusel, lf.-rf.	3	0	1	1	0	Bluege, ss.	5	0	0	1	7
Wilson, lf.-cf.	5	1	1	4	0	Taylor, 3b.	2	0	0	0	3
Jackson, ss.	6	0	0	1	4	Miller, 3b.	2	0	0	1	1
Gowdy, c.	6	0	1	8	0	Ruel, c.	5	2	2	13	0
Barnes, p.	4	0	0	1	2	Ogden, p.	0	0	0	0	0
McQuillan, p.	0	0	0	0	0	Mogridge, p.	1	0	0	0	0
Nehf, p.	0	0	0	0	0	Marberry, p.	1	0	0	1	0
Bentley, p.	0	0	0	0	0	Johnson, p.	2	0	0	0	1
Groh	1	0	1	0	0	Tate	0	0	0	0	0
Southworth	0	0	0	0	0	Shirley	0	0	0	0	0
						Leibold	1	1	1	0	0
Totals	45	3	8	*34	15	Totals	44	4	10	36	14

Meusel batted for Terry in 6th.
Groh batted for McQuillan in 11th.
Southworth ran for Groh in 11th.
*One out when winning run was scored.

Tate batted for Marberry in 8th.
Shirley ran for Tate in 8th.
Leibold batted for Taylor in 8th.

NEW YORK	0	0	0	0	0	3	0	0	0	0	0	0—3
WASHINGTON	0	0	1	0	0	0	2	0	0	0	1—4

Errors—Jackson (2), Gowdy, Judge, Bluege (2), Taylor. Earned runs—Washington 4, New York 1. Runs batted in—Harris 3, McNeely 1, Meusel 1. Two-base hits—McNeely, Goslin, Ruel, Leibold, Lindstrom. Three-base hit—Frisch. Home run—Harris. Double plays—Kelly to Jackson, Jackson to Frisch to Kelly, Johnson to Bluege to Judge. Bases on balls —Off Ogden 1, Mogridge 1, Marberry 1, Bentley 1, Barnes 1, Johnson 3. Struck out—By Ogden 1, Mogridge 3, Marberry 3, McMillan 1, Barnes 6, Johnson 5. Hits—Off Ogden 0 in 1-3 inning, Mogridge 4 in 4 2-3 inning, Marberry 1 in 3 innings, Johnson 3 in 4 innings, Barnes 6 in 7 2-3 innings, Nehf 1 in 2-3 inning, McQuillan 0 in 1 2-3 innings, Bentley 3 in 1 1-3 innings (one out in 12th). Winning pitcher—Johnson. Losing pitcher—Bentley. Umpires—Dinneen (A), Quigley (N.), Connolly (A.), Klem (N.). Time—3:00

and do you know that before we were through with our dinner 200 telegrams had been delivered there. I never thought so many people were pulling for me to win, because the Giants were pretty popular. When we packed up and went home to Kansas we had three trunks full of letters from fans all over the world. Mrs. Johnson answered about 75 every day for me . . . and we still didn't finish until after Christmas.

MORTON COOPER

as told to
JOHN P. CARMICHAEL

Morton Cooper was the National League's "winning-est" pitcher for the last two seasons. In 1942 his earned run average was 1.77, lowest in the league since Carl Hubbell of the Giants compiled 1.66 in '33. Cooper has been rejected for military service.

My biggest, and saddest, baseball day was also the longest day day I eve put in and you might know which one it always will be. That day was October 6, 1943, the second game of the last World Series, and it began without warning at 6 o'clock in the morning. My wife and I were asleep in our New York hotel when the phone rang. It was long distance ... asking for Mr. Cooper. I answered, and you can tell how sound asleep I'd been when I didn't even recognize the voice.

It was my oldest brother, Bob, and I didn't know it, I said: "This is Mort," and the voice said: "Oh, pardon me, I wanted Walker Cooper ..." and the line went dead. I climbed back to the hay and it wasn't until around 9 o'clock that we went down to breakfast, joining Walker and Johnny Hopp and their wives. There was something wrong with Walker. Then, of course, I didn't know what, but I accused him of being afraid of the Yanks and he just grinned feebly and let it go at that.

We'd just about finished eating when Walker's wife said to me: "You and Walker go on ahead upstairs ... Billy Southworth wants to see you both in your room." Well, we walked out and left the women folks there and I said to my brother: "Wonder what Billy wants ... I'll bet he's heard from the slack people." (We'd signed with some company that made slacks for advertising purposes, you know.) But Walker shook his head. "No it ain't," he answered abruptly. I looked at him funny ... he seemed too tight-lipped and sort of cold looking and he walked straight ahead of me and never looked around.

We got in the room and I started to flip on the radio, but Walker told me to turn it off. Billy was there and we all sat down and suddenly Walker spoke. I remember he talked real slow as though the words wouldn't come out. "Mort," he said, "somebody's got to tell you. Dad died today." I sat there. Nobody said a thing for what seemed an hour ... only it wasn't even a minute. Southworth told me later I said: "No ... no"; but I didn't know I did. But I heard Walker say: "Yes, that's the phone call you got this morning.

"R. J. (that was my older brother) got you by mistake. He didn't want to tell you, because he knew you were pitching today. If we only could have kept it quiet until afterward ... but the newspapers have it ..." and my brother let the sentence trail off. The writers gave me all the credit after that game, but it belonged to Walker. He's the kid who deserved any honor. He not only had the same burden to share that I did, as a brother, but he had to keep me together, too. I had to pitch. Walker had all the grief and me on top of it to shoulder. He was the strong man ... carrying me along.

Billy (Southworth) sat there quietly and let it sink in and when he spoke it was hardly more than a whisper. "Mort," he told me, "you're my pitcher today. Do you want to go?" That seemed to wake me up. Walker said my voice filled the room. "Yes, sir," I told Billy.

Joe Gordon

"The lid is off now. The worst has already happened to me. Nothing else can hurt and besides you don't think for a minute dad would want me to miss this game?"

I saw Billy and Walker exchange quick looks and I felt better. So did Walker. . . . I could see that. Billy said good-by and left and in a few minutes the women folk came in. By this time my wife knew what had happened, but they tried to act real casual-like and we all went to the park early. Some of the Yankees had heard about it and when I met them they all stopped to tell me they were sorry. Afterward, when we got home for the funeral, there were only two big sprays of flowers on the casket . . . one at the top from the Cardinals, one at the bottom from the Yankees. Dad would have been pleased.

That's the only game I ever beat the Yankees; the only game I ever licked an American League club in what is it . . . five starts? But somehow it comes back to me sort of piecemeal, even now. I guess because of the circumstances, it was too big for me to appreciate right away. But I remember saying to Walker in our clubhouse meeting: "Bill Dickey's the guy we have to stop, don't forget that. Remember last year?" My brother did. We pitched harder to him than anybody and still couldn't get him out.

"He's the hardest man to fool I ever pitched to. You can even cross him up and he'll get a piece of the ball. He's a helluva guy too . . . don't forget it. When he hit that home run off me in the fifth game, to win the series, I told him: 'If I had to lose that way, I don't know anybody I'd rather have beat me' and he came right back with: "I hit it off the best pitcher in the league, Mort . . .' and then he invited me to come down bird-hunting with him in Arkansas. I'd rather take a chance with

Charley Keller anytime than **Dickey . . . yet it was** Keller who almost beat me in that second game.

We started the game. I never pitched more carefully in my life. I wasn't in a daze, but I felt all alone out there. Once I caught myself nodding to Walker, down there behind the plate, when he wasn't even giving me a sign. He straightened up and took a couple of steps as if to come out to me, but I knew what he meant and I nodded and waved him back. Well, as you know, we got off in front and going into the ninth, the Cards led 4-1. Every time I came by third base to pick up my glove, I'd get thinking about dad and I'd say to myself:

"I can't think of him now . . . the ball game comes first. He knows that."

That way I went along. Then Bill Johnson doubled in the ninth and Keller hit for three bases. One run was home, another on third. It was my own fault although to people who've asked me from time to time why I threw a fast ball to so-and-so or a curve or anything else and let 'em hit me, I always say: "Listen, don't take credit away from me . . . give those fellows some. After all they're good hitters . . . probably as good as I am a pitcher, or better. It's as much their fault as mine."

But in this case I got carried away by the fact that it was the ninth inning. I told myself: "Now I've got you guys, after all this time and I'm going to pour it on." I did. Instead of going along like I had been, I decided to show off. That's what it amounted to. So Johnson hit and Keller hit. You can't throw the ball past those guys and I knew it. They'd hammered me the year before. But in my moment of triumph as I thought, I forgot.

Southworth came running out on the field. Probably everybody thought he was going to yank me because there was nobody down and the tying run was coming to plate. But he wouldn't have taken me out . . . I know that. "Mort, Mort," he said to me. "Listen. Pitch your natural game. Don't go overboard now. Settle down. You got a two-run lead." I nodded and grinned at him and he wagged a finger and ran back to the bench. The other guys returned to their positions and I looked at the plate. Who was there but Dickey!

I recalled that in the '42 series we'd pitched him 11 straight curve balls to try and catch him waiting for a fast one and still we didn't get him out. Here he was again, in his own park with that short right-field fence. There was only one thing to do . . . try and make him hit it on the ground. If it got through, only one run scored anyway; if it went anywhere near a fielder, the guy could kick the ball a little and still be able to get Bill, who isn't fast. So I shook Walker off until he called for a screwball. It was as perfect a pitch as I threw all day, knee-high over the outside corner and still he got a hold of it.

What's more he got that bat around so fast he actually pulled the ball between first and second. He smacked it on a line too but right into the hands of Lou Klein for the first out. Then Nick Etten was at

Walker Cooper

bat. I slowed up on him for the "good pitch" and he grounded to Klein as Keller scored. It was 4-3 with two out and Joe Gordon hitting. He was crouched over the plate, expecting the same kind of outside treatment I'd given the other two. And that's what he was going to get . . . but the pitch slipped . . . !

That was the worst ball I threw in the whole series, both games. Instead of getting it low and away, it boomed in there high and inside, exactly the pitch for a guy like Gordon to belt out of the lot. Walker knew it too . . . and he jumped up and acted like he was going to dash out in front of the plate and head it off. And Gordon? He saw what was coming before it got there and tried desperately to pull back and swing hard. He swung, but he was too close and the ball ticked off the handle end of his bat and sailed high to the left of the plate . . . a foul.

I can see Walker and Kurowski going for it yet. My brother got it . . . but it jiggled in his glove just a little, he squeezed it so hard. But I don't think it would have fallen even if it had jumped free. Kurowski would have had it. We won . . . I won . . . Walker won, mostly . . . the Cardinals won. But I guess Dad won, in the long run, because maybe I'd a' got licked again if that hadn't happened to him. I'm not being sentimental when I say that I truly believe Dad died so I could win that game.

THE BOX SCORE
(October 6, 1943)

ST. LOUIS	A.B.	R.	H.	P.	A.	NEW YORK	A.B.	R.	H.	P.	A.
Klein, 2b.	4	0	1	4	4	Crosetti, ss.	4	1	2	2	2
Walker, cf.	5	0	1	5	0	Metheny, rf.	3	0	0	2	0
Musial, rf.	4	1	1	2	0	Johnson, 3d.	4	1	2	0	1
W. Cooper, c.	3	0	1	5	0	Keller, lf.	4	1	1	3	0
Kurowski, 3b.	4	1	1	0	1	Dickey, c.	3	0	0	9	2
Sanders, 1b.	3	1	1	8	0	Etten, 1b.	4	0	0	4	0
Litwhiler, lf.	3	0	0	3	0	Gordon, 2b.	4	0	1	4	0
Marion, ss.	3	1	1	0	3	Stainback, cf.	3	0	0	3	0
M. Cooper, p.	3	0	0	0	0	Bonham, p.	2	0	0	0	0
						Murphy, p.	0	0	0	0	1
Totals	32	4	7	27	8	Wetherly	1	0	0	0	0
						Totals	32	3	6	27	6

Wetherly batted for Bonham in 8th.

ST. LOUIS	0	0	1	3	0	0	0	0	0 — 4
NEW YORK	0	0	0	1	0	0	0	0	2 — 3

Errors—Walker, W. Cooper. Runs batted in—Marion, Kurowski, Sanders (2), Keller (2), Etten. Two-base hit—Johnson. Three-base hit—Keller. Home runs—Marion, Sanders. Stolen base—Marion. Sacrifices—W. Cooper, M. Cooper. Earned runs—St. Louis 4, New York 3. Left on bases—St. Louis 7, New York 4. Bases on balls—Off Bonham 3 (Sanders, Klein, Marion), Murphy 1 (Litwhiler); M. Cooper 1 (Dickey). Strikeouts—Bonham 9 (Walker, Kurowski), (3), Litwhiler (2), M. Cooper (2), Sanders; M. Cooper 4 (Etten, Gordon, Steinback, Crosetti). Hits—Off Bonham, 6 in 8 innings; Murphy, 1 in 1 inning. Umpires—Reardon (N. L.), plate; Rue (A. L.), first base; Stewart (N. L.), second base; Rommel (A. L.), third base. Losing pitcher—Bonham. Time—2:08. Attendance—68,578.

Durocher and his team

LEO DUROCHER

as told to

JOHN P. CARMICHAEL

Leo "The Lip" Durocher, although owning a lifetime batting average of only .247, still ranks as one of baseball's brilliant shortstops. Born at West Springfield, Mass., on July 27, 1906, Lippy is only 5 feet 6 inches today, and his first nickname was "Speedy" until he became the scourge of umpires—hence his new monicker of "The Lip." Came up to the Yanks in 1928 after a year at St. Paul, then to Cincinnati in 1930. Became manager of the Brooklyn Dodgers Oct. 12, 1938, and has held the post since.

Y ou mean the day I'll never forget? That's easy, brother! We've only got to go back to 1941 when Brooklyn won the pennant. It was my first flag as manager, too, and I was fired before the day was over. That's right. Won a pennant and I was fired as manager the same day. Put that down in the books.

In the first place, I didn't think I'd live to get to Boston, where we clinched the flag. I couldn't sleep nights. If you recall we played a double-header in Philly the Sunday before and we won the first game easy and I was all set to let Curt Davis go in the second one, when Larry MacPhail came in the clubhouse and asked: "Who yuh workin' this game . . . Luke Hamlin?" I said: "No, Davis," and he didn't say nothin' and walked out.

Well I got thinkin' about Davis and Hamlin and whipsawin' myself and finally wound up with Hamlin and Litwhiler hit a homer off him with the bags loaded in the first inning and we blew it. I was afraid to shave that night because I couldn't stop shakin' and finally I went to a barber and I thought of Casey Stengel as I got in the chair; the time he dropped two in one afternoon, walked into a shop, sat down and told the guy:

"Once over and never mind cutting my throat. I may do that myself later in the evening."

That just shows you how things were going when we got to Boston for those two games. We won the first, thanks to "Dixie" Walker's three-run triple in the eighth, and that only made things worse. I didn't close an eye all night. "Peewee" Reese had booted one to give Boston the lead and I lay awake wondering if maybe I hadn't better take him out the next day and play myself. I got up outta bed four times . . . the last time at a quarter after 5 . . . and made out different lineups. Finally I just stayed up.

Oh, how that morning dragged. Every time I picked up a paper I read where if we won and the Cards lost we were "in" and then I'd have more coffee. It was a helluva relief to get into the uniforms; just putting it on seemed to quiet me a little and I'd keep telling myself, "What you worryin' for: Wyatt's pitching and he's beaten these mugs five straight times. He'll handcuff 'em." I remember as we were walkin' out on the field, ol' Whitlow came by and maybe he figured the skipper could stand some cheering up and he put a hand on my shoulder and said: "Get me one run today. They won't score!" That's all.

We got him one right off the bat. Walker singled, went to third on two infield outs and then Medwick topped a ball toward third. I saw

Frank Demaree

it might be a hard play for Tom Early, the Boston pitcher, and hollered to Joe: "Run for your life." I thought afterwards that must have sounded funny as hell, because what else would he do, but anyway he beat the play by a step and Walker came home. In the next inning Owen was on second with two out and took third as "Dixie" singled again...too short for Mickey to score. But Walker got himself trapped off first and maneuvered around long enough to let Owen count before he was caught.

I was feeling a little better by then •and so help me if that Rowell, at second, didn't make three straight errors in the third and give us another run. You'd a thought those guys were winning a pennant. They were so damn anxious to beat us, like everybody else in the league, and they blew up. He kicked Camilli's grounder, just an easy roller, and then threw it away and he fell all over Medwick's ball and Dolph scored from second. About the time Reiser hit that homer in the seventh to make the score 5 to 0, the guys in the press box were hollerin' down that the Cards were losing 3 to 1 and somebody on our bench let out a yip and I shut him up. It was too soon to shake hands with ourselves.

That Wyatt was beautiful to watch. They got three hits off him in seven innings and not a man reached third. I never said a word to him at any time, nor to any man on the club, except to yell and holler, "Keep the 'pepper' up." Whitlow was my best pitcher. If we couldn't win with him, the chances were we couldn't win at all. The same went for the whole team. There it was on the field, the best we had. The fourth hit off Whit came by Rowell in the eighth and they sent up

Frank Demaree to pinch hit. He was ready and he hit one. I can close my eyes now and see Billy Herman going for that ball.

Larry MacPhail

He made the (deleted by censor) stop I've seen in many a day. He just dove, almost full length, after it and still kept his feet. That was the end. We were home. I started to laugh, like a kid who knows Santa Claus is coming that night. Wyatt went through the motions in the ninth and we carried him into the clubhouse. It's funny to see big, swearing men cry, but they did. Everybody was tired and worn and happy.

That ride to New York was something! We had a special train. We drank up $1,400 worth of beer, Scotch and champagne on the trip. Well, you were on it . . . remember when Tony Martin, the movie guy, got up to make a speech and somebody hit him smack in the face with a hot steak? The gang yelled: "Sit down, you bum, this isn't your party," and from then on it was a riot.

At New Haven the conductor got a wire from MacPhail telling him he'd board the train at 125th Street in New York. I didn't know anything about a wire, but the conductor came to me and asked if we wanted to stop there. I told him no. We knew there'd be a mob in Grand Central Station and some of the fellows wanted to get off at 125th and slip home, but I vetoed that. I told them: "I don't care if they tear your clothes off. We belong to those fans. They've been waiting 21 years for this chance to celebrate and we've gotta go through with it. There'll be no stop."

We went right on through. MacPhail was standing on the platform with Sam Breadon and Branch Rickey. They were on their way to see Rochester in the playoffs. We passed 'em up, just like that; went roaring right on and I got a glimpse of MacPhail and I said to myself: "Oh, oh, there'll be hell to pay about this." There was. I met him in a Hotel

New Yorker elevator. He never said a word. Didn't congratulate me or the team or a thing; just looked at me. We got off at the same floor, walked into the same suite together, never talked.

People began to come in and he called me into another room. Still didn't say anything about the pennant. "Why didn't you have the train stopped at 125th?" he shot at me. I told him I didn't know he'd sent a wire; I told him why we decided to go on through, so the players wouldn't get off. He was plenty mad. Told me I might have called him up and asked and a lot of junk and finally I said I was runnin' the team, not the (deleted by censor) train and he barked back:

"Well, you're not even runnin' the team any longer. You're fired!"

So I said "all right" and walked out and went up to my own room. Somebody sent up word the newsreel men were waiting below and I refused to come down. I never did, either. They had to use Joe Meddick and I never saw the pictures afterward. Maybe they didn't use 'em. I stayed where I was and finally went to bed. I was so tired I coulda slept standin' up. About 3 o'clock in the morning the phone rang and it was MacPhail.

THE BOX SCORE
(September 25, 1941)

BROOKLYN DODGERS	A.B.	R.	H.	P.	A.
Walker, rf.	5	1	3	3	0
Herman, 2b.	4	0	0	2	2
Coscarart, 2b.	1	0	0	0	0
Reiser, cf.	3	1	2	2	0
Camilli, 1b.	4	1	0	10	0
Medwick, lf.	4	0	1	1	0
Lavagetto, 3b.	2	1	0	1	4
Reese, ss.	3	0	1	2	0
Owens, c.	4	1	1	5	0
Wyatt, p.	4	1	1	1	0
Totals	34	6	9	27	17

BOSTON BRAVES	A.B.	R.	H.	P.	A.
Sisti, 3b.	3	0	0	1	4
Dudra, 3b.	1	0	0	0	0
Cooney, c.	1	0	0	0	0
Moore, cf.	3	0	0	0	0
Hassett, 1b.	4	0	0	9	2
Waner, rf.	3	0	1	1	0
West, lf.	4	0	2	3	0
Miller, ss.	3	0	0	3	0
Roberge, 2b.	0	0	0	1	0
Rowell, 2b.	3	0	2	2	0
Berres, c.	2	0	0	5	2
Johnson, p.	0	0	0	0	0
Earley, p.	2	0	0	1	3
Masi, c.	1	0	0	1	0
Total	31	0	5	27	19

Demaree batted for Berres in the 8th.

BROOKLYN	1	1	1	0	0	0	2	1	0 — 6
BOSTON	0	0	0	0	0	0	0	0	0 — 0

Errors—Miller, Rowell (3). Runs batted in—Medwick, Reiser (2). Two-base hit—West. Home run—Reiser. Stolen base—Owen. Double plays—Herman to Reese to Camilli, Hassett to Miller to Hassett, Miller to Rowell to Hassett, Johnson to Miller to Hassett. Left on bases—Brooklyn 7, Boston 5. Bases on balls—Off Wyatt 1, Earley 5, Johnson 1. Struck out—By Wyatt 5, Earley 5. Johnson 1. Hits—Off Earley, 8 in 8 innings; Johnson, 1 in 1 inning. Losing pitcher—Earley. Umpires—Reardon, Goetz and Stewart. Time—2:08. Attendance—10,096.

"You comin' by the office in the morning?" he asked.

Twice as mad now, because I'd been asleep, I yelled into the phone: "What for, to get my money?" and hung up. In about two minutes it rang again.

"No," he said, "I want to talk over some things about the series with you." I said: "Okay," and went back to sleep.

That's it!

ROGERS HORNSBY

as told to
BILL VAN FLEET

(*Sketch by Hod Taylor*)

Rogers Hornsby led the National League in batting seven times. Played 11 seasons with the Cardinals. In addition to serving as manager of the latter team also piloted Braves, Cubs and Browns.

The peak of my whole baseball career came in that seventh game of the 1926 World Series. That game, and that series, is an old, old story by now because it has been told so often, but that day always will be my greatest. As playing manager of the Cardinals, I won St. Louis' first pennant in history and beat one of the finest of all Yankee teams in the same year. You couldn't ask for anything more to remember.

Mechanically, I may say right here, I played a very ordinary game. I got two singles, but neither figured in the scoring. I handled five chances without an error, but not one was a hard play. So it wasn't what I did, but what WE did, as a championship team, that will never be forgotten. Personally, I came as close to being one of the all-time goats as eventually winding up with the temporary rank of first-class hero.

Just to start from the beginning, our club was rated well from opening day that season, but for a long time we couldn't get going. We really didn't move into contention for the flag until early in September. With about two weeks to go we won two out of three from the Reds and went into the lead, but then lost three out of four in Boston and fell into second place. In Philly we rallied for five out of six and it was September 27, or thereabouts, that we beat the Giants a double-header to clinch the title. This was the team destined to outfinish the mighty Ruth and Gehrig and Bob Meusel and Lazzeri.

No question but what fandom was pulling for us. We were the new-comers to championship circles. We were brash Davids throwing rocks at the Yankee Goliaths and nobody can say we didn't give 'em a battle. The only real "cleaning" we got was the day in St. Louis when Ruth hit those three homers to score four runs and drive in four more. The other Yank wins were by Herb Pennock, 2-1 and 3-2, while Jess Haines and old Pete Alexander packed away three for us. It was Alex who had simply breezed to a 10-2 triumph in No. 6. Old Pete didn't have to bear down at all and suddenly we were at the climax. It was now or never for both. There'd be no tomorrow for either. Jess Haines, who had hurled the only shutout of the series in whipping "Dutch" Reuther, was my choice; Waite Hoyt drew the Yankee assignment. You can imagine the scene in Yankee Stadium. The very air tingled. You couldn't step on that field without experiencing a feeling that this whole setup was a grand, grand thing.

The Yanks got a run in the first. We got three in the fourth on sin-gles by Tommy Thevenow, "Chick" Hafey and Jim Bottomley, thanks to a couple of timely Yank misplays. Even when Joe Dugan's single and a two-bagger by Hank Severeid gave the American Leaguers another run in the sixth, I didn't particularly worry. Haines was the kind of a pitcher who could hang onto a one-run lead if it came down to it. Then he unaccountably grew wild. Standing back there as he walked the first man in the seventh I wondered if, finally, the strain was beginning to tell.

With two out, he walked three men to fill the bases. I was thinking he ought to get one out of four out, even with Lazzeri up, then I figured something had happened to Jess. I walked over to him and asked. It had. A blister had broken on the first finger from the pressure of throw-ing his knuckler. Because he couldn't roll the ball over that raw spot without flinching a bit, he'd lost control. We were in a tight spot. Bases full of Yanks and a fellow waiting to hit who might have extended Haines even when Jess was in perfect shape. I made the only choice I could; the only selection any manager could make. I called Alexander.

It was no spot for youth and sheer speed even if I'd had some in the bull pen. You couldn't throw the ball past the Yanks then any more than in recent years. You couldn't afford to make a mistake in this clutch and the only man available was Alex. You should have heard the rumbling through the stands.

One minute the fans had seen Alex sitting in the sun out yonder, apparently oblivious to what was going on; the next he was shambling toward the mound, the biggest man in America . . . the man of the day and the hour and the moment. What the fans didn't know was that Alex never warmed up much. He never had to. He took his time getting to the hill and, of course, what I said to him and what he answered has been written before. "We're in a tough spot," I told him, "and there's no place to put this guy." He twisted his lips into that slow, tilted smile and nodded in complete understanding of the situation as he replied: "I'll take care of that," just like he was accepting a chore to do for an old friend.

There are a few things I'd like to say about Alexander. Almost every fan has heard stories of that game, about how he still was reeling from a celebration the night before and a lot of other things. Some fans have even told me, to my face, that I had to send a cab to get him out of a barroom after the game had started. That, of course, was a downright lie. After the sixth game some friends picked Alex up and they had a few drinks at a hotel. That was only natural, and I knew where they were. But Alex was as sober as I was for the final game and everybody who knows me knows I never took a drink in my life. He never gave me a bit of trouble.

Well, there was Alex in the sunlight and there was Lazzeri. There were the base-runners straining at leashes. There was that great crowd just about smothered by the tenseness of the spot. I moved back to position and waited. The first pitch came in low and inside, a curve. As Alex threw I couldn't help noticing the honest-to-God elegance ... that's the only word to describe it ... with which he pitched. He was more than graceful ... he was a gesture of perfection itself. Just the same, Lazzeri swung and got his meat-end of the bat around in time. The ball sailed for the left-field bleachers and my heart came as close to stopping as it ever will before it never beats again.

It curved foul. Not by much. No more than two feet at the most. We had been given a new lease on life; the title hadn't yet slipped out of reach. As if the pitch was something Alex had to get out of his system before he could go about his work, he mowed down Tony on two more tosses and the danger was over. The greatest pitcher of them all didn't allow a ball hit out of the infield the next two innings, but there still was a little excitement in the guise of anticlimax to come. Ruth came up in the ninth with two out and nobody on.

The count reached three and two and the Babe chose to let the sixth pitch go by. Umpire Bill Klem called it a ball and for a minute there was an argument at the plate. Bob O'Farrell, our catcher, thought it caught a corner, but, of course, the decision stood, and Meusel was next. Nobody ever doubted but what he could blast with the best on occasion. We were scared all over again, but the Yanks came to our rescue. They decided to let Ruth run.

He went down on the first pitch just to make the surprise move as effective as possible, but O'Farrell's throw had him by 10 feet. I'll always remember putting the ball on him. He didn't say a word. He didn't even look around or up at me. He just picked himself off the ground and walked away to the dugout and I had lived through the greatest day any man could ask.